A Study on Chinese Translation of
ANGLO-AMERICAN
LEGAL TERMS

英美法律术语汉译研究

张法连 ◎ 著

北京大学出版社
PEKING UNIVERSITY PRESS

图书在版编目 (CIP) 数据

英美法律术语汉译研究 / 张法连著 . —北京：北京大学出版社 ,2022.9
ISBN 978–7–301–33387–7

Ⅰ.①英… Ⅱ.①张… Ⅲ.①法律 – 英语 – 名词术语 – 翻译 – 研究 Ⅳ.① D90

中国版本图书馆 CIP 数据核字 (2022) 第 175447 号

书　　　名	英美法律术语汉译研究 YING-MEI FALÜ SHUYU HANYI YANJIU
著作责任者	张法连　著
责 任 编 辑	郝妮娜
标 准 书 号	ISBN 978–7–301–33387–7
出 版 发 行	北京大学出版社
地　　　址	北京市海淀区成府路 205 号　100871
网　　　址	http://www.pup.cn　　新浪微博：@ 北京大学出版社
电 子 信 箱	bdhnn2011@126.com
电　　　话	邮购部 010-62752015　发行部 010-62750672　编辑部 010-62759634
印 刷 者	北京圣夫亚美印刷有限公司
经 销 者	新华书店
	720 毫米 ×1020 毫米　16 开本　16.5 印张　330 千字 2022 年 9 月第 1 版　2022 年 9 月第 1 次印刷
定　　　价	66.00 元

未经许可，不得以任何方式复制或抄袭本书之部分或全部内容。
版权所有，侵权必究
举报电话：010-62752024　电子信箱：fd@pup.pku.edu.cn
图书如有印装质量问题，请与出版部联系，电话：010-62756370

前　言

　　法律翻译中术语的翻译具有特别重要的意义。术语翻译的准确与否常常关系到翻译质量的好坏,翻译不当甚至会酿成法律纠纷。英美法的国际影响力较大,我国的司法体制改革吸收了不少英美法的先进司法理念;法律英语专业也是以英美法为载体,所以英美法律术语的汉译是法律英语翻译中的核心问题,直接影响到我国司法体制改革能否充分借鉴域外先进法治经验和中国法治国际传播的效能。

　　随着对外开放向纵深发展,我国对外交往日益增多,法律活动日益频繁,因而对法律翻译的需求空前旺盛。但是受法律翻译人员专业水平的影响,我国法律翻译质量不容乐观。有些法律文本的翻译,特别是法律术语的翻译,没有体现出源语法律文本的专业性和规范性,源语文本中的同一法律术语,在目的语文本中经常用多个不同的法律术语来翻译。术语是法律语言的基本组成部分,它包括俚语、外来语、行话等。为了提高法律翻译的质量,需要在了解法律术语分类及含义的基础上,研究探讨其翻译方法。

作为一种比较特殊的英语文体,法律英语语言表述用词准确,表意严谨。而法律英语术语是法律英语语言的精髓,它是用来准确表达特有的法律概念的专门用语,具有明确的、特定的法律含义,其他词汇无法替代。正确理解和应用法律英语术语是做好法律翻译工作的关键。

依据来源的不同,法律英语术语可分为来自普通英语的法律术语、来自古英语的法律术语、来自其他语言的法律术语、来自法律行业习惯的法律术语和来自其他专门领域的法律术语;依据使用范围的不同,法律英语术语可分为专用法律术语和非专用法律术语;依据表述词义的准确程度的不同,法律英语术语可分为模糊法律术语和精确法律术语。同义反复的法律英语术语,即两个同义词或近义词并列在一起而组成的特殊法律术语,是法律英语中的一个特殊语言现象。上述法律英语术语的分类是相互联系,相互作用的。它们之间有特定的语义联系,构成独特的法律英语术语体系,所以,我们应该既要看到每种术语的鲜明特征也不要忽略法律术语的体系性。

本书聚焦英美法律术语的汉译问题研究。理解是翻译的前提,准确理解英美法律术语的含义也是法律英语证书(LEC)考试必考内容。看到英美法律术语,要经过什么样的思考路径将其准确译为汉语?保障"准确"的依据是什么?书中都有详细论述,这是作者多年法律翻译实践的总结,不当之处,祈请方家不吝赐教。

本书成书过程中,作者参考了大量中英文相关资料,在此向原作者表示感谢。本人指导的博士研究生蒋毓婧、孙贝、陆贝旎以及LEC办公室姜芳、汤文华老师帮助作者查找资料、校改清样,在此对她们的辛苦付出深表谢意。本书是我访美归来,在上海隔离的日子里定稿的,也算是给我的"有天无日"带来了一丝的轻松,以此纪念。

2022 年 3 月 6 日于上海希尔顿逸林酒店

目 录

第一章 法律英语术语特征 …………………………………… 1
第二章 英美法律术语汉译策略 ……………………………… 12
第三章 法律翻译中的文化传递 ……………………………… 24
第四章 法律英语术语误译解析 ……………………………… 35

附录一 常见美国法引证缩写 ………………………………… 224
附录二 常用法律缩略语 ……………………………………… 229
附录三 WTO法常用术语 ……………………………………… 247

参考文献 ………………………………………………………… 250
索 引 …………………………………………………………… 253

第一章 法律英语术语特征

法律工作自身的严肃性使法律工作中的专门化行业语汇具有类似科技术语的精密明确、用法固定、语义单一的特点。法律语言专业术语数量大，应用范围广，其词汇术语体系主要由法律专业术语、法律工作常用词语和民族共同语中的其他基本词汇和非基本词汇构成，而法律术语是法律语言语汇体系中的核心内容。

词义的单一性——科技术语最突出的特点是词义单一而固定，在这一点上，英汉法律术语是一样的。因此，在具体运用过程中，任何人在任何情况下都必须对其统一的解释。法律专业术语的单一性主要表现在两个方面。一是每个专业术语所表示的都是一个特定的法律概念，在使用时其他任何词语都不能代替。例如：过失——negligence，而非 mistake；谋杀未遂——uncompleted murder 而非 failure in murder。"故意"不能用"存心""特意"代替，"犯罪嫌疑人"不能用"犯罪可疑人"替换。二是某一个专业术语即使在民族共同语中属多义词，一旦进入法律语言作为专业术语出现时，也只能保留一个义项。

词语的对义性——词语的对义性是指词语的意义互相矛盾、互相对立,即词语所表示的概念在逻辑上具有一种矛盾或对立的关系。如"一般"与"特殊"、"上面"与"下面"等。在民族共同语中,这类意义相反或对应的词属于反义词的范畴。在法律语言中,我们称之为对义词。之所以这样称呼,是因为法律工作必须借助一组表示矛盾、对立的事物或表示对立的法律行为的词语来表示各种互相对立的法律关系。在这一点上,法律专业术语中,英语和汉语有一致性。

使用上的变异性——法律专业术语的变异性是指有些术语的使用与民族共同语的语言习惯有所不同。如"不作为""不能犯"这两个法律术语,在民族共同语中属动词词组,在句子中常充当谓语。而在法律语言中,作为法律专业术语的"不作为""不能犯"不再是动词词组,而是具有动词功能的法律概念,在句中常常充当主语和宾语,而不能充当谓语。英语中也存在这种现象,但与汉语比起来要少得多。例如:在"not proven(证据不足)"的结构中,not 是副词,proven 是由动词 prove 转化而来的过去分词,具有形容词的功能,意思是"未证实的"。在英语中,proven 只能做表语和定语。但作为法律专业术语,它已名词化,在句中可以做主语和宾语。

词语的类义性——类义词是指意义同属某一类别的词。英汉法律专业术语存在大量的类义词是其又一大特点。如:"car(小汽车)""bus(公共汽车)""truck(卡车)""train(火车)"等都属于"vehicle(车辆)"类的类义词。类义词是概念划分的产物。归属于同一义类的词则分别表示同一属概念之内的若干种概念。如"crime(罪,罪行)"就是一个属概念,人们可以根据犯罪行为的不同性质将其划分为许多种类的罪,这许多种类的罪就成为种概念。

法律专业术语中存在许多类义词,是因为法律所面向的是整个社会,其调整的对象是全体公民、法人、机关、团体等各种各样的法律关系。而表示这些法律关系的概念必然有大有小,有属有种。在使用这些概念的过程中,为了明确其外延的范围,就要从不同角度、不同层次上根据其各自的属性进行门类的划分,然后用适当的词语加以确定,以避免理解上的任意扩大或缩小,于是就产生了不同层次上的属概念和种概念,而表示这些概念的词语就是不同层次上的类义词。

法律英语是法律科学和英语语言学交叉产生的新兴交叉学科,属于应用语言学的范畴,是一种具有法律职业技能特征的行业语言。词汇术语是法律英语语言的基本组成部分,它包括俚语、外来语、行话等。法律词汇术语也是法律英

语证书(LEC)全国统一考试的必考内容。法律英语术语特征明显,具体表现在以下几个方面:

一、普通词汇表法律新意

词汇分两种,一种叫普通词汇,一种叫专业词汇。普通词汇有全面性、稳定性和造词能力强等特点。法律语言中有大量的普通词汇。法律专业词汇是人们在长期使用民族共同语的过程中,根据立法、司法工作的实际需要而逐步形成的一套具有法律专业特色的词汇和术语。《牛津法律英语大词典》指出:法律语言部分地是由具有特定法律意义的词组成,部分是由日常用语组成,但这些日常词汇往往具有特定法律意义。我们将这一现象称之为具有普通词形态而无普通词意义的法律词汇。请看以下的例子:

例1

He was awarded a scholarship.

This earthquake caused great damage.

Plaintiff was awarded ＄36,900 damages for the injury he suffered in the car accident.

作为普通词汇,award 通常指给予某人的"奖励",damage 是造成的"损坏"。但对于法律英语学习研究者,一看到句子的第一个单词 plaintiff(原告)就要断定这是一个法律英语句子,其中有些普通词汇可能被赋予了法律意义。所以,award 应理解为"法庭宣判",damages(复数)为其所宣判给付的"赔偿金"。该句应译为:原告因车祸而得到36900美元赔偿金。

这类需要一定语境或上下文才能确定词义的词汇,通常都是普通英语词汇中的多义词。又如:

例2

Thank you for your consideration.

He showed great consideration to her.

No consideration, no contract.

作为普通词汇,consideration 通常指"考虑""体贴",前两个句子中的 consideration 都表示的是普通意义。第三句是法律英语句子,句中的

consideration 却是"对价""约因"的意思,所以该句应译为:没有对价就不构成合同。

例 3

The testator died without <u>issue</u>.

The parties could not agree on the <u>issue</u>.

The passport was <u>issued</u> by the foreign ministry.

issue 既是一个普通词,又是法律词汇。其法律上的含义主要通过语境来确定。上述三个句子中画线的 issue,只有在第一句和第二句中才是法律术语的用法,专指遗嘱中的"子嗣"和富有争议性的"问题"。第三句中的 issue 是普通词汇的用法,意思是"颁发"。

二、古旧词汇依然活跃

古英语词汇在现代英语中已很少使用,但在法律性文件中依然随处可见。尽管在英美国家要求法律语言"简明化"的呼声颇高,但为了使法律文件句子简练、严谨,反映出法律文句正规、严肃、权威等文体特征,适当使用古旧词汇是必要的。请看下面的例句:

例 4

The following terms used in these rules shall have the meanings <u>hereunder</u> assigned to them.

古英语词汇 hereunder 是副词,意为"在下面",them 代表 the following terms。该句应译为:本细则下列用语的含义是……。本句用上 hereunder 一词使句子法律味道浓厚。

例 5

A contract shall be an agreement <u>whereby</u> the parties establish, change or terminate their civil relationship.

在本句中,古英语词汇 whereby＝by which,引导定语从句,其中 which 代表 an agreement。该句应译为:合同是当事人之间设立、变更、中止民事关系的协议。如果原文中缺少了 whereby,整个句子就不能成立。

例 6

Provided further that this Policy shall be subject to the Conditions herein contained and to any Memoranda endorsed hereon and such Conditions and Memoranda are to be taken as part of the Policy and the observance and performance by the Insured of the times and terms thereon contained so far as they relate to anything to be done by the Insured are of the essence of this contract and shall be conditions precedent to any liability on the part of the Insured under this Policy.（薛华业，1993：98）

本例是合约条款,选自一份现代的保险合约,但其中 herein, hereon, such 以及 thereon 全是普通英文中废弃的典型的古英语词汇（主要用作副词），而其他旧式用法还有 provided that, subject to 等。

三、频繁使用外来词或短语

法律英语词汇的一个重要特点是大量地引进外来语。这些外来词汇主要来自于拉丁语,包括成语和短语。法律英语中广泛使用拉丁词和拉丁词源的词使语言严肃冰冷。法律英语还广泛地采用法语借词,使法律语言显得高贵典雅。法律英语中的拉丁语自公元 597 年基督教传入英国后逐渐渗入而来,而法律英语中的法语主要是 11 世纪诺曼底人征服英国后逐渐从法语中的法律词汇借入的。

法律越来越融入人们的生活,日益成为现代人们生活的一部分,一些法律文献上常用的标准外来词已经在人们的日常生活中得到认可,其词源渐渐被人们淡忘。由于法语词汇形态和发音与英文词汇极其相似,故没有受过词源学方面专门训练的人士一般无法辨识这些词的来源。比如：

拉丁语外来词

affidavit 誓章，证明　　　　　　alieni juris 受他人监护的
alibi 不在犯罪现场　　　　　　　bona fide 真诚
de facto 事实上　　　　　　　　habeas corpus 人身保护令
in rem 对物权　　　　　　　　　prima facie 表面的
quorum 法定人数　　　　　　　 sine die 无期限

法语外来词

estoppel 禁止反言　　　　　　lien 留置权,扣押权
void 无效的　　　　　　　　　voir dire 陪审团成员资格审查
jury 陪审团　　　　　　　　　fee 律师费
breve 法院的令状　　　　　　quash 废除,撤销

四、大量使用专业术语

法律英语专业术语具有明确的、特定的法律含义,它们可以非常准确地表达复杂的法律概念,其他词汇无法替代。这类词词源复杂,可以是正宗的英语词、法语词,也可以是拉丁词。它们在法律英语中数量也比较可观。

根据意义结构或语义范围,这类专门用语可分为常用术语、排他性专门涵义术语、专门法律术语和借用术语四种形式。

1. 常用术语

法律英语常用术语有两层含义:1)不明确表示特定的法律概念,语域比较广,既常用于法律语言中,也是社会日常生活各方面不可缺少的词语,在两种语域中无语义差别,而且通俗易懂。例如:conduct(行为),write(签字),witness(证明),signing(签署),insurance(保险),marriage(婚姻),divorce(离婚)等等。2)表示特定的法律概念,但是随着应用范围的扩大和全民词汇发生密切联系而经常互相交换与影响,结果由原来只有法律工作者知晓的术语扩伸到全民词汇领域中。例如:murder(谋杀),crime(罪行),will(遗嘱),fine(罚款),punishment(惩罚),sentence(判决),judgement(审判),robbery(抢劫)等等。法律英语常用术语由于法律和全民通用,所以其最大特点就是常用性及适用场合广。据此,这类术语一般文体信息较少,具有中性文体意义效果。另外由于这类术语都是常用词,所以其构词能力较强,如 law lawful 和 lawyer, crime criminal, contract contractual,而且有的具有多义性,应用时要注意词形变化和语境。

2. 排他性专门涵义术语

这种术语指排斥与法律概念无任何联系的一般涵义而保留特定的法律专门涵义的法律专门用语。这类术语有两种涵义:一是法律方面的;二是普通意义方

面的。由于两种涵义截然不同,所以必须通过排斥与法律无关的普通涵义才能明晰地揭示特定的法律专门涵义。这类术语的多义现象主要是由于词义范围在历史演变中扩大或缩小而产生的。据此,可将其分为两类形式:1) 词义外延术语:许多专门创造的法律专门术语由于词义从原先表示的单一概念扩大到表达外延较宽广的概念而越出其使用范围,渗透到日常生活中,例如 alibi 是一个法律专门术语,意为"不在犯罪现场",现在词义已扩大为"借口,托词",甚至还转化为动词"为……辩解"。statute 法令,成文法,(公司、学校等的)章程,条例;jury 陪审团,(竞赛时)评奖团;code 法典,法规,密码,电码;2) 词义缩小产生的术语:与第 1 类相反,许多法律专门术语不是专门创造的,而是由于全民的原始词义外延缩小,从日常生活转用到了法律方面形成的,即在原先含有一般词义的旧词基础上赋予其表示法律概念的新义。例如日常生活用词 box 表示"盒,箱"之义,现在已具有法律涵义,成为法律专门术语,表示"证人席,陪审席"。parole(俘虏)假释;complaint 报怨,控告,起诉;deed 行为,契约。排他性专门涵义术语由于表示法律专门概念,使用频率高,所以构成法律英语专门术语的主体部分。这类术语虽然从词形看许多都是常用词,但是在语义方面由于它是由一般词义和法律专门涵义两类不同语义内容构成,所以一般只有精通法律英语的法律工作者才能懂得术语所揭示的特定法律概念,而多数人一般只了解其一般涵义。法律英语用词的最大特点就是准确。这类术语有一词多义的特点,所以在实际应用中切不能望词生义,一定要借助语境正确理解,以免误用。

3. 专门法律术语

这类术语因为符合术语的单义性、准确性和所表达的概念严格区分三个根本特征,所以是严格意义上的标准术语。这类术语概念非常确切,词义明确,不会一词多义。如 plaintiff(原告),defendant(被告),recidivism(累犯),bigamy(重婚罪),proximate cause(近因),negligence(疏忽),以及 foreseeability(可预见性),都只有专门的法律上的意义。这些词"词简意赅",法律资讯负载量很大;用一个非常简单的词汇能表达一个相当复杂的概念。单义性的实际意义在于它可有效地防止误解,即使在较小的语境中也是如此。

4. 借用术语

随着政治、经济和科技的发展,法律调整的内容越来越多,门类的划分也日趋细密,目前已发展成为一个体系庞大、门类众多、结构严密的学科。一些新的法律分支学科和边缘学科应运而生,相关领域内的专门术语大量涌入法律英语专门术语,其中许多术语已站稳脚跟,占有非常固定的一席之地。例如:sadism(性虐待狂)源自心理学,abortion(堕胎)源自医学,artistic work(艺术作品)源自艺术,continental shelf(大陆架)源自地理学,heredity(遗传)源自生物学,ratio(比率)源自数学,incest(乱伦罪)源自社会学,monogamy(一夫一妻制)源自人口学,tariff(关税)源自经济学,average(海损)源自运输,claims(索赔)源自对外贸易,life insurance(人寿保险)源自保险等等。

五、经常使用正式词汇

为了体现法律语言的严肃性,法律英语的措辞风格以严谨、庄重为主,多采用正式书面体。除了使用上述各类非普通英语用词外,经常使用正式程度较高的词汇也是实现这一风格的措施之一。所谓法律文书中的正式词汇,不但指相对于口语用词而言的书面语用词,尤指普通书面语体中不常用的正式程度较高的词汇或短语。如任何书面语体中都会使用 according to(按照),with regard to,regarding 或 concerning(有关)。但在法律文体中,更常用的、表达相同概念的是正式程度较高的词汇 in accordance with,pursuant to 及 in respect of。这类词汇还包括许多委婉语(词)。例如,死去的人(the dead),在法律英语中会用 the deceased 或 the decedent。请看以下的例子:

例 7

This law is promulgated with the purpose of regulating insurance activities, protecting the legitimate rights and interests of the parties involved, strengthening supervision and regulation of the insurance industry and promoting its healthy development.

上面例句中的 promulgate, regulate, supervision 等词都是非常正式的书面语词汇,句子里也没有任何修饰或夸张成分。全句可译为:为了规范保险活动,保护保险活动当事人的合法权益,加强对保险业的监督管理,促进保险事业的健康发展,制定本法。

日常英语词汇	法律英语词汇
come here	approach the bench
before	prior to
after	subsequent
end	termination
begin	commence
if	where, provided that
obey	comply with
think	deem, hold
for	for the purpose of

六、故意使用模糊词汇

一般来讲,法律语言要求表达清晰、准确甚至精确,法律文书的写作要力求避免含糊其辞或模棱两可。但是,在有些情况下恰恰是为了表现法律语言的严谨性,我们不得不使用一些意义模糊、灵活的词语去准确表达某些需要模糊或灵活的法律概念或事实。

汉英两种法律语言各自都有不少模糊词汇。比如汉语中常用到"大约、若干、严重、从重、从轻、恶劣、合理的、数额巨大"等等。英语中常用到 about, further, general, reasonable, necessary, properly, perfect, within, possible, approximately 等等,这类词汇和短语数量相当可观。法律英语中的这些模糊词汇不仅具有概括性、灵活性的特点,而且还具有丰富的法律内涵,留给司法人员更大的空间发挥其能动的认识把握,从而更好地发挥法律的调节功能。具体来说,在下列情况下常用模糊语言:

1. 体现法律条文的预见性及适用性

《香港合约法纲要》(Digest of Hong Kong Contract Law)中规定:要约在要约人规定的期限内有效。如果要约人没有规定期限,要约在合理的期限内有效。合理的期限(a reasonable time)在此是一个事实问题,受要约规定的条件影响。英国上诉法院曾裁定:在能够合理地推定受要约人已经拒绝要约之际,合理期限即告结束。澳大利亚高等法院曾裁定:在可以推定要约人已经撤回要约之际合理期限即告结束。

2. 体现礼貌原则

在法庭辩论中的控辩双方律师或合议庭中的法官出于对他人的尊重及体现自身的修养,常使用委婉语或非直接用语以表述自己的不同意见。如:my lord, I take the strongest possible objection to the course proposed by my learned friend. 在此,strongest /objection 表达了不同意见,而 possible/learned/friend 显示了对他人的尊重。

3. 自我保护

在诸多合同关于数量、性质、时间的条款中,模糊词常被使用,主要是为了日后产生纠纷时能有效地保护自己。如一房地产商在其格式合同中写道:The greenery coverage will be between 25%～35%。在此,房地产商就有较大的余地来确定绿地覆盖面积。

4. 故意隐瞒信息

当一项交易涉及国家机密、商业秘密以及个人隐私时,其书面文字就可能含有模糊词。此外,一些虚假的商业广告也常用模糊语言。

七、近义词的重复使用表单一法律含义

法律英语经常用两个或三个意思相近或相同的赘词构成一个短语以表达法律上本来只需要一个词就能表达的概念。这也是法律英语词汇的重要特征之一。近义词的重复使用体现了法律语言的严肃性和法律用词的准确性和严密性,避免意思曲解。请看例句:

例 8

It is the intent of the parties that all documents and annexes forming part hereof shall be read and taken together and that each and every provision or stipulation hereof be given full force, effect and applicability. However, in the event that one or more provisions or stipulations herein be declared null and void by the courts, or otherwise rendered ineffective, the remaining provisions and stipulations shall not be affected thereby.

(陈建平,2007:14)

本句中同义词的重复使用多达七处。each and every, provisions or stipulations, null and void 等均属典型的同义重复使用。

例 9

It is an offence for any person taking part in a riot to unlawfully and with force (a) <u>prevent, hinder or obstruct, or attempt to prevent, hinder, or obstruct</u>, the loading or unloading, or the movement of; or (b) <u>board, or attempt to board</u> with intent to do so; <u>any motor vehicle, tramcar, aircraft, train or vessel</u>.

另外,如在租赁合约中,通常都会包含这样的条款,即 well and sufficiently repair, uphold, maintain the premises。其中 well 修饰 repair 已经 sufficient (足够),sufficiently 其实是完全多余的。而另外三个同义的动词——repair, uphold, maintain,只要保留其中的最简单、最常用的 repair 就足以表达合同的一方要求另一方妥善维修房屋的意图,但法律语言偏偏要重复使用这些词,使句意达到高度完整、准确。请看下面的例子:

terms and conditions	obligation and liability
interpretation and construction	acknowledge and confess
alter and change	cease and desist
fraud and deceit	free and clear
keep and maintain	fair and equitable
full and complete	save and except

法律英语术语在法律英语的学习中起着举足轻重的作用。对于广大的法律英语爱好者来说,了解和研究法律英语术语的特点和文体特征具有十分重要的意义。

第二章　英美法律术语汉译策略

法律术语是法律语言最重要的组成部分,术语翻译的精确性直接体现司法的权威公正性。准确严谨是法律术语翻译的灵魂。本章结合法律翻译的实践,探讨了英美法律术语汉译的思维过程,给出了相应的翻译策略并指出译者应该认真对待三种法律语言现象:注意法律语言的与时俱进,注重汉语法律术语的表达习惯,尊重约定俗成的翻译。中文法律语言素养是英美法律术语汉译成功的关键。

一、概述

十八届四中全会提出加强涉外法律工作,我国的司法体制改革正处于攻坚阶段。英美法体系是世界上最成熟的法律体系之一。因其示范作用,我国近年学习研究英美法的高潮迭起,但英美法的汉译,尤其是英美法律术语的汉译乱象丛生,值得关注。

法律术语具有法定的语义,有法定的适用范围,要求特定的语境。法律术语的正确使用是法律严肃性和准确性的保证。法律术语所表达的概念限定在法律范围内,所指称或反映的现象和本质是从法律角度观察和理解的。因此,理解和使用法律术语必须以整个法律系统为参照系。关于法律翻译,David M. Walker 指出:不同法律体系中没有完全对等的法律概念和分类体系是最大的困难之一。法律翻译中术语的翻译具有特别重要的意义。

二、英美法律术语汉译过程

法律翻译不再被认为是语言转换的过程,而是在法律机制中进行的交际活动,旨在翻译中实现法律功能(legal function)的对等。所谓法律功能对等就是源语和译入语在法律上所起的作用和效果的对等,目标是使译入语精确地表达源语的真正内涵。法律翻译在跨法系交际中,要重点实现对语言表象背后的没有用文字表述出来的法律文化和法律规约清楚表述。中国基本属于大陆法系,而英美两国属于普通法体系,法系的不同使得汉语和英语中的法律术语有很大差异,这就给译者提出了更高的要求:不仅要精通汉英语言,还应掌握充分的中美法律文化知识,并必须熟悉待译双语中的法律术语内涵及外延。

基于法律语言庄重、严谨等特点,准确严谨是法律翻译最基本的原则,术语翻译也不例外。英美法律术语汉译一般应遵循以下三个步骤:

(一)根据具体语境弄清英美法律术语的准确定义,切忌"望文生译"。

比如 final judgement 经常被翻译为"终审判决",很显然,这是望文生义的翻译。译者首先应了解其英语定义:Final judgment refers to a court's last action that settles the rights of the parties and disposes of all issues in controversy, except for the award of costs (and, sometimes, attorney's fees) and enforcement of the judgment. This is also termed as final appealable judgment or final decision or final decree or definitive judgment or determinative judgment or final appealable order. 在汉语语境中,终审判决是法院对案件的最后一级判决。我国实行两审终审制,中级人民法院、高级人民法院和最高人民法院的第二审就是终审。最高人民法院的第一审也是终审。终审判决是不可以上诉的。但根据定义,final judgment 是 appealable,很显然译为"终审判决"是误译,而应译为"最后判决"或者"判决"。judgment of last resort 才对应"终审判决"。

把 personal jurisdiction 译成"属人管辖权""人事管辖权"是否正确?判断

翻译正确与否的首要标准是弄清源语术语的准确含义。请看英美法上的定义：Personal jurisdiction or in personam jurisdiction is the jurisdiction, over the person of the defendant, which can be acquired only by service of process upon the defendant in the state to which the court belongs or by his voluntary submission to jurisdiction. The court must have in personam jurisdiction over a person in order to try a case against that specific individual. In addition to the mandatory requirement of having subject-matter jurisdiction, a court needs to acquire in personam jurisdiction over the respondent/defendant. Any order issued by a judge in the absence of both subject-matter jurisdiction and in personam jurisdiction is void, or of no legal force or effect. Personal jurisdiction is obtained when the respondent/defendant is properly served with a summons and complaint either by certified mail, by personal service, or by publication (only rarely used and only when the address of the respondent/defendant is unknown).

将 personal jurisdiction 译为"属人管辖权"或"人事管辖权"均不妥，一是因为属人管辖权在我国已有特定含义：属人管辖权又称国籍管辖权，是指国家对于具有本国国籍的人，无论在国内还是国外，都有行使管辖的权力。二是因为"人事"(personnel)这一概念在我国已有约定俗成的特定内涵，与其管辖权制度中的含义不符，personnel 与该术语中的 personal 字面含义也不相同。"人事管辖权"也会被误认为是"人事争议仲裁管辖权"的简称。另一种常见的译法"对人管辖权"是正确的吗？美国各州对被告有两个管辖依据：一是针对被告的人身，传统上这种管辖依据用拉丁文 in personam 表示。因此这种建立在被告人身基础上的管辖权也就被称为 in personam jurisdiction。二是针对被告的财产(rem)。由于以被告的财产作为管辖依据时有的是针对财产本身的所有权，有的仅是以该财产来偿还债务。所以又进一步将其分为两类：对物管辖权(in rem jurisdiction)，准对物管辖权(quasi-in-rem jurisdiction)。

可见，personal jurisdiction 是一个统称。从当事人的角度看，既包括对原告的管辖权也包括对被告的管辖权。就对被告的管辖权而言，根据管辖权依据的不同，又包括三大类：对人管辖权、对物管辖权和准对物管辖权。所以将 personal jurisdiction 译为"对人管辖权"至少不准确，不能体现 personal jurisdiction 是对人管辖权、对物管辖权和准对物管辖权三种管辖权的上位概念。根据定义，personal jurisdiction 决定被告在哪个州被起诉，是属地管辖。译为"对人管辖权"并将其与作为对物管辖权和案件类别管辖权（subject-matter jurisdiction）相对应的概念，显然不能体现概念中的属地性质。将 personal jurisdiction 与对物管辖权以及案件类别管辖权相并列也不符合美国的立法实际。在美国立法中，与 personal jurisdiction 相并列的应是案件类别管辖权和审判地（venue），它们三者共同构成美国民事诉讼中具体法院选择的三个标准。所以，将 personal jurisdiction 译为"州域管辖权"或"区域管辖权"比较合适。

英美法中还有个常见术语 next friend，如果不看其英语定义，译者根本无从下手。A next friend is someone who, without being formally appointed guardian, acts for the benefit of an infant, married woman, or other person who is unable to act independently. It is a person who is appointed by or admitted to a court to act in behalf of a minor or other party under legal disability. 分析其定义内涵，我们也就不难把 next friend 译为"（未成年人、已婚妇女或其他无民事行为能力人的）诉讼代表人"。

法律术语都有特定的概念和意义，不可随便改变。因此译者应该尽可能地寻求和源语对等或是接近对等的术语进行翻译，但前提是首先搞清源语术语的准确定义。再比如 brief 一词，Black Law Dictionary 对该词的定义是 It is a document prepared by a counsel as a basis for arguing a case. 所以并不能简单地将其译成"案情摘要"。在美国诉讼实务中 brief 一般指诉讼双方律师撰写的向法院提交的一种重要法律文件，包括 trial court brief 和 appellate court brief 两大类，并有严格的格式要求（一般包括 statement of issue, statement of the case, statement of the facts, summary of the argument, argument, standard of review, conclusion 等几部分），所以译为"律师辩论书"是合适的。在英国 brief 是事务律师委托出庭律师出庭的聘书，有时也指"案情摘要"。

看到美国法中的 Attorney-General 不要匆匆将其译成"大律师""检察长"等。美国没有检察院，其检察功能合并在司法部内，这就是我们常说的美国实行的是"大司法"，我国实行的是"小司法"。Attorney-General 应该翻译成"司法部长"而非其他。所以，英美法律术语汉译要根据术语所处的具体语境和定义确定合适的翻译。

(二)要谙熟中国法律语言和文化,切忌生搬硬套。

英美法律术语汉译要求译者一定熟悉中国法的有关内容。英语和汉语中的法律术语都各有其特定的法律上的意义,不可随便改变形式。为了达到法律上的功能对等,译者应尽量寻求在本国法律中与源语对等或接近对等的正式用语,而不是任意创造,以免引起歧义。

我们常见到把 reckless driving 译成"危险驾驶罪"。乍一看上去,好像是非常精准的翻译,先了解一下中国法的危险驾驶罪的定义:危险驾驶罪是指在道路上醉酒驾驶机动车,或者在道路上驾驶机动车追逐竞驶,情节恶劣的行为。再比较一下 reckless driving 的源语定义:Reckless driving refers to driving with a willful or wanton disregard for safety. It is the operation of an automobile under such circumstances and in such a manner as to show a willful or reckless disregard of consequences. In such cases the driver displays a wanton disregard for the rules of the road; often misjudges common driving procedures and causes accidents and other damages. It is usually a more serious offense than careless driving, improper driving, or driving without due care and attention and is often punishable by fines, imprisonment, and/or driver's license suspension or revocation. As a general rule something more than mere negligence in the operation of an automobile is necessary to constitute the offense. Many U.S. states have reckless driving statutes and specifics vary from state to state. Where statutes proscribed reckless driving by use of the terms "careless manner," "carelessly and heedlessly," "carelessly," or "careless, inattentive, or imprudent manner," it has been held that they are constitutionally valid, in that their terms are well known and clear, giving definite warning of the proscribed activity, and that they set forth the necessary elements of the offense. As a general rule, what constitutes reckless driving is to be determined from all the surrounding circumstances, at least where the statute does not specifically declare what particular acts shall constitute the offense.

通过比较,这两个定义内涵差别还是比较大的,把 reckless driving 翻译成

"危险驾驶罪"是不准确的。能否译成中国法中相近的"交通肇事罪"？译者需考查一下交通肇事罪的定义：指违反交通运输管理法规，因而发生重大交通事故，致人重伤、死亡或者使公私财产遭受重大损失的行为。显然，译成"交通肇事罪"也不合适，所以我们只能谨慎地创造个新罪名"鲁莽驾驶罪"来完成任务。

再比如，我们常把美国宪法中的 police power 译为"警察权"。尽管我们熟悉这三个汉字，但我们很难理解什么是警察权。请看源语术语的定义：In the United States constitutional law, <u>police power is the capacity of the states to regulate behavior and enforce order within their territory for the betterment of the health, safety, morals, and general welfare of their inhabitants.</u> Under the Tenth Amendment to the United States Constitution, the powers not specifically delegated to the Federal Government are reserved to the states or to the people. This implies that the Federal Government does not possess all possible powers, because most of these are reserved to the State governments, and others are reserved to the people. Police power is exercised <u>by the legislative and executive branches of the various states through the enactment and enforcement of laws.</u> States have the power to compel obedience to these laws through <u>whatever measures they see fit</u>, provided these measures do not infringe upon any of the rights protected by the United States Constitution or in the various state constitutions, and are not unreasonably arbitrary or oppressive. Methods of enforcement can include legal sanctions, physical means, and other forms of coercion and inducement. Controversies over the exercise of police power can arise when its exercise by the federal government conflicts with the rights of the states, or when its exercise by federal or state authorities conflicts with individual rights and freedoms.

根据定义，所谓的警察权包括政府的安全、健康、道德、教育等权力。根据美国宪法，州拥有非列举权力。联邦政府拥有列举性的权力，而没有在宪法中明确列举的权力留给各州行使。美国宪法第十条修正案主要用于保护州的权力不受联邦政府侵害。在这个条款之下，联邦政府拥有列举权力和由此而引申出来的暗含的权力，其他权力归人民和州政府。联邦宪法及其修正案的诸条款确立了美国的联邦制原则。法律文本列举的内容是有限的，但社会生活涉及方方面面，经济发展、文化教育、安全卫生、社会福利等等都是每个政府要面对的问题。根据联邦制原则，所有这些具体问题的管理和规范都由各州承担。在美国宪法性法律中，州管理经济和社会各个方面的权力综合到一起就是 the police power。

在汉语语境中，我们正好有个"社会治安综合治理"概念，指的是在党委、政府统一领导下，在充分发挥政法部门特别是公安机关骨干作用的同时，组织和依靠各部门、各单位和人民群众的力量，综合运用政治的、经济的、行政的、法律的、文化的、教育的等多种手段，通过加强打击、防范、教育、管理、建设、改造等方面的工作，实现从根本上预防和治理违法犯罪，化解不安定因素，维护社会治安持续稳定的一项系统工程。所以，我们不妨把 police power 译为"社会治安综合治理权"。

我们常把 presumption of innocence 译成"无罪推定"或"疑罪从无"，其实这两个术语还是有区别的：无罪推定是刑事诉讼的一般原则和精神，较为抽象，适用于判决前的各个诉讼阶段，是一种假定；而疑罪从无则是一个操作性的原则，很具体，主要适用于事实存在疑问的情况，是一种解决方法；无罪推定是判决确定有罪前，推定为无罪，主要作用是防范错案，并防止司法人员先入为主，事实上就是要求要客观中立地办案；而疑罪从无是在具体事实搞不清楚的情况下，做有利于被告人的推定，即视为没有发生过这种事实，事实上就是要求宁可放纵犯罪，也不能冤枉无辜。无罪推定是英美法术语，疑罪从无是我们自己的法律概念，不能混淆。拉丁语 in dubio pro reo 正好对应"疑罪从无"，也可译成 innocent until proven guilty。

再比如 unjust enrichment 可直译为"不当得利"，但其法律含义却比《中华人民共和国民法典》（以下简称《民法典》）中的不当得利宽泛得多，不但包含了《民法典》中第九百八十五条"不当得利"、第九百七十九条"无因管理"，而且还有违反信托义务（fiduciary duty）和侵犯他人知识产权所取得的利益。agreement 和 contract，可分别译为"协议"和"合同"，在中国法律中似乎没有什么区别。但根据英美法规定，有要约和承诺，便是 agreement，而 agreement 只有在采取书面形式或有对价（consideration）支持的情况下，才能成为 contract，具有法律效力。所以，译者一定要熟悉中国法的内容，按照法律英文原意进行准确翻译。

(三)如果在中国法语境里无法找到合适的对等术语,就要敢于合理创造。

中国法学的语言环境是一个外来语世界,外来语构成了中国法学的主要常用术语。在 20 世纪的最后 20 年里,大量英文法学著作翻译成中文,中国法律又出现了许多来自英文的外来语。在 1999 年颁布的新合同法里,可以看到来自德文、拉丁文和英文的外来语混合在一起,例如:同时履行抗辩(exception on adimpleti contrattus)、不安抗辩(unstable counter-argument right)、代位权(right of subrogation)等等。

加强涉外法律工作,推动司法体制改革,中国需要借鉴援引英美法国家的立法经验,适时地援引英美国家司法活动中有关的法律术语。因为很多英美法中的术语所涉及的概念、制度在汉语法律语言里根本就不存在接近对等和对等的词,所以,译者可以在正确理解源语词义的基础上,进行合理创造。像专利(patent)、巡回法庭(circuit court)、地役权(easement)等早已进入汉语法律语言。

法律翻译的创造性主要体现在法律术语或概念的翻译方面。对跨法系的法律术语进行翻译的难点在于如何找到或创造出与源语法律功能对等的法律术语。译者可以通过给普通语言或其他专业领域中现有的术语赋予法律涵义,使用别的法律制度中现有的术语或者创造新的术语。在法律翻译中最常见的是使用源语法律制度已有的术语直译对等词,例如,把 reasonable doubt 译为"合理怀疑",把 Miranda Warning 译成"米兰达警告",fruit of the poisonous tree 译成"毒树之果",equity court 译成"衡平法院"等等就是使用了直译对等词。中国法律制度中没有"米兰达警告""毒树之果"和"衡平法院"这些概念,因此可以说直译对等术语是创造新术语的一种形式,但是创造新的法律术语必须谨慎,译者要尽可能掌握第一手材料,正确理解源语术语的真正含义。法律翻译权威机构应制定统一标准,定期向社会公布标准译文,以使新的法律术语的翻译统一而规范。

三、术语翻译应该注意的三种语言现象

要做好英美法律术语的汉译工作,还应注意以下三种法律语言现象:

(一)要注意英美法律术语的与时俱进

英美法律语言也在循序演变的过程中。英美法中的 burglary 一词曾被定

义为 the breaking and entering of the dwelling house of another person at night with the intention to commit a felony of larceny inside,即行为人以犯重罪或盗窃为目的破门窗闯入他人住宅的行为。曾被译为"夜盗行为""夜盗罪"。当今的美国刑法对 burglary 的定义已有了很大的修订:the entry into a building illegally with intent to commit a crime, especially theft; the crime of so doing。时间不局限于夜间,地点不仅是住宅,也可以包括其他建筑物等等,美国《统一刑事案例汇编》(Uniform Crime Reports)(1998)甚至对 burglary 的定义简单到"为犯重罪或偷窃而非法进入某一建筑内",也不管进入该建筑内是否使用了暴力。为了伤害、强奸甚至杀害某人而进入他人住宅或其他建筑物(不一定是使用暴力的强行闯入),同样也构成 burglary。所以,burglary 一词可译为"恶意侵入他人住宅罪"。现在再把 burglary 译成"夜盗罪"显然是不合适的。

看到 enterprise crime 不要直接翻译成"企业犯罪",谁都不明白企业犯罪到底是一种什么犯罪。原来 enterprise crime 是由 organized crime 发展而来的。在英美国家,organized crime 固属"有组织的犯罪"之列,但人们心目中的 organized crime 按已经形成的语言习惯却是专指帮会犯罪,如三 K(KKK)党等,因此英美法律工作者在20世纪80年代别出心裁,又创造了 enterprise crime 一词来专门表示"有组织的犯罪"。请看定义:Enterprise crime is any organized or group of persons engaged in a continuing illegal activity which has as its primary purpose the generation of profits. Beside the main activities being illegal under various state and federal laws, there are also laws which deal with money laundering from organized crime activities. Criminal organizations keep their illegal dealings secret, and members communicate by word of mouth. Many organized crime operations have profitable legal businesses, such as licensed gambling, building construction, or trash hauling which operate alongside and provide "cover" for the illegal businesses.

法律术语的含义在不断发展演变。administrator 原指任何"管理人",自从20世纪80年代以来,在英美获得新义"法庭指定的破产公司管理人"。法律翻译工作者对新词的内涵及生成背景要高度重视。译者必须注意运用那些能确切表达原文本产生时其内在意义的术语。如果译者忽略了法律术语的与时俱进,则会导致严重的后果。这是发生在纽约的真实案例:澳大利亚当局授权原告与其配偶 scheidung 的判决已经生效,按规定对判决进行了翻译。由于判决是在 1938 年以前做出的,scheidung 在当时澳大利亚法律中根本不像今天是 divorce(离婚)的意思,而是分居。然而译者用了 divorce 这一词,由于译者的错误,尽管原告只是从法律意义上与第一个妻子分居,但他还是被允许在纽约重新结婚。

(二)要注重汉语法律术语语言表达习惯

英美法律术语汉译一定要注重汉语法律术语的表达习惯和语言内涵。"海商"与"海事"是海商法理论与实践中使用频率颇高的两个词,作为一对词义相近,又相互包含与交叉的概念,使用时要避免混淆。伴随航运立法国际统一化的趋势,众多的国际公约不加区别地使用 maritime law 和 admiralty law,使得两词含义逐渐趋同。请看英美法上的定义:Admiralty law or maritime law is the distinct body of law (both substantive and procedural) governing navigation and shipping. Topics associated with this field in legal reference works may include: shipping; navigation; waters; commerce; seamen; towage; wharves, piers, and docks; insurance; maritime liens; canals; and recreation. Piracy (ship hijacking) is also an aspect of admiralty.

按照我国海商法学界的习惯,通常将 admiralty 译为"海事",将 maritime 译为"海商"。虽然两词在英美国家的含义已经基本等同,但作为外来语译入词,"海商"与"海事"在融入中国本土化语境的过程中,其字面含义以及在中国法律体系中的用语解释却衍生出了自己独特的内涵。最典型的就是对两个词所做的狭义和广义的理解。所谓狭义的"海事",通常指造成航海财产损失或人身伤亡的事故,包括船舶碰撞、海难救助、残骸打捞、共同海损等;而广义的"海事",则泛指与海有关的活动。狭义的"海商",一般是指与海相关的商业活动,如海上货物运输及旅客运输、船舶租赁、海上保险等;广义的"海商"则是指与海上运输或船舶有关的活动,侧重于商业行为,但不限于商业范畴。人们在使用这两个词的时候,根据特定的情形,取其特定的含义。一般来说,海商法是专指以法典形式存在的法律,是法律的一个部门。海事法不是法典的名称,也不是一个独立的法律部门,而是一类法律的总和或者概括。海商法和海事法是两个独立的不同概念,翻译时要严加注意。

英美法律术语汉译需要认真取舍不同的汉字所表示的内涵，做到咬文嚼字，对汉语言文字要高度敏感。比如"黑车"和"黑色车"含义是不同的；legal person 到底翻译成"法人""法定代表人"还是"法定代理人"？这三个术语所表述的内涵都是不同的；silent partner 应该译成"隐形合伙人"，而不是"隐名合伙人"或"隐性合伙人"。这类译例不胜枚举。英美法律术语汉译一定要注意汉语法律术语的表述习惯。

（三）要尊重约定俗成的翻译

英美法律术语汉译过程中出现了一些翻译欠妥的译例，有些翻译甚至就是错误的，但我们要尊重接受这些约定俗成的翻译。比如把 intellectual property 译成"知识产权"就是不妥当的。这个术语不论从字面看、按含义译都不能译为"知识产权"。intellectual 一词根本没有"知识"的意思，它与"知识"是两个完全不同的概念。作为名词 intellectual 指"知识分子"，但是在 intellectual property 术语中 intellectual 显然是形容词而不是名词，何况"知识分子"与"知识"并不能画等号。从定义上看（Intellectual property (IP) is a term referring to creations of the intellect for which a monopoly is assigned to designated owners by law. Some common types of intellectual property rights (IPR) are trademarks, copyrights, patents, industrial design rights, and in some jurisdictions trade secrets: all these cover music, literature, and other artistic works; discoveries and inventions; and words, phrases, symbols, and designs.) intellectual property 指对于智力劳动所创造的智力产品或智力成果的权利，主要包括版权、专利权、商标权等，所以应该译为"智力产权"，在中国台湾和香港，则通常称之为"智慧财产权"或"智力财产权"。

我们要了解并接受诸如此类的约定俗成的误译。比如 common law 译成普通法是误译，我们没必要一定要将其更名译为"共同法"，也没必要一定要正名把美国的 Department of State 翻译为美国外交部。

四、结语

译者应该在法律术语翻译原则指导下，积极学习掌握法律语言的规律特点，努力提高法学素养，机动灵活地运用上述翻译策略，出色完成英美法律术语的汉译工作。中国法律语言素养是英美法律术语汉译成功的关键。法律翻译界要加强法律术语的规范和统一工作。只有规范以法律术语为核心的法律翻译,才能保证有效的中美司法交流,推动我国的司法体制改革,提升我国法治国际传播效能,提高我们在国际法律事务中的话语权。法律术语翻译乱象必须得到有效整治。

第三章　法律翻译中的文化传递

　　法律语言是法律文化的载体,法律文化是法律语言形成的基础环境。法律翻译跨越语言学、法学和翻译学三大领域,是沟通不同法律体系的重要途径,是语言转换和文化移植的双重过程,直接影响着不同法律文化间的交流效果。因此,在法律翻译过程中,译者必须注重文化考量,充分了解中外不同法律文化的基本内涵和特色,语言文化双管齐下,从而实现等效法律翻译。

一、法律文化与法律翻译

　　"一带一路"建设日益推进,众多中国企业参与国际竞争。由于中外法律体系、文化观念、价值理念等客观因素的差异,中国企业在与国际企业合作中,因翻译不当导致的冲突时有发生,遭受了巨大经济损失。这一现象已经引起企业界和学术界的高度关注。

　　十八届四中全会对发展涉外法律服务业、培养涉外法治人才队伍做出了重要部署,提出了明确要求。《教育部、中央政法委关于坚持德法兼修实施卓越法治人才教育培养计划2.0的意见》提出加快培养涉外法律人才。培养合格的涉外法律人才,尤其是"精英明法"的国际化人才,国家需要大批高素养的法律英语翻译人才。法律翻译,特别是法律英语翻译是涉外法律工作的重要内容之一,其重要性是由英语法律语言的国际通用语地位决定的。在当前国内涉外法律人才奇缺的情况下,涉外法律工作必须借助法律翻译才能完成,所以,可以说法律翻译人才是涉外法律人才的一种。

(一)法律文化的内涵

20世纪80年代末,伴随我国的对外开放和司法体制改革,作为舶来品的"法律文化"(legal culture)一词才开始在法学界走红。法律文化是文化的一种具体形态。由于"文化"概念本身错综复杂,对法律文化的解释,学者们观点莫衷一是。在西方,首创"法律文化"一词的是美国学者劳伦斯·弗里德曼,他在《法律文化与社会发展》一文中最先提出并界定了法律文化的含义,"法律文化是指公众对法律制度的了解、态度和行为模式。法律文化是与整个文化具有有机联系的有血有肉的习惯……"(Friedman,1969);英国学者拜尔对这一概念进行了更加宏观的阐述,"法律文化包含历史、制度环境、立法与司法活动、法律行为者的观念和态度、法律职业者、构成性规范和价值等,它包括全部法律现象"(Bell,2001:12)。我国学者也从不同角度对法律文化进行了定义:"法律文化是人类文化系统中不能缺少的一个组成部分,是社会精神文明的重要构成;法律文化是人类在漫长的文明进步过程中从事法律活动所创造的智慧结晶和精神财富,是社会法律现象存在与发展的文化基础;法律文化是法律意识形态以及与法律意识形态相适应的法律制度、组织机构等总和"(刘作翔,1992:36);"所谓法律文化,既是一种现象,又是一门科学,还是一种方法。谈论法律文化,首先是把法律作为一种文化现象来把握。任何一种有效的法律,都必定与生活于其下的人民的固有观念有着基本协调的关系"(梁治平,1987)。

文化先于制度。尽管以上对法律文化的定义表述不一,但都赞同法律文化受各个国家、地区或民族文化的影响而具有独特性,可涉及历史、环境、习俗、社会制度、意识形态、价值观念等方面。法律就是文化,法律制度的移植或借鉴离不开法律文化。因此,法律翻译要做到等效,译者必须重视中外法律文化的差异性。

(二)法律翻译的文化性特征

法律翻译是一种跨文化交流活动,法律文化可具体为源语和目的语中的法律制度、规范、组织,法律心理、思想、习惯以及整个法律运行环境。法律文化融于整个社会文化系统,但又自成体系。法律文化与一个国家的文明发展程度紧密相关,法律翻译要适时传递法律文化信息。

法律翻译作为涉外法律工作的重要内容之一,目的语语言表述准确甚为关键。法律翻译之所以难,是因为法律语言反映法律文化,并受法律文化的制约。要有效地从事法律翻译活动,译者不但要有相关法律知识、双语能力,而且还要有法律相关的双文化乃至多文化知识,特别是对两种法律语言的民族心理意识、文化形成过程、历史习俗传统、宗教文化,甚至地域风貌特征等一系列互变因素均要有一定的了解。这是法律翻译的文化特征决定的。

二、影响法律翻译的文化因素

语言的发展常常折射文化的变迁。翻译是通过语言机制的转换连接或沟通自身文化和异域文化的桥梁,它不仅涉及两种语言,而且还涉及两种社会文化,并受到多种因素的影响。

(一)词源因素

法律英语主要指英美等普通法国家在立法、司法过程中使用的专业语言。法律英语术语大多来自于日常用语,也有专门术语、行话和借用术语,其中外来法律术语主要来源于法语和拉丁语。例如,来源于法语的 jury(陪审团)、de facto marriage(事实婚姻)、voir dire(挑选陪审员过程)等;来源于拉丁语的 ad hoc(专门的)、custody(拘留)、appeal(上诉)、ex post facto(追溯)等。此外,法律英语中也在使用很多古英语词汇,它们在长期的使用过程中已经形成了为人们所公认的特定含义,例如,herein(此处)、whereby(由此)、hereto(至此)、aforesaid(上述的)等。中国的法律术语中也存在着古词语,如"大赦""诉状""自首"等以及一些文言虚词,如"兹""上述"等。

(二)法系因素

目前,世界上影响最大的两个法系是大陆法系和英美法系。大陆法系主要以德国、法国为代表,比较注重法典的编纂,将成文法典作为最关键的法律渊源。英美法系以美国、英国为代表,比较注重判例。两个法系的根本区别在于法律观念的不同,大陆法系注重理性,英美法系强调经验。此外,法系的差异还反映在诉讼程序上，英美法系的诉讼程序复杂，例如审前证据开示(discovery)流程，在大陆法系中就不存在。英国和美国属于同一法系，两者在法律渊源、司法程序和法律适用等方面存在共性，但在具体的法律体制上也存在着许多差异，如司法机关的名称、设置、职能等。

(三)思维因素

西方国家从思维形式上侧重于抽象思维。早在罗马时代，就已经有了契约、侵权责任、不当得利等法学概念。同时，西方国家的思维也是一种"求异"思维，注重逻辑，这种方式导致了整个社会鼓励创造，推崇创新。而中国则惯于形象思维，相信"人之初性本善"，注重道德培养，强调法律的感情因素。因此，由于思维方式不同，英汉民族在观察事物和现象时的角度会有所不同，甚至是相反的。这种思维上的差异也表现在语言上，例如法律英语中的 Law of Unfair Competition 译成"反不正当竞争法"；Statute of Frauds 译成"防止欺诈条例"。英美法律文件中的 Put an ×，不能直译为"打×号"，应译为"打√号"或"签字画押"。

(四)历史宗教因素

各国的法律都与本国历史紧密相连。要理解法国对宗教的规范措施，就必须了解1789年大革命前的法国及19世纪后期的政治斗争，否则，就不可能真正理解法国法律。不了解英国18和19世纪在印度扮演的角色，便无法理解印度的法律。不了解英国历史，就很难理解大宪章(The Great Charter)。

外国法律与宗教密不可分。今天德国的平稳状态是基督教徒与天主教徒大体势均力敌的结果，但这曾是激烈斗争的根源。英美国家受基督教影响最大，连美元上都印有"我们相信上帝"(In God We Trust)，新任美国总统要手按圣经宣誓就职。基督教文化相信"人性本恶""人生来都是有罪的"，所以极力推崇法律，不注重道德说教。美国宪法第一修正案规定了政教分离和宗教自由，这是文明国家第一次用法制的形式把政教分离问题法律化、明确化。

三、文化缺省下的法律术语误译

术语翻译是法律翻译的关键。术语翻译的准确与否直接关系到翻译质量的优劣。术语翻译错了，就极可能造成误解，甚至酿成纠纷。下面仅举数例"没文化"的误译：

（一）望文生义导致的误译

把 attorney in fact 译成"实际律师、事实律师"，这是望文生义的逐字硬译。精准汉译英美法律术语，可靠的方法当然是查阅该术语的源语释义：An attorney who may or may not be a lawyer who is given written authority to act on another's behalf esp. by a power of attorney. 指经授权委托书授权主要从事非诉讼活动者，多在庭外处理委托事务，不一定具有律师资格。所以 attorney in fact 应译为"委托代理人"。attorney at law 才是我们通常意义上讲的"律师"。类似的例子还有 death benefit，不要轻率地将其译为"死亡利益、死亡好处费""丧葬费"等，根据其定义：Amount paid under insurance policy on death of insured. A payment made by an employer to the beneficiary or beneficiaries of a deceased employee on account of the death of the employee. 所以，death benefit 应译为"死亡抚恤金；死亡保险金"；Death grant（State grant to the family of a person who has died, which is supposed to contribute to the funeral expenses.）才是"丧葬费"。有人把 Federal Public Defender Office 译为"联邦安全办公室"，其实应该译为"联邦公共刑辩律师办公室"；美国法中常见到 reasonable person，在法律语境下，应译为"普通正常人"，国内法学教材中译为"理性人"是欠妥的。

（二）法律文化差异导致的误译

在美国，州最高法院一般都称为 the Supreme Court，但纽约州例外，其最高法院叫 the Highest Court，而 the Supreme Court 在该州却指初审法院。美国法庭上，律师通常称法官 Your Honour 或 Judge，例外的是按洛杉矶高等法院的规矩，不能当面称呼法官 Judge。在联邦最高法院，大法官必须被称呼为 Justice，首席大法官为 Chief Justice。美国的 associate justice 常被译为"副法官""助理大法官"或"陪审大法官"，其实都是误译。associate justice 与 justice 同义，都指大法官，只是和 chief justice（首席大法官）相对应而已，是不担任院长或审判长的大法官。

英国法官的称呼更加讲究，与法官所在法院的级别有密切关系。御前大臣（也称大法官 Lord Chancellor）为英格兰首席法律官员，同时兼任内阁成员及上议院议长;皇家首席大法官 Lord Chief Justice 为上诉法院刑事庭庭长,兼任高等法院王座庭庭长。在英格兰和威尔士,只有高等法院 High Court 以上的法官才被称为 My Lord /My Lady,有时也称 Your Lordship /Your Ladyship。一般的 Crown court 的首席法官因具有高等法院法官的地位才被称为 My Lord。我国香港律师对法官的称呼承袭了英国传统。在高等法院,诉讼双方都会尊称法官为 My Lord /My Lady 或 Your Lordship;在区域法院,则称法官为 Your Honour;在裁判法院会称裁判官为 Your Worship 或 Sir。

我们常说美国实行三权分立,其中的"司法权"是从 judicial 翻译过来的,但是中文语境下的"司法"包括公检法司,而美国法语境中的 judicial 仅指法院的审判权及法律解释权,这显然和中文的"司法"内涵不对应。此外,美国法中的 Attorney General 不能译成"大律师""检察长"等,应译成"司法部长"而非其他(张法连,2016),和 Chief Justice 应表述为"美利坚合众国首席大法官"一样,Attorney General 应表述为"美利坚合众国司法部长"而不是"美利坚合众国司法部部长"。

(三)一词多义导致的误译

issue 这个词在不同的语境下有不同的含义:He died without an issue. 中的 issue 应译为"子嗣";而在 What's the issue of this case? 中,issue is a legal term, refers to sth. to be decided by a judge,应译为"纷争点、争议点",所以需要特别指出的是"台湾问题"应译为 Taiwan Question 而不是 Taiwan Issue,否则台湾问题就成了国际问题,需要国际法庭法官裁判。再比如 He was awarded $1,000 damages for the injury he suffered in the accident. award 在普通英语中意为 to officially give a prize or money to someone for a special reason,而在法律语境下意为 judged by the court。

common law 也属一词多义现象,不能在任何语境下都译为"普通法"。从英美法系的发展史来看,该术语在不同语境中应作不同解释。common law 的本意是指在 1066 年英格兰被诺曼人征服后,英王派自己的法官到各个领主区域的法院,依据当地的习惯并参照诺曼人的法律观念审理案件,并将判决的内容用文字完整记载下来,成为日后相似案件判决的基础和参考。该法律的适用有一致的法律标准,且在全英国范围内具有普遍的约束力,故首先 common law 应译为"普遍法"或"共同法"。也有人认为与 civil law（大陆法）相对，把 common law 译为"海洋法"，也是欠妥，因现代法律体系中已有专门的海洋法（ocean law）。其次，当与 equity（衡平法）相对而言时，应译为"习惯法"。再次，当与 statutory law（成文法）相对而言时，应将 common law 译为"不成文法"，因前者以抽象法律条文为特征，而后者则以法院判决内容这种不成文的法律方式作为法律规范。最后，当与 cannon law 或 ecclesiastic law（教会法）相对而言时，应将 common law 译为"世俗法"。

（四）法系差异导致的误译

大陆法系与英美法系在法律渊源、法律结构、司法组织、诉讼程序和法官权限等方面存在着明显的差异，并体现在法律文化上。

cross-examination 这个词常被误译成"盘问""盘诘""反复讯问"。按照英美法系的审判制度，起诉方和被告方均可要求法院传唤证人出庭作证，在庭上先由要求传证人的一方向证人提问，然后再由对方向证人提问，也就是起诉方询问被告方的证人或被告方询问起诉方的证人，即双方交叉询问证人，所以 cross-examination 最好译成"交叉询问"。deposition 是英美诉讼法上特有的制度，可以由双方当事人在审判前互相询问对方或其证人进行采证，发生在审判前，而且是在庭外进行的（通常在一方律师的办公室举行），一般译作"庭外采证"或"庭外采取（的）证词或供词的笔录"。该词不同于中国法律制度中的"证词"或"法庭作证"，因而不能译成"录取证词"或"在法庭上作证"。把 jury 译为"陪审团"是典型的误译，请看其定义 jury：a body of citizens sworn to give a true verdict according to the evidence presented in a court of law。所以，jury 应译为"公众裁判团"。当然这一类误译已是"约定俗成"。

我国的人民陪审员制度与美国的陪审制度均被称为"陪审"，但是由于两大法系的渊源、文化历史传统等因素的差异，两者虽然中文名称相同但有实质差异。法律英语中的 juror 专指英美国家的陪审员，中国的陪审员应译成 judicial assessor，以示区别法系差异。我国刑事诉讼法中"取保候审"是否和美国刑事诉讼法中的 bail 相对应？二者具有相同点：都是刑事诉讼法概念，形式都为提供保证人或交纳保证金，对象都是犯罪嫌疑人，目的都是让犯罪嫌疑人随传随到，给予其一定程度的自由。二者不同点在于："取保候审"属于强制措施，虽程度较轻,但价值取向是限制犯罪嫌疑人自由,体现公权力;bail 体现的司法理念是无罪推定,是对民权的保护;批准主体不同,"取保候审"是公检法机关均有权决定,而 bail 一般由法官决定;实施细节不同,"取保候审"的保证金一般为现金,而 bail 也可为不动产。所以,把"取保候审"译为 bail 是欠准确的,用 post a bail and await trial with restricted liberty of moving 或 obtain guarantor pending trial 翻译"取保候审"则更好体现了中美法系的差异。

(五)词义相近导致的误译

英汉法律术语中存在着大量的类义词,即意思相近甚至同义,翻译时稍不注意就会混淆。法律翻译要做到正确措辞,准确理解术语的含义是前提。

美国侵权法中的 battery 和 assault 是对人身的故意侵权(intentional torts to a person)行为,包括殴打、威吓、非法监禁以及精神伤害等。A battery is the actual infliction of unlawful force on another person. battery 指被告故意对他人人身进行伤害性的、冒犯性的接触,其涵盖面广,只要碰到他人的身体以及与身体相连的东西,就算殴打或恶意触碰。battery 可译为"殴打""恶意触碰"。In the law of tort, an assault is an act that causes another person to apprehend the infliction of immediate unlawful force on his person. 在美国侵权法中,assault 指引起他人对即将发生的殴打产生合理警觉的行为。也就是说,被告的行为引起了他人对即将要发生的伤害的警觉,至于其行为是否伤害了原告,甚至是否触碰到了原告,法律并没有要求。因此,将 assault 译成"威吓、恫吓"更准确一些。这正是两个术语间的主要区别:殴打必须有身体上的接触,威吓则没有接触。殴打和威吓容易混淆,就是因为二者在时空上常同时出现,且相互转换。murder, manslaughter 和 homicide 通常都可译作"杀人",其实它们有很大区别。murder 指"故意杀人",即"谋杀",专指"有预谋的蓄意谋杀"(premeditated and deliberate murder),常可按情节分为一级和二级等多种等级的谋杀。manslaughter 指"过失杀人"或"误杀",着重于没有预谋的杀人,它分为无故意非预谋杀人罪(involuntary manslaughter)和非预谋但故意杀人罪(voluntary manslaughter)。manslaughter 是一种犯罪,应译成"防卫过当致人死亡罪"。homicide 指一个人的作为或不作为导致或促使他人的死亡,并非就道德或法律判定该行为一定为犯罪或有过错。所以,homicide 泛指所有的杀人,既包括意外的过失杀人,也包括故意杀人。在刑法上他杀可分为无罪杀人(lawful homicide)和有罪杀人(felonious homicide)两种。

中文法律语言中也含有大量的词义相近的法律术语,翻译时一定要先搞清楚其具体含义,否则做出的翻译就和源语大相径庭了。比如"交代"还是"交待"?在说"交代罪行""坦白交代"的时候,宜用"交代";在说吩咐、安排、总结工作等事情的时候,宜用"交待"。所以,"交代(罪行、问题)"可译为 confess 或 admit;"交待(工作)"则要译为 arrange。"吊销、撤销、注销"也有不同的含义:吊销是一种行政处罚行为,具有强制性和制裁性;撤销是一种对行政许可的法律收回行为,具有剥夺性和不可逆转性以及补救性;注销在一定程度上也是一种法律行为,具有程序性质,有时带有一定的惩罚性。所以翻译选词上要格外小心:注销登记 nullify the registration,吊销许可证 cancel/revoke a license,撤销案件 dismiss/withdraw a case。"被告"与"被告人"也是两个不同的概念。被告与原告相对应,是民事诉讼法律术语;而被告人与被害人、公诉人相对应,属刑事诉讼法律用语。所以"被告"只可译为 defendant,"被告人"也可译为 the accused。

四、法律文化考量下法律翻译策略

法律翻译比一般的语言翻译更为复杂,因为"法律翻译并不是用译入语中的概念和制度来替代原来的法律体系中的概念和制度的简单过程,而是一个包含语言转码和法律转码的双重解码过程"(Susan Sarcevic,1997)。因此,译者必须在两种文化之间找到相对应的语言表达方式,做出相应的转换。

(一)概念对等时使用确切对等词

中国属于大陆法系,如果其法律渊源中存在着与英语法律术语相对等的术语,则直接进行翻译,实现目的语词与源语词的一一对应。例如 plaintiff(原告),will(遗嘱),criminal law(刑法),等等。同时,还要注意法律英语中"近义词并用"的惯用法,如 null and void(无效),terms and conditions(条件),rights and interests(权益),等等。

(二)接近对等时使用功能对等词

如果汉语或英语中没有确切的对等词,译者可以在忠实原文的基础上选择功能对等词。例如英语中的 jail 和 prison,人们习惯于把两个词都译成"监狱"

而不加区分是不对的。jail 的用法更倾向于口语化,一般关押的是等待审讯的或者已判轻罪的犯人,更接近于中国的"看守所,拘留所";而 prison 关押的是已判刑,而且刑期较长的犯人,其功能对等词应该是"监狱,牢狱"。因此,选择功能对等词可以保证在没有确切对等词的情况下法律翻译的正确性和可接受性。

(三)部分对等时扩充词义

如果某个汉语功能对等词不能用来翻译源术语,此时可以用扩充词义的方法来限定或扩大对等词的意义。例如法律英语中 barrister 和 solicitor 两个术语都可译成"律师",但在英国英语里,barrister 的含义是指有资格在任何法庭作辩护的出庭律师;solicitor 的含义是一般事务性律师,不能出庭辩护。所以这两个术语分别译为"出庭律师"和"事务律师"意义就非常明确了。

(四)完全不对等时使用释义、中性词或新词

释义是指直接用译入语把源语中的意图内涵表达出来,这是解决缺少确切对等词的有效手段之一。例如,把法律英语中的 sunset law 译成"日落法"很令人费解,虽然译成了汉语,中国人却看不懂。这个术语的英语定义为:a statute that includes provision for automatic termination of a government program, agency, etc., at the end of a specified time period unless it is reauthorized by the legislature。意为"定期审查政府机构工作以便决定是否保留该机构或其工作计划之法律",即"定期废止法律",这样就一目了然了。采用释义法翻译,目的语读者能更好理解源术语的准确含义。

由于法律文化的不同,不少法律英语中的概念在汉语中找不到确切对等或接近对等的概念,只能用汉语中的某些中性词来翻译。例如在英美法系中,libel 和 slander 是侵权法的概念,而不是刑法的概念,对于侵害他人名誉者,受害人可以提起损害赔偿的诉讼。中国没有专门的侵权法,只有《侵权责任法》,有些侵权行为根据其严重程度分别由民法和刑法来调整,但中国有诽谤罪,可以译作 defamation。libel,slander 和"诽谤罪"显然不是对等的法律概念,这种情况下就要分别使用中性词"书面诽谤"和"口头诽谤"来翻译。

法律翻译过程中,当使用释义、中性词、扩充等都不能实现功能对等时,就需要创造新词。比如美国法中的 plea bargaining,指被告人就较轻的罪名或数项指控中的一项或几项做出 guilty plea(有罪答辩,指刑事被告人理智自愿地在法

庭上正式承认犯有受指控的罪行)就可以换取检察官的某种让步。这种检察官和被告人律师之间经过协商达成某种协议,通常是被告人获得较轻的判决或者撤销其他指控的有效途径,所以该术语可创造性地译为"认罪协商"。中国的司法体制改革借鉴域外经验,我们也建立了相应的"认罪认罚"制度。

五、结语

新时代背景下法律翻译工作日显重要。法律文化概念改变了人们对法律性质过于简单的理解。法律文化是法律语言之魂,任何一部法律的产生都伴随相应的法律文化背景。法律翻译是两个法律体系间的语言转换,是法律语言文化的跨语系交际行为。法律语言的翻译其实就是法律文化的翻译。法律翻译一定要注重法律文化的准确传递,只有这样,我们才能提高国家法律翻译能力,讲好中国法治故事。

第四章 法律英语术语误译解析

access right

该术语常被误译为"出入权""通行权""接触权"。很显然,误译的原因就是"望文生译"。根据前面章节提到的翻译策略,我们首先应该去查找该术语的源文英语解释,这才是法律术语翻译的基础和依据。

通过查阅《布莱克法律词典》(*Black's Law Dictionary*, 9th Edition),access right 的英语释义为:A right, granted in an order or agreement, of access to or visitation of a child. 并且还发现另一个相关术语及释义:

Right of Way: a person's legal right, established by usage or by contract, to pass through grounds or property owned by another.

根据源语的释义,access right 是美国家事法(Family law)术语,指离婚父母对不属于其监护的子女的一种见面、看望的权利。根据"以术语译术语"的原则,这时还不好确定到底是译成"探望权"还是

"探视权"。

查阅《民法典》第五编相关章节得知：探望权，又称见面交往权，是指离婚后不直接抚养子女的父亲或母亲一方享有的与未成年子女探望、联系、会面、交往、短期共同生活的权利。《民法典》婚姻家庭编：

> 第一千零八十六条　离婚后，不直接抚养子女的父或者母，有探望子女的权利，另一方有协助的义务。
>
> 行使探望权利的方式、时间由当事人协议；协议不成的，由人民法院判决。
>
> 父或者母探望子女，不利于子女身心健康的，由人民法院依法中止探望；中止的事由消失后，应当恢复探望。

查阅有关资料表明，"探视权"与"探望权"是一样的，只是名字不同罢了。探视权（探望权）是一种身份权。亲权是父母基于其身份所有的权利义务。探望权属于亲权范畴，探望权产生的基础是父母对子女享有的亲权，其权利的主体是离婚后不直接抚养未成年子女的父或母，是父母对未成年子女的特有权利，因此是一种身份权。

尽管如此，根据法律术语翻译的精准严肃性原则，最好将 access right 译为"探望权"，因为《民法典》条文里并没有提到"探视权"，况且在我国《监狱法》相关条款里提到了"探视权"。

根据英语解释，right of way 可译为"通行权"。另外，美国财产法还有一个常见专业术语 easement(the privilege of using another's land as a right of way to your own land)，可译为"地役权"，指在他人拥有的土地上通行经过的权利。

administrative revocation

该术语从字面来看就是"行政撤销"或"行政撤回"。中国的法律条款中有"行政许可的撤销""行政行为的撤销"等表述。行政许可的撤销，是指做出行政许可决定的行政机关或者其上级行政机关，根据利害关系人的请求或者依据其职权，对行政机关及其工作人员违法做出的准予行政许可的决定，依法撤销其法律效力的行为。根据《中华人民共和国行政诉讼法》第七十条的规定，行政行为有下列情形之一的，人民法院判决撤销或者部分撤销，并可以判决被告重新做出行政行为：1. 主要证据不足的；2. 适用法律、法规错误的；3. 违反法定程序的；4. 超越职权的；5. 滥用职权的；6. 明显不当的。

administrative revocation 到底有什么涵义，我们不能根据字面意思胡乱猜测，保险的做法是查找该术语的英文释义：

> Administrative revocation means termination of the arrestee's license pursuant to this part and does not include any revocation imposed under section 291－4.

这是美国夏威夷州的法律规定。基于英语释义我们可以确定的是该术语是对驾驶人员驾驶执照的吊销。可参照《英美法律术语辞典（英汉双解）》的译法，将该术语译为"吊销驾驶执照"。该术语不能译成"撤销驾驶执照"，吊销主要是针对严重违法行为或者重大事故主要责任以上的情况。撤销主要是针对业务程序过程中的不当或违法。

我们不妨多了解一下与 administrative revocation 密切相关的法律程序：Administrative hearing. (a) If the director administratively revokes the arrestee's license after administrative review, the arrestee may request an administrative hearing to review the decision within six days of the date the administrative review decision is mailed. The hearing shall be scheduled to commence no later than twenty-five days from the date the notice of administrative revocation was issued. The director may continue the hearing only as provided in subsection (d). 被捕的驾驶人员可以申请行政听证。

...

(d) The director shall conduct the hearing and have authority to：

(1) Administer oaths and affirmations；

(2) Examine witnesses and take testimony；

(3) Receive and determine the relevance of evidence；

(4) Issue subpoenas, take depositions, or cause depositions or interrogatories to be taken；

(5) Regulate the course and conduct of the hearing; and

(6) Make a final ruling.

由此可知，被捕人被吊销驾驶执照，被捕人在一定的时间期限内可以申请行政听证。这类听证是由法院的行政人员或其他司法机关的人员来进行的，并非法官主持。

advocate general

该术语从字面上理解很容易翻译为"大顾问""法律总顾问"；此外还有"护法顾问""大律师""法务助理""法律顾问官"等译法。我国的法律语境中并没有"大顾问""法律总顾问"等类似表述，上述译法不仅没有展现出该词的真正含义，还会使读者云里雾里，难以理解该词的具体指向。

《布莱克法律词典》对该术语的定义是：An officer appointed under the Scotland Act of 1998 to advise the British government on Scotland and to represent it in court.

Oxford Dictionary of Law（Oxford University Press，5th edition，2003）对该术语的定义：An assistant to the judge of the European Court of Justice whose function is to assist the court by presenting opinions upon every case brought before it. The Advocate General acts as an amicus curiae in putting forward arguments based upon his own view of the interests of the European Union, although it is not open to any of the parties to the legal action to submit observations on his opinion.

维基百科提供的定义：… in the European Union and some continental European jurisdictions, the officer is a neutral legal adviser to the courts.

根据以上定义可知 advocate general 主要使用于两种语境：其一，在法庭上代表英国政府并为其提供建议；其二，充当欧洲法院法官的助理，其职责是协助法院就提交的每个案件提出意见，但 advocate general 并不是代表欧盟利益的检察官或委员，总体上来说角色更贴近于法官但并不完全代表法官立场。

再者，还应了解该术语产生的背景以及其背后的法律制度。其一，advocate general 在英国通常被称为 King's/Queen's Advocate，通过任命状（letters patent）设立，为王室的首席法律官员，其在海事法院和教会法院中的职责是就民法、教会法和国际法方面的问题向王室提供咨询意见。该职位从未被正式废除，但自 1872 年起便一直空缺。在 1857 年律师公会（College of Advocates）被废除之前,其人选全部来自该公会。其二,1951年制定《欧洲煤钢联营条约》时,由于当时的共同体法律尚不成熟,法官不可能熟悉每个成员国的法律背景,因此欧洲法院参照了法国行政法,创造性地设立了 advocate general 一职,让本身具有成员国法学专业背景的 advocate general 参与到庭审程序中。advocate general 以其个性化的见解,为案件的解决方案提供建议。伴随着新成员国的不断加入,advocate general 制度吸收了不同成员国的国内法律乃至不同法律体系中的精华,形成了自己独具一格的意见书。advocate general 既不是代表当事人利益的律师,也不是代表欧盟利益的检察官或委员(欧盟委员会官员),更不是法官;他就是一个独立的个体,像法庭上的第四人,客观地以其所学协助法官做出合适的判决。

综上,advocate general 应根据不同的使用语境对应不同的译文:(英)王室首席法律顾问官;(欧盟法院)法务官。

agency of necessity

《英汉汉英双向法律词典》将该术语译为"必需代理",此种译法并不能让读者清楚其真正内涵。中国法律条款中没有完全同义等值的术语。

查阅《布莱克法律词典》可知,agency by necessity 与 agency of necessity 同义,agency by necessity 的英语释义是:A doctrine, esp. in English law, that confers authority to act for the benefit of another in an emergency without having obtained the latter's express consent; the relation between the person who so acts and the one to whom the benefit accrues. This is a quasi-contractual relation formed by the operation of legal rules and not by the agreement of the parties. —Also termed agency from necessity; agency of necessity.

该术语是指行为人在面临紧急情况时即使没有委托人的授权,也可视为被授权为委托人的利益而从事行为。这是依据法律规定的而不是委托人授权的代理行为。《元照英美法词典》将其译为"紧急事务的代理",意思比较接近,但未体现 without having obtained the latter's express consent。

这其实是中国法律中有关特殊代理权的一个问题。根据《民法典》第一百七十二条的规定,行为人没有代理权、超越代理权或者代理权终止后,仍然实施代理行为，相对人有理由相信行为人有代理权的，代理行为有效。委托代理权的取得根据是被代理人的授权行为。授权行为相当重要。重大事务的授权，以用书面形式为妥。用书面形式授权即签署授权委托书，授权委托书应当记载代理人的姓名或者名称、代理事项、代理权限及期限。《民法典》第一百六十九条规定：代理人需要转委托第三人代理的，应当取得被代理人的同意或者追认。转委托代理经被代理人同意或者追认的，被代理人可以就代理事务直接指示转委托的第三人，代理人仅就第三人的选任以及对第三人的指示承担责任。转委托代理未经被代理人同意或者追认的，代理人应当对转委托的第三人的行为承担责任；但是，在紧急情况下代理人为了维护被代理人的利益需要转委托第三人代理的除外。

根据前述法律术语翻译原则，如果在目标语法律体系中没有完全对应的法律术语，就要大胆创新，敢于创造一个新术语。所以 agency of necessity 可译为"紧急无授权代理"。

amicus curiae

该术语来源于拉丁语，因其英文释义为 friend of the court，故通常被译为：法庭之友、法院之友，此译法完全依照了英文释义的字面意思而进行翻译，属于"转译"，难免会忽略该拉丁语本身的丰富内涵。

《布莱克法律词典》对该术语的解释为：A person who is not a party to a lawsuit but who petitions the court or is requested by the court to file a brief in the action because that person has a strong interest in the subject matter。由此可见，amicus curiae 参与到诉讼中主要通过两种方式：主动向法庭提出请求，或者受法庭要求而加入。除此之外，实践中 amicus curiae 也可以基于对案件的浓厚兴趣或基于对公共利益的考虑而提交意见书，目的在于协助法院更公正地做出裁决。

《元照英美法词典》给出的译文及解释为：法庭之友，对案件中的疑难法律问题陈述意见并善意提醒法院注意某些法律问题的临时法律顾问；协助法庭解决问题的人。

amicus curiae 制度起源于古罗马法，经历了漫长的历史发展，早期运用于英国普通法中，然后运用于美国法律并且由此逐渐发展开来，当前国际、区域司法机构或贸易协定中也会频繁引用该制度。amicus curiae 制度通常指案件当事人之外的个人、团体或政府机关，对特定案件的事实或法律问题具有专业特长或独到见解，在法庭做出裁判（一般限于二审程序）之前，就法院所面临的法律等问题向法院提供意见。amicus curiae 为法院提供了不同于当事人的观点、意见、补充性事实和论据，目的在于帮助法庭做出公正合理的判决，而提交的意见则表现为支持一方当事人的主张或完全从公共利益的角度出发向法院提交意见。

综上，amicus curiae 完全是案件双方当事人之外以及法庭之外的独立个体，立场中立，不代表任何一方利益，"法庭之友""法院之友"的译法虽然明确了 amicus curiae 同法院一道属于中立方，但此种表述不能指明 amicus curiae 的职能且不具有法律语言的庄严性，显得过于随意。此外 amicus curiae 并不出现于所有案件中，法官可根据自由裁量权决定是否采用 amicus curiae 出具的意见（amicus brief）。我国的司法实践中虽然没有直接引入 amicus curiae 制度，但是存在"鉴定人""有专门知识的人""专家证人"等说法，他们协助解决案件疑难问题，与 amicus curiae 制度的价值考量有异曲同工之处。

综合考量，可参照《英美法律术语辞典》的译法，将该术语译为"法官顾问"。

apparent authority

该术语根据字面意思易被译为"明显的权力"，但这并非该术语的真实含义。

《布莱克法律词典》中的释义为：Authority that a third party reasonably believes an agent has, based on the third party's dealings with the principal, even though the principal did not confer or intend to confer the authority. Apparent authority can be created by law even when no actual authority has been conferred. Also termed ostensible authority; authority by estoppel. 指第三人从委托人的行为中合理推断或认为代理人应当享有的权限，即便无真正授权也可依据法律予以推定。

《路易斯安那法律评论》(*Louisiana Law Review*)[①] 第 33 卷中讲解 Apparent Authority in a Civil Law Jurisdiction 时提到第三人善意地认为代理人有权代表委托人行事且基于此信赖而造成自身的损失。The doctrine

---

① https://digitalcommons.law.lsu.edu/cgi/viewcontent.cgi?referer=https://www.google.com/&httpsredir=1&article=3916&context=lalrev

protects innocent third persons who have reasonably relied to their detriment upon the representations of those whom the principal holds out as possessing authority to act for him.

我国《民法典》第一百七十二条规定：行为人没有代理权、超越代理权或者代理权终止后，仍然实施代理行为，相对人有理由相信行为人有代理权的，代理行为有效。《民法典》无更改地继承了《民法总则》关于表见代理的规定。《民法典》实施后表见代理的构成要件为：1.无权代理人没有获得委托人的授权，表见代理属于无权代理的范畴；2.代理人与第三人的民事法律行为须有效；3.代理权具有外观上的表象，使第三人足以相信代理人有代理权；4.第三人须善意且无过失。

综上可发现国内表见代理制度与 apparent authority 构成要件类似，根据"以术语译术语"的原则，该术语可以译为"表见代理权"。

appellate record

该术语仅从字面上理解很容易译为"上诉记录"。我们有必要通过其源语英文释义理解其具体所指。

《布莱克法律词典》中 appellate record 与 record on appeal 同义，定义为：The record of a trial-court proceeding as presented to the appellate court for review. 由此可见，译为"上诉记录"与实际含义不符。

《元照英美法词典》虽然也将该术语译为"上诉记录"，但其给出的解释可以帮助理解该术语的内涵：指初审法院报送上诉法院的关于具体案件的各种文件，即初审时各诉讼程序的记录，包括诉状、书证、物证、询问证人记录、法庭裁定等。

此外，美国《联邦上诉程序规则》（Federal Rules of Appellate Procedure）中，Rule 10 是关于 The Record on Appeal 的，其第一款内容如下：

Composition of the Record on Appeal. The following items constitute the record on appeal:

(1) the original papers and exhibits filed in the district court;

(2) the transcript of proceedings, if any; and

(3) a certified copy of the docket entries prepared by the district clerk.

由上述规定可知,record on appeal 包括地区法院接收的原始的书证、物证、诉讼过程中的笔录,地区法院书记员提供的摘录文件的经鉴定的复印件等。这些文件都是要送交上诉法院的。中文的"案卷"一词或许可以很好地概括。

《英汉法律用语大辞典》(第 2 版)将 appellate record 译为"上诉案卷材料",此译法具有参考价值。

此外,在查阅资料过程中,发现 appeal record 似乎与该术语意思相同。不列颠哥伦比亚上诉法院(British Columbia Court of Appeal)官网上为上诉人提供的指南(Guidebook for Appellants)里将 appeal record 定义为:a bound book containing filed copies of the initiating documents, order and reasons for judgment of the lower court or tribunal, as well as the notice of appeal. An appeal record contains key documents about the previous hearing.《美国联邦法规》(45 CFR § 155.500)规定:Appeal record means the appeal decision, all papers and requests filed in the proceeding, and, if a hearing was held, the transcript or recording of hearing testimony or an official report containing the substance of what happened at the hearing, and any exhibits introduced at the hearing。该术语的一种译法为"基层法院庭审记录",但容易误导读者以为仅包含法庭审判过程中的庭审记录,导致对该术语包含的内容理解得不够全面。

综上,appeal record 与 appellate record 指向的内容相差无几,建议将它们译为"基层法院上诉案卷材料"。

assignment of error

该术语仅从字面意思理解无法确定其真正含义,会错译成"错误的分配"或"错误的任务",与原文的真正含义相差甚远。要翻译该术语,首先必须查看其源语英文释义。

《布莱克法律词典》中的释义为:a specification of the trial court's alleged errors on which the appellant relies in seeking an appellate court's reversal, vacation, or modification of an adverse judgment。

该术语是指上诉人可依据下级法院对其初审判决中的错误所做出的陈述,要求上级法院推翻、撤销、修改下级法院的判决或命令并重新审判。

美国弗吉尼亚州最高法院 Rule 5:17(c)(1)(Rules of the Supreme Court of

Virginia)规定:an assignment of error must do more than just state "that the judgment or award is contrary to the law and the evidence."; an assignment of error should be concise and "without extraneous argument."; an assignment of error must "address the findings, rulings, or failures to rule on issues in the trial court or other tribunal from which an appeal is taken."据此可以看出，assignment of error 是一份相对正式的文件且其中内容有较为明确的规定，必须简洁且直接指明初审法院的错误之处。

《元照英美法词典》给出的译文为"错误陈述"，该译文不易使读者一目了然地了解到什么是"错误"的。《英汉法律用语大辞典》中译为"审判错误陈述"；《英汉法律词典》（第四版）中译为"原审错误陈述书"，这两种译法都可以让读者直观了解到是"审判"出现了错误，而非其他错误。

综上，建议将该术语译为"初审错误陈述书"。

attorney-in-fact

该术语仅从字面意思容易理解为"事实代理人"，该术语背后所指到底是什么样的代理人还需进一步了解其英文源语释义及背后的制度理念。

《布莱克法律词典》中对 attorney-in-fact 的释义为：Strictly, one who is designated to transact business for another; a legal agent. Also termed private attorney. 即一方被另一方指派并代为进行交易。

美国康奈尔大学法学院法律信息机构（Legal Information Institute，后文简称康奈尔法学院 LII）搭建的在线数据库平台①根据以往的判例给出了更为详细的解释及示例：An agent authorized to act on behalf of another person, but not necessarily authorized to practice law, e.g. a person authorized to act by a power of attorney. An attorney in fact is a fiduciary. Also known as attorney in fact or private attorney. For example, Person A might give a power of attorney to Person B that allows Person B to manage Person A's bank accounts. In this example, Person A is the principal, and Person B is the attorney-in-fact.

---

① https://www.law.cornell.edu

综上，attorney-in-fact 的释义可以总结为：一方接受委托人授权成为法律事务代理人，但不一定具有律师资格且主要从事非诉业务（多在庭外处理委托事务）。可见 attorney-in-fact 的权限范围仅取决于委托人的授权，不得越过授权范围。

此外，attorney-at-law 则指具有律师资格而从事诉讼实务代理者。《布莱克法律词典》中对 attorney-at-law 的释义为：A person who practices law; lawyer. —Also termed public attorney。可见 attorney-at-law 就是我们通常所称的"律师"。

我国《民法典》第一百六十三条规定：代理包括委托代理和法定代理。委托代理人按照被代理人的委托行使代理权。法定代理人依照法律的规定行使代理权。综合《民法典》第一编第七章关于"代理"的有关规定，attorney-in-fact 可以翻译为"委托代理人"，但切记不可将 attorney-at-law 按照字面意思翻译为"法定代理人"，二者的概念内涵和外延并不完全相同。

bad title

《布莱克法律词典》中对 bad title 的释义有：

1. 与 defective title 同义，即 a title that cannot legally convey the property to which it applies, usually because of some conflicting claim to that property。

2. 与 unmarketable title 同义，即 a title that a reasonable buyer would refuse to accept because of possible conflicting interests in or litigation over the property. Also termed unmerchantable title; nonmerchantable title。

上述两个释义表达的意思几乎没有差别，都表明某财产因为存在潜在的利益冲突和诉讼风险，从而导致财产不能转让（defective title）或买家拒绝接受交易（unmarketable title）。

需要注意的是，还应明确 bad title，defective title，unmarketable title 中 title 的含义，《布莱克法律词典》对这三个术语中的 title 的释义为：Legal evidence of a person's ownership rights in property; an instrument（such as a deed）that constitutes such evidence. 即证明某人拥有财产的所有权的法律证据；构成此类证据的文书（例如契据）。根据《元照英美法词典》的释义，title 一词虽然使用频繁，但缺乏明确统一的定义，它通常指一个人对财产，尤其是土地等不动产所拥有的组成所有权(ownership)的各项权利,有时也被用来指所有权本身。这一解释与《布莱克法律词典》中给出的示例表示的意思相同。严格意义上,title并非所有权,而是所有权的证据和基础,是构成所有权的全部要素的集合。产权人和所有权人是两个不同的概念,所有权人对财产的占有正当合法、具有绝对效力;产权人对财产占有的范围更广一些,包括抵押(mortgage)、占用(occupancy)或单纯占有(bare possession)等,甚至包括非法占有人或侵权行为人的占有,只不过这一占有可以被合法权利人依法剥夺。换句话说,真正的所有权人可以对抗一切他人对物的权利;即所有权人的权利是绝对的所有权,而产权人的权利则是相对的。因此,bad title、defective title、unmarketable title 中 title 应该译为"产权",而非"所有权"。

理清 title 的含义后,bad title 可以根据具体使用的语境进行翻译,如果使用的场景符合 defective title 的内涵,强调财产因某原因导致不可转让,则译为"有瑕疵产权";如果使用的场景符合 unmarketable title 的内涵,强调买方因产权存在瑕疵而拒绝接受交易,则译为"不可交易产权"。

bench

该术语属于典型的"普通词汇表示特定法律含义"的词汇,绝不能按字面意思理解为法庭上的长凳或长椅,也不指法庭里的观众席。

《布莱克法律词典》对 bench 的释义有:1. The raised area occupied by the judge in a courtroom,比如法官在法庭上会对双方律师说 approach the bench;2. The court considered in its official capacity,比如 remarks from the bench;3. Judges collectively,比如 bench and bar;4. The judges of a particular court,比如 the Fifth Circuit bench。

《元照英美法词典》针对上述释义给出了对应的译文:1.(法庭上的)法官席;2.法庭、裁判庭,即法官行使裁判权的地方;3.(总称)法官;4.(某一特定法院的)全体法官,比如 the Fifth Circuit bench 指第五巡回法庭的全体法官。

此外,不妨多了解几个相关术语。比如:bench trial,《布莱克法律词典》解释为:A trial before a judge without a jury. The judge decides questions of fact as well as questions of law. 也称 trial to the bench; nonjury trial; court trial; trial before the court (abbr. TBC); judge trial。该术语映射了英美法的审判制

度,英美法国家对案件的审理通常分为由法官审理或者由陪审团审理,法官审理即为 bench trail,法官既裁决案件事实又适用法律;陪审团审理即为 jury trail,陪审团负责裁决案件事实,法官负责适用法律。

bias crime

该术语按照字面意思容易翻译为"偏见犯罪",具体指何种犯罪还是要先了解其英文释义。

查阅有关资料后发现 bias crime 与 hate crime 同义,《布莱克法律词典》将 hate crime 定义为:A crime motivated by the victim's race, color, ethnicity, religion, or national origin. 一些群体也期望法规中能够将因残疾、性别或性取向歧视为动机的犯罪纳入到 hate crime 的法定范围内。美国联邦以及各州对 bias crime 或 hate crime 的范畴分别有详细规定,比如美国俄勒冈州司法部(Oregon Department of Justice)官网上将 hate crime 定义为:A hate crime, known as bias crime under Oregon law, is a crime motivated by bias against another person's race, color, disability, religion, national origin, sexual orientation, or gender identity. 这些犯罪行为的表现形式有:口头行为、肢体行为或视觉行为。

综合有关资料给出的示例及上述定义,可以将 bias crime 或 hate crime 的定义概括为:针对某一特定社会群组成员歧视性的犯罪行为。这种歧视性的犯罪行为通常因种族、宗教、性取向、身心障碍、族群、国籍、年龄、性别、性别认同及政党等问题生恨而引致(包含但不限于)凌辱、攻击甚至是谋杀等罪行。总而言之,该犯罪行为最大的特征是基于 bias 而实施的犯罪行为。

有关资料表明,美国 45 个州及华盛顿所在地哥伦比亚特区都已经通过了针对歧视性犯罪行为的法律。这些州都将因种族和宗教信仰歧视而导致的犯罪行为列为打击目标,这其中还有 32 个州针对残障歧视犯罪立法,31 个州针对性取向歧视犯罪立法,28 个州针对性别歧视犯罪立法,14 个州针对变性或性别认同歧视犯罪立法,13 个州针对年龄歧视犯罪立法,5 个州针对政治背景或政治立场歧视犯罪立法,另有 3 个州及哥伦比亚特区还特别针对无家可归者的歧视犯罪立法。

综上,相较"偏见犯罪",读者对 bias crime 或 hate crime 较为熟悉的译法是"仇恨犯罪",为了更能凸显出该犯罪行为的犯罪动机,建议将其译为"歧视性犯罪"。

bill of indictment

《布莱克法律词典》对该术语的解释为:An instrument presented to a grand jury and used by the jury to declare whether there is enough evidence to formally charge the accused with a crime. 首先,该术语指明的是某种法律文书,不可看到 bill 就理解为这是某种法案;其次,该文书要呈交给大陪审团(grand jury)且由其决定是否可正式对被告人予以起诉。值得注意的是,因为大陪审团是在刑事法庭审案期间由行政司法官选定并召集,受理刑事指控,听取控方提出的证据,从而决定是否将犯罪嫌疑人交付审判,由此可以判定 bill of indictment 只适用于刑事案件中,所以该术语可以译为"大陪审团刑事起诉书"。

如果大陪审团经过审查且由足额陪审员同意通过,认为提出的犯罪指控有充分证据而签署认可的起诉书称为 true bill,即大陪审团签署的正式起诉书。如果大陪审团的多数成员认为犯罪未得到充分的证明,即在申请起诉书上签署"不予起诉"(No true bill; Not a true bill; Not found),并释放被指控人。

此外,还应区分 bill of indictment 与 information 以及 complaint。对被指控人刑事犯罪的正式指控始于政府向有管辖权的法院提交起诉书。在美国刑事司法实践中,起诉书分为刑事控告书(complaint)、检察官刑事起诉书(information)和大陪审团刑事起诉书(indictment)三种。

根据美国《联邦刑事诉讼规则》(Federal Rules of Criminal Procedure)的相关规定,警察或检察官会基于合理根据(probable cause)向有管辖权的地方基层法官(magistrate judge)或其他地方司法官员(state or local judicial officer)提交陈述犯罪事实的指控文书,即刑事控告书(complaint)。之后地方基层法官会据此决定是否签发逮捕令(warrant)或签发传票(summons)。在之后的刑事诉讼程序中,对重罪的起诉(felony prosecution)应启用大陪审团,检察官首先应向大陪审团提请大陪审团刑事起诉书(bill of indictment);不经由大陪审团审查的刑事案件中,比如美国大多数州规定轻罪案件(misdemeanors)不启用大陪审团,由检察官直接以州或国家名义提起刑事指控,该类文书称为检察官刑事起诉书(information)。

bona fide purchaser

bona fide 这一拉丁语词汇表示"善意地"之意,该术语大家比较熟悉的译文是"善意购买人""善意第三人"。根据《布莱克法律词典》的释义,bona fide purchaser 与多个术语表示同一含义:bona fide purchaser for value, good-faith purchaser, purchaser in good faith, innocent purchaser, innocent purchaser for value。

传统的普通法规则认为,没有人可以转让不属于他本人所有的商品。但在实践中,若某人确实不知该商品存在权利瑕疵,且为之付出了对价(consideration),那么该人即为 bona fide purchaser,且对于所购商品享有对抗一切先在物主的所有权(a bona fide purchaser is one who does not know of the seller's wrong doing but has a good faith belief that the seller has title, and in addition pays valuable consideration)。美国《统一商法典》第 2-403 条后段的规定即体现了这一原则:"… a person with voidable title has power to transfer a good title to a good faith purchaser for value. When goods have been delivered under a transaction of purchase the purchaser has such power even though (1) the transferor was deceived as to identify of the purchaser, or … (4) the delivery was procured through fraud punishable as larcenous under the criminal law."依该条规定,只要购买人出于善意且支付了对价,即使因受骗而不知卖方真实身份或者交付货物系通过欺诈取得,交易货物交付后,bona fide purchaser 即取得所有权。1979 年《英国货物买卖法》规定:如果货物是在公开市场上购买的,根据市场惯例,只要买方是善意的,没有注意到卖方的权利瑕疵,就可以获得货物完全的权利。这也体现了对 bona fide purchaser 原则的确认。

在美国法的善意取得中,适用范围明确规定为"货物(goods)",所以善意取得适用于动产交易中。由于房屋、土地等不动产交易适用登记制度,通过既定的登记公示方法使第三人直观了解到不动产物权变动的事实,因而不存在无所有权人或者无处分权人处分不动产所有权的可能性,也就不存在适用善意取得的必要前提,故各国立法通常规定只有动产交易适用善意取得制度。

我国《物权法》第一百零六条打破善意取得限于动产的传统,将善意取得扩展到不动产交易领域。我国《民法典》继续沿用了这一规定,第三百一十一条,第三百一十二条,第三百一十三条给出了善意取得制度的相关规定,其中能够与

bona fide purchaser 相对应的概念在《民法典》中表述为"善意受让人"。

"善意购买人"的译法没有体现出 bona fide purchaser 可以对抗一切先在物主的所有权,如译为"善意受让人",能够让读者一眼便知第三人已善意取得物的所有权。

breach of the peace

该术语非常容易被当作普通短语误译为"破坏和平",这时就需要通过查阅专业的法律词典了解其在法律语境下的含义。

根据《布莱克法律词典》的释义,breach of the peace 与 breach of peace, disturbing the peace, disturbance of the peace, public disturbance 同义,意思为: The criminal offense of creating a public disturbance or engaging in disorderly conduct, particularly by making an unnecessary or distracting noise. 通过其英文释义可以发现该行为会扰乱公共秩序和社会治安,属于刑事犯罪。《元照英美法词典》中列举了一些示例,如:在公共场所高声叫喊、谩骂、争吵、打斗以图引起骚乱。美国一些州的法规中也对 breach of the peace 做出了界定,比如:内布拉斯加州(Nebraska)规定,故意扰乱社区和平与安宁的人被判三级轻罪(详见 NE Code § 28-1322 (2019))。在怀俄明州(Wyoming),如果一个人不合时宜地外放音乐,使用威胁性语言或暴力行为,并且该人应当知道这些行为会扰乱他人,该行为即属 breach of the peace(详见 WY Stat § 6-6-102 (2019))。根据佛蒙特州(Vermont)的规定,如果某人在日落和日出间制造过多噪音,或袭击他人、使用通信工具骚扰他人等,该行为即属 breach of the peace(详见 2020 Vermont Statutes, Title 13 — Crimes and Criminal Procedure, Chapter 19)。由此可见,各州对于 breach of the peace 的范围规定不一,界定模糊,但所列行为均属于扰乱社会安宁和公共秩序的行为,给他人的正常生活造成了不良影响。

《中华人民共和国刑法》(以下简称《刑法》)中规定了"危害公共安全罪",但它是指故意或者过失地实施危害不特定多数人的生命、健康或者重大公私财产安全行为。该术语不能用于翻译 breach of the peace,两者虽然都属于刑事犯罪,但很明显"危害公共安全罪"对公共安全的侵害程度远大于 breach of the peace 对社会安宁和公共秩序的破坏程度。我国《刑法》第六章第一节规定了"扰乱公共秩序罪"的各种具体情形及具体罪名,比如第二百七十七条规定了妨害公务罪、袭警罪;第二百七十八条,煽动暴力抗拒法律实施罪等;仔细分析后会发现其内涵远大于 breach of the peace 的内涵,因此"扰乱公共秩序罪"也不能和 breach of the peace 画等号。

法律翻译中经常会出现源语概念在目标语文化中找不到对等概念的情形,在查清楚源语概念的内涵后,译者可以根据差异采取补偿策略,依据源语的概念创造新的译文。

综上,建议将 breach of the peace 译为"妨害治安罪"。

breaking bulk

《布莱克法律词典》对该术语的解释为:Larceny by a bailee, esp. a carrier, who opens containers, removes items from them, and converts the items to personal use. Also termed breaking bale. 我们有必要先了解术语 larceny 的含义,即以非法占有为目的,未经所有人同意而取走他人财物的行为,通常译为"盗窃罪"。因此,breaking bulk 指受托人,特别是承运人的行为构成普通法意义上的盗窃罪(larceny),比如:承运人拆卸其负责承运的物品包装,转移其中物品并挪作自用。

网络上对 breaking bulk 的译文有"盗窃托管物品罪",我们可以进一步了解 breaking-bulk doctrine。根据《布莱克法律词典》的释义,该原则指 a bailee who had lawful possession of property delivered in bulk and wrongfully took the property committed larceny only if the bailee broke the container open and took part or all of the contents. If the bailee wrongfully took the property without opening the container, the act was theft but not larceny. Also termed breaking-bale doctrine. 如果受托人违法拆卸包装,盗窃部分或全部受托物品即构成普通法上的盗窃罪(larceny);如果受托人只是盗窃走受托物品但没有拆卸包装则构成制定法上的盗窃罪(theft)。根据前文的解释,breaking bulk 指承运人拆卸了物品包装的盗窃行为,因此将 breaking bulk 译为"拆包盗窃罪"更为合适。

此外,《英美法律术语辞典》中指明:受托人应尽到对受托管财物保管的义务,如果受托人擅自拆开被托管的财物,部分或者全部挪作他用,均可以盗窃罪论处。结合前文释义,将 breaking-bulk doctrine 译为"受托人义务原则"比按照字面翻译为"包装拆卸原则"更能体现该原则映射的对受托人的义务规定。

brief

有些词典中将 brief 翻译为"案情摘要",该译法容易使读者误以为 brief 仅仅是对案件情况的简单介绍,没有体现出 brief 中所包含的丰富内容。

《布莱克法律词典》的释义为:1. A written statement setting out the legal contentions of a party in litigation, esp. on appeal; a document prepared by counsel as the basis for arguing a case, consisting of legal and factual arguments and the authorities in support of them. Also termed legal brief; brief of argument. 2. English law. A solicitor's document that abstracts the pleadings and facts to inform a barrister about the case。

根据上述释义可知,在美国,brief 指律师向法庭提交的表明其对案件的观点的书面辩论文件。通常包括对案件事实的概述、相关法律及关于对案件事实如何适用法律以支持律师主张的争论。在英国,brief 指事务律师(solicitor)为出庭律师(barrister)代理当事人出庭而准备的简要的说明性文件,通常包括案件事实叙述及适用的相关法律,并附有律师意见、重要文书的副本、正式诉状、证人证词等。因此,根据其功能以及准备该文件的主体可以将 brief 译为"律师辩论书"。

在英美法国家,律师辩论书是诉讼双方律师撰写并向法院提交的一种重要的法律文件,包括初审法院辩论书(trial court brief)和上诉法院辩论书(appellate court brief)两大类,有严格的格式要求。一般包括七个部分:争议焦点(statement of issue)、案件历程(statement of the case)、案件事实(statement of the facts)、辩论概述(summary of the argument)、辩论(argument)、审查标准(standard of review)和结论(conclusion)。"律师辩论书"也是控辩双方律师在上诉法院口头辩论的基础。有时,上诉法院根本不用开庭,直接在双方律师提交的辩论书基础上做出判决。

burden of proof

《布莱克法律词典》对该术语的解释为:A party's duty to prove a disputed

assertion or charge. The burden of proof includes both the burden of persuasion and the burden of production. Also termed onus probandi.

由上述释义可知,burden of proof 指当事人有义务证明其在争议中提出的主张或指控。它包含两个方面：burden of persuasion 和 burden of production。《布莱克法律词典》对这两个概念进一步进行了解释：

burden of production 指 the burden of going forward with the evidence,指当事人就自己主张的事实或提出的争点(issue)提出充分证据予以证明的责任,以证明其主张的事实成立。若当事人未能履行其举证责任,将会承担败诉的风险。通常在诉讼过程中双方当事人都承担举证责任。所以该术语应翻译为"举证责任",强调当事人提出证据进行证明的责任。

burden of persuasion 指 a party's duty to convince the fact-finder to view the facts in a way that favors that party,指说服事实认定者(法官或陪审团)确信其所提证据指向的事实或要件(如犯罪要件)为真实情况的责任。若当事人未能履行其说服责任,事实认定者须就该事实或要件做出对该当事人不利的裁决。所以该术语应翻译为"说服责任",强调当事人要提出证据说服事实认定者的责任。

综上,当事人的 burden of proof 包含了"举证"和"说服"的双重特性,大家普遍将其译为"举证责任"的译法实则"窄化"了其内涵,翻译为"证明责任"更为合适。

在英美法系,刑事诉讼中实行无罪推定(presumption of innocence)原则,公诉方要证明被告人有罪,须遵循排除合理怀疑(beyond a reasonable doubt)证明标准。民事案件中遵循优势证据(preponderance of evidence)原则,证据的分量、可靠程度和价值决定其是否具有"优势",而非靠数量取胜。英美证据法上的一般规则是"谁主张,谁举证",所以无论是刑事还是民事案件,提出控诉的一方,都负有举证的责任,即向法庭提出证据,支持控诉和申索的事由。虽然在一般情况下,向法庭举证是主控方和原告的责任,但如果被告在刑事案中被法庭判罪之后,再被受害人以民事追讨赔偿,在有关的民事诉讼中,如果被告否认他对受害人的损失负赔偿责任,被告便有责任向法庭举证来支持他的抗辩。这种情况下,按比例分配的举证责任就落在被告身上。英美证据法中证明责任的多层学说总体看来是科学的。它基本反映了审判实践中各方当事人在不同情形下承担的证明责任,不仅有利于证明责任的理论研究,而且有利于指导诉讼实践。

bylaw

《布莱克法律词典》对 bylaw 的解释义项有两个:

其一,通常用作复数形式,即 bylaws,在美式英语中指 a rule or administrative provision adopted by an organization for its internal governance and its external dealings。它属于会议法(Parliamentary law, the collection of laws, rules and procedures that organizations use to conduct business)之下的概念,即隶属于一切议事机构(比如公司的股东会或董事会)所遵循的开会及议事规则中的一种。结合《元照英美法词典》中的释义可知,bylaws 是社团或公司等为内部管理而制定的规章、命令、规则或制度,所以可译为"内部管理章程"。它可以确定公司机构中各类职员、组织的权利和义务,规定处理诸如召开会议等日常事务的规则。虽然内部管理章程可能是某组织机构内部最权威的规范性文件,它仍然要遵循该组织机构依法制定的"章程"(charter or articles of incorporation or association or to a constitution),此"章程"和"内部管理章程"分别独立存在。

我们可以看《英美法律术语辞典(英汉双解)》提供的一个例子:Under the company's bylaws, he can continue as chairman until the age of 70.(根据该公司的内部规定,他可以继续担任董事长一直到 70 岁。)在这个例子中,company's bylaws 指公司的内部规定。而我们通常所说的"公司章程"是指公司依法制定的、规定公司名称、住所、经营范围、经营管理制度等重大事项的基本文件。bylaws 和公司章程是两个不同的概念。

其二,也可以拼写为 by-law 或 byelaw,在英式英语中与 ordinance 同义。结合《元照英美法词典》中对 ordinance 的释义可知,英式英语中的 bylaw 指由市政法人(municipal corporation)的立法机关通过的法规,可译为"条例"或"地方法规"。

check

personal check, cashier's check, certified check, money order 这几种 check 都可以笼统的叫作"支票",让我们通过了解其源语释义从而对以上几种支票进行区分。

《布莱克法律词典》对 personal check 的定义是 a check drawn on a person's

own account，即以个人账户开立的支票。通常翻译为"个人支票"，它是基于个人信用来开具的，办理前个人需要接受银行部门的审查。这种支票类型在我国存在但并不是十分流行，因为在生活中个人支票的局限性较大，比如：由于商家无法确定个人支票账号里是否真的有钱，所以不接受个人支票；某些特定的大宗交易（买房买车等）也不接受个人支票；易于伪造。总之，由于个人支票缺乏第三方的担保，大众较难接受使用个人支票。

《布莱克法律词典》对 cashier's check 的定义是：A check drawn by a bank on itself, payable to another person, and evidencing the payee's authorization to receive from the bank the amount of money represented by the check; a draft for which the drawer and drawee are the same bank, or different branches of the same bank. 指银行签发，支付给另一人的支票，证明收款人有权从银行收到支票所代表的金额；出票人和受票人需在同一家银行或同一家银行的不同分行进行操作，是由银行在见票时按票面金额付款的票据。鉴于此类型支票由银行签发，有银行见票即付，因此通常翻译为"银行支票"。银行支票可以用于转账，注明"现金"字样的银行支票可以用于支取现金。

《布莱克法律词典》对 certified check 的定义是：A depositor's check drawn on a bank that guarantees the availability of funds for the check. The guarantee may be by the drawee's signed agreement to pay the draft or by a notation on the check that it is certified. 指银行在支票上加盖"承兑"或"保付"字样并签字的支票，从而保证支票上资金的可用性。银行对这种支票承担绝对的付款义务，指银行开出的存款支票，保证支票资金的可用性。鉴于银行保证一定付款的特征，经常将其翻译为"保付支票"。它比 cashier's check（银行支票）具有更高的安全性，因为在开具的时候需要有银行方面的背书，一旦钱款出现问题，其责任需要银行和购买保付支票的人一起承担，因此对于收款人的保障是最高的。

此处可以多了解几个与"保付"相关的概念：del credere①（保付代理商），指的是保证买方有支付能力的代理商。他接管并占有被代理方用于销售的财物，

---

① A del credere agency is a type of principal-agent relationship wherein the agent acts not only as a salesperson, or broker, for the principal, but also as a guarantor of credit extended to the buyer. 参见 https://www.qidulp.com/question/2091/answer/2143。

保证每一个赊购财物的买方都会实时付款,保付代理商为此收取较高的销售佣金。保付代理商又称为 del credere agent。与之类似的搭配还有 del credere commission 保付代理佣金①;del credere agreement 保付货款协议②。

《布莱克法律词典》对 money order 的定义是:A negotiable draft issued by an authorized entity (such as a bank, telegraph company, post office, etc.) to a purchaser, in lieu of a check to be used to pay a debt or otherwise transmit funds upon the credit of the issuer. 由授权实体(如银行、电报公司、邮局等)签发给买方的可转让汇票,代替支票用于支付债务或以其他方式在发行人的信用证上转账。由此可见 money order 的发行人不一定是银行。我国于 2017 年正式实施《公共服务领域英文译写规范》,汇票的标准英文为 Money Order。我国的《票据法》第十九条规定:"汇票是出票人签发的,委托付款人在见票时或者在指定日期无条件支付确定的金额给收款人或者持票人的票据。"由此可见,money order 与中文"汇票"的概念内涵相同,都是一种委付证券,基本的法律关系最少有三个人物:出票人、受票人和收款人。它和 cashier's check 的机制类似,也是去银行办理;区别是 money order 往往有额度限制,如果你想用它支付巨额金钱恐怕不行。

check fraud

查阅相关资料显示,check fraud 的源语定义③是:Check fraud (American English) or cheque fraud (British English), refers to a category of criminal acts that involve making the unlawful use of cheques in order to illegally acquire or borrow funds that do not exist within the account balance or account-holder's legal ownership. Most methods involve taking advantage of the float (the time between the negotiation of the cheque and its clearance at the cheque writer's financial institution) to draw out these funds. Specific

---

① 在货物买卖中,卖方因保付代理商(del credere agent)保证买方到期即支付贷款而额外支付给该代理商的佣金。参见 https://www.qidulp.com/question/2091/answer/2143。

② 保付代理人与卖方之间签订的协议。约定保付代理人担保买方有能力清偿卖方赊销的货款而收取额外的佣金,在买方违约或无力清偿时由保付代理人赔偿。参见 https://www.qidulp.com/question/2091/answer/214。

③ https://www.miteksystems.com/blog/what-is-check-fraud

kinds of cheque fraud include cheque kiting, where funds are deposited before the end of the float period to cover the fraud, and paper hanging, where the float offers the opportunity to write fraudulent cheques but the account is never replenished. 它指的是涉及非法使用支票的犯罪行为,以非法获取或借入账户余额或账户持有人合法所有权范围内不存在的资金。大多数方法涉及利用浮动时间(支票议付和支票签发人的金融机构清算之间的时间)提取这些资金。写空头支票(cheque kiting)也属于check fraud的一种表现形式,即在浮动期结束前存入资金以掩盖欺诈行为。随着现代科技的发展,check fraud也更加不易被识别。

《元照英美法词典》提供的解释是:由在银行或在付款人处开有合法账户的人签发作为合法的正式票据支票、汇票或汇款单,如果该票据的签发人或使用人事前明知银行或付款人将因存款不足或账户已结清而拒付,则该签发或使用票据的行为就构成支票诈骗。非法印制支票或签发不属于自己的账户的支票构成伪造罪(forgery)。

综上可见,fraud check指利用支票而进行的欺诈行为,可将其翻译为"支票欺诈"。

community service

该术语在普通英语中表示"社区服务"之意,那在法律语境中是否具有特殊含义呢?

《布莱克法律词典》的释义为:Socially valuable work performed without pay. Community service is often required as part of a criminal sentence, esp. one that does not include incarceration.

由此可见,community service 在法律语境中指:法庭可要求刑事罪犯从事一定时间的无偿劳动,以替代对罪犯的其他处置方式。因此,不能将该术语翻译为普通英语中的"社区服务"。

《英美法律术语辞典(英汉双解)》进一步补充了community service的背景知识:法庭可以做出使罪犯提供community service的命令,但需要罪犯的同意,并在其要工作的社区提供相应的准备。该罪犯必须完成特定小时数的劳动,其间他可能受到相关官员的指导。如果该罪犯未能遵守命令和要求,或不能令人满意地完成被要求从事的劳动,则他可以被带到地方法庭处以罚金,或受到他本来应该受到的处罚。法庭做出的 community service 命令可以被改正或撤销。由此可见,community service 是对罪犯的一种"替代性"的司法救济和制裁方式(judicial remedies sanctions),罪犯如果按照命令提供了特定小时数的服务,则不需要再接受其他处罚。

根据维基百科给出的释义可知,在美国,community service 的具体形式也会根据罪犯的犯罪行为做出调整,比如:因乱扔垃圾受处罚的人可能需要清理公园或马路;酒驾者要在学校等公众场合解释为什么酒驾是种犯罪行为。

综上,可以总结出 community service 的特征:适用于罪行较轻的刑事犯罪分子;具有刑罚性质;对犯罪分子不予关押,不剥夺其人身自由;需借助社会力量。这些特征与我国《刑法》中规定的"管制刑"较为相似,但二者的产生机理以及在刑罚体系中发挥的作用并不相同。此外,它也不同于我国已经废止的"劳动教养制度"。建议将 community service 译为"社区服务刑"以突出其作为一种刑罚手段的特征。

conjugal rights

《布莱克法律词典》的释义为:The rights and privileges arising from the marriage relationship, including the mutual rights of companionship, support, and sexual relations. Loss of conjugal rights amounts to loss of consortium. 这里提到的 loss of consortium 指:A loss of the benefits that one spouse is entitled to receive from the other, including companionship, cooperation, aid, affection, and sexual relations. 由此可知,conjugal rights 指夫妻间应当相互陪伴支持、拥有性关系的权利。结合《元照英美法词典》的释义可知,由于他人的侵权行为而致某人的相伴、相爱、互助、同居、性关系等权利丧失,即 loss of conjugal rights 或 loss of consortium。

我国《民法典》第一千零四十三条提出了对婚姻家庭的倡导性规定,倡导"夫妻应当相互忠实,互相尊重,互相关爱",该条文与英美法律体系中规定的 conjugal rights 背后的法律精神高度吻合,但我国《民法典》中该条款仅具有倡导性,并不具有强制约束力,非属必须遵守的义务;而 conjugal rights 是一种因婚姻关系而产生的权利和特权(rights and privileges),属夫妻间应当遵守的义务。查阅《民法典》婚姻家庭编的规定后,并未发现能够与该术语内涵匹配的义务规定。

国内提及该术语时,通常译为"夫妻同居权",事实上,我国法律体系中也并未明确提出"同居权"。关于"同居"一词的含义,可以通过《最高人民法院关于适用〈民法〉婚姻家庭编的解释(一)》第二条有关"与他人同居"的规定中得以确定,即:有配偶者与婚外异性,不以夫妻名义,持续、稳定地共同居住。由此可见,conjugal rights 的内涵远大于"同居"内涵。

《牛津高阶英汉双解词典》(第 8 版)对 conjugal 的定义为:connected with marriage and the sexual relationship between a husband and wife,指"夫妻间的、婚姻的"。那么 conjugal rights 可否翻译为配偶权呢?仅从中文词义来看,夫妻与配偶两个词并没有太大差别,似乎是合理可行的。但我们需要将 conjugal rights 和 spouse rights 进行对比与区分。

spouse rights 或 spousal rights 常译作"配偶权",这一概念由英美法系国家率先提出并日臻完善。配偶权是指基于合法婚姻关系而在夫妻双方之间发生的、由夫妻双方平等专属享有的要求对方陪伴生活、钟爱、帮助的基本身份权利[①]。由此可见,二者在概念上有一定重合的地方。但与 conjugal rights 相比,配偶权是基本身份权,是基于法律规定的夫妻身份地位而产生的,还包括诸多派生的身份权,比如夫妻姓名权、住所决定权、同居义务、贞操忠实义务以及日常事务代理权。由此可见,配偶权涵盖的范围比 conjugal rights 要大得多。因此,仅从 conjugal 一词出发,把 conjugal rights 简单的翻译为配偶权也是不恰当的。

排除了以上两种不恰当的翻译,结合 conjugal rights 的英文释义,我们可以将 conjugal rights 直译为"夫妻权利"。

constructive acceptance

《布莱克法律词典》对 constructive 的释义为:Legally imputed; existing by virtue of legal fiction though not existing in fact. Courts usu. give something a constructive effect for equitable reasons. 比如:the court held that the shift supervisor had constructive knowledge of the machine's failure even though he did not actually know until two days later. 通过该释义可知,constructive 作为

---

① 马强.试论配偶权.法学论坛,2000(02):49—57.

形容词在法律语境下的含义是指"法律推定的",虽不一定是事实,但因法律拟制而产生法律效果。比如:法院会推定认为值班主管对机器的故障应当有所了解,即便事实上该主管并不明知机器有故障。法院做出这样的推定通常是出于公平考量。

熟悉英美法体系的人都知道 acceptance 在合同法中有"承诺"之意,但这并不意味着 constructive acceptance 就可以按照字面意思翻译为"推定承诺"。通过查阅有关资料可知,"推定承诺"是各国刑法理论和实践所普遍接受的一种正当化事由。大陆法系国家和地区的刑法著作中一般都有关于推定承诺的行为的论述,是指行为时虽然没有被害人的承诺,但为救助被害人的紧急事项,可以推定如果被害人知道行为时的紧急情况就会当然做出承诺,而法律上认可基于对被害人意思的推定而实施的行为①。通过阅读一些相关刑法案例可知,该语境中的"承诺"其实更偏向于取得被害人的"同意(consent)"。

英文法律词典中虽然未收录 constructive acceptance 这一词条,但在具体实践中,constructive acceptance 使用较多的法律场景有:1. constructive acceptance of goods,美国《统一商法典》第 2—606 条规定了推定买方接收货物的各种情形,比如:尽管买方表示货物不符合合同,仍将收取或保留货物;买方未能做出有效拒收等。2. 合同中的 constructive acceptance,比如联邦政府与企业签订的建筑合同中,如果政府代表人没有在合理时间内明确表示接受或者拒绝(accept or reject),即推定为接受(constitute a constructive acceptance)②。

此外,《元照英美法词典》中也提供了 constructive acceptance 的另一个使用情景,即 constructive acceptance 是构成默示的财产寄托人与被寄托人(bailor and bailee)关系的要素之一。当某人偶然发现和占有他人财物时,或当顾客或病人将其衣物遗留在商店、办公室或其他经营场所时,即产生 constructive acceptance,成立寄托代管关系。该情景中,被寄托人被视为"接受"应当保管寄托人财物这一事实,负有保管义务。

综上,根据 constructive acceptance 在法律实践中的使用情景,可翻译为"推

---

① 田国宝. 论基于推定承诺的行为[J]. 法学评论,2004(03):133—138.
② Edited by Kelleher, Thomas J.; Mastin, John M.; Robey, Ronald G. *Smith, Currie & Hancock's Common Sense Construction Law: A Practical Guide for the Construction Professional* (4th edition), Wiley.

定接受",但注意 accepatnce 指什么还是要看具体的使用情景。

count

根据《布莱克法律词典》的释义,count 做名词和动词时含义不同,结合《元照英美法词典》的释义,其具体含义如下:

count 做名词:1. The part of an indictment charging the suspect with a distinct offense,即(大陪审团)刑事起诉书(indictment)中分别指控被告人犯有一项独立的罪行的部分。可以通过《英美法律术语辞典》提供的例句进一步了解其含义:He was indicted by a grand jury on two counts of murder。因此,可译为"一项指控"或"一项罪名"。2. In a complaint or similar pleading, the statement of a distinct claim,即民事起诉状或刑事控告书(complaint)或类似的诉讼文件(pleading)中,提出权利请求的陈述,因此该含义可译为"权利主张"或"权利请求"。3.(古)The plaintiff's declaration, or initial pleading, in a real action,指不动产诉讼中原告的起诉状(declaration)或最初的权利请求。普通法上原告开始其诉讼的第一份诉状,应按照规定的格式,条理清楚地陈述作为其诉因的事实和情况。它通常包括几个部分,称为诉讼理由(counts)。这个意义上的 count 可译为"起诉状"。4. 专利法中,count 指 the part of a patent application that defines the subject matter in a priority contest (i. e., an interference) between two or more applications or between one or more applications and one or more patents。即在专利申请书中,对多个专利申请之间或专利申请与已有专利之间的优先性争议进行阐释的部分。在数人就同一发明申请专利时,专利局可以依此决定如何授予专利权。因此,count 在专利法语境中应译为"在先发明陈述"。

count 作动词:1. In pleading, to declare or state; to narrate the facts that state a claim,即在诉答程序中,当事人陈述事实并阐明各自的诉求。2.(古)To plead orally; to plead or argue a case in court,据此释义,可译为"辩论"。

crossed check

《布莱克法律词典》对 crossed check 的定义是:A check that has lines drawn across its face and writing that specifies the bank to which the check must be presented for payment. The same effect is achieved by stamping the bank's name on the check. The check's negoliability at that bank is unaffected, but no other bank can honor it. 即在支票正面(左上角)划两条并行线,并在并行线之间记载收款银行的名称,或在支票上盖上银行的名字也能达到同样的效果。因此类支票经常被称为"划线支票"。根据《元照英美法词典》的解释可知,此支票类型起源于英国。只能向横线内指定的银行付款的支票为特别划线支票(special crossing);也可以在并行线之间记载"与公司"(and Co.)字样或不作任何记载而只有两条并行线,这时,只能付款给银行,即通过银行账户转账,此为普通划线支票(general crossing)。

划线支票必须由银行做付款提示,由其他人提示时则必须拒绝付款,因此划线支票的开立者可以保护转账金额不被未经授权的人兑现或偷取。划线支票的这种格式在其格式或声明的性质上可能因国家而异。由于划线支票只能通过银行账户支付,受益人的交易记录可以在之后查到,以便进一步查询和说明。由此可见,划线支票是一种较为安全、可靠的方式,减少了因支票遗失、被窃或因欺诈而造成损失的风险。

custodial parent

《布莱克法律词典》中对 custodial parent 的释义为:The parent awarded physical custody of a child in a divorce. 这其中要注意两个要点:其一,限定了使用情景,即离婚关系中;其二,离婚父母一方获得孩子的 physical custody。根据《布莱克法律词典》的释义,physical custody 指:在美国《家事法》(Family law)中,也称 residential custody,法庭判决父母一方获得照顾和监管子女的权利。根据源语的解释,让人联想到我国法律体系中的"监护"一词,custodial parent 是否可以译为"监护父母"呢?

我国《民法典》总则编对父母的监护权做出了规定,比如:

  第二十六条 父母对未成年子女负有抚养、教育和保护的义务。
  第二十七条 父母是未成年子女的监护人。

《中华人民共和国妇女权益保障法》第四十九条规定:父母双方对未成年子女享有平等的监护权。

综上可见，父母是未成年人的法定监护人，他们对未成年人的监护是基于父母子女关系而产生的，父母双方对子女的监护权是平等的。非因法定事由限制或剥夺，父母任何一方都享有孩子监护权。无论离婚与否，父母双方都对未成年人有监护权和承担监护人义务。

因此，"监护父母"既包含父母婚姻关系存续期间父亲和母亲对子女共同享有的监护权，同时也包含父母婚姻关系结束后，取得子女监护权的一方之涵义。准确严谨是法律翻译必须遵循的首要原则，继而才可追求言简意赅，不妨将 custodial parent 翻译为"离婚父母监护权"，这样才能体现该术语的真实含义，以免产生歧义使读者理解错误。

daisy chain

普通英语中，daisy chain 有"雏菊花环"之意。根据《布莱克法律词典》，该术语在法律英语中的释义为：A series of purchases and sales of the same stock by a small group of securities dealers attempting to drive up the stock's price to attract unsuspecting buyers' interest. Once the buyers have invested (i.e., are caught up in the chain), the traders sell for a quick profit, leaving the buyers with overpriced stock. This practice is illegal.

从以上英文释义并结合《元照英美法词典》的解释可知：daisy chain 是证券法中的概念，指由一小撮证券经纪人对同一股票进行连续的买进和卖出，从而引诱购买者"落入圈套"，继而从中获利。该行为属非法行为。

没有学习过法律英语的读者，仅从 daisy chain 的字面意思来看，很难理解其背后的法律含义。而了解了该术语的法律含义后，会发现 daisy chain 这一说法十分生动形象。"雏菊花环"由许多雏菊花朵穿线而成，常佩戴于脖颈等部位，而这里所意指的一系列非法股票交易行为是在多个证券经纪人相互串通之下，吸引投资者上套，可以说是让投资者在证券经纪人编织的美丽幻景下"上套"。

因此，综合该术语的字面意思和蕴含的法律含义，可以将 daisy chain 翻译为"雏菊套环"或"雏菊套锁"，既保留了该术语本身的字面含义，也暗指这种股市交易连环套的非法行为。

damn-fool doctrine

damn-fool doctrine 也称 damned-fool doctrine，查阅《布莱克法律词典》可知，该术语是保险法中的概念，指 the principle that an insurer may deny (esp. liability) coverage when an insured engages in behavior that is so ill-conceived that the insurer should not be compelled to bear the loss resulting from the insured's actions。由此可见，该术语指的是保险公司对于因投保人一系列不符合保单规定的行为而引发的事故，承保人有权不承担相关责任，也不需要赔偿相应的保费。

一般来说，damn-fool 是一种口语化表达，用于责备对方是"彻头彻尾的傻瓜"，并且言辞较为激烈。而就其法律涵义而言，damn-fool 实际表达了法律上对于投保人离谱、不着边际行为的谴责与反对，在法律上可将此类行为判定为无效。因此也可以算作是一个双关语，一方面，借用了这一口语化表达自身所带的感情色彩；另一方面，可以理解为"谴责愚蠢骗保行为"。

根据源语的解释，保险公司将投保人一系列不符合保单规定的行为视为无效，通不过理赔稽核的行为——即未通过事故损失后对赔偿情况的监督与检查的行为。

综上所述，damn-fool doctrine 可以翻译为"稽核无效不理赔原则"。

dawn raid

通过查阅英语源语资料发现，dawn raid 的适用语境有：

1. If police officers carry out a dawn raid, they go to someone's house very early in the morning to search it or arrest them[①]。即警方凌晨突袭进行搜查或逮捕。

2. If soldiers carry out a dawn raid, they attack enemy soldiers very early in the morning[②]。即军队拂晓突袭，袭击敌军。

3. A dawn raid refers to the practice of buying up a large amount of shares right at the open of the day's trading. The goal of a dawn raid is to amass a

---

① https://www.collinsdictionary.com/dictionary/english/dawn-raid
② Ibid.

large number of shares in a target company by one company to influence a potential takeover of the target. Due to the rapid dissemination of price data and exchange and securities regulations, it is actually quite difficult to achieve the purpose of a dawn raid in practice.① 即个人或公司在当天交易开始时立即购买大量股票的做法。潜在投标人试图在市场开放后的短时间内收购目标公司的大量股份,从而影响对目标公司的收购。但在实践中由于价格数据以及交易所和证券监管的迅速传播,实际上很难在实践中达到 dawn raid 的预期目的。

4. In the context of competition law, a surprise inspection carried out by the officials of the competition authorities at the premises of the business or businesses suspected, to obtain incriminating evidence.② 在竞争法(也称反垄断法)领域,指反垄断主管部门人员对涉嫌垄断市场的一家或多家企业的经营场所进行突击检查,以获取有罪证据的行为。Winston & Strawn LLP 的律师事务所发布的一篇文章里也对 dawn raid 做出了解释:Dawn raids are unannounced inspections of offices or residences by competition or other regulatory authorities to look for evidence of antitrust violations. Typically, dawn raids result in the seizure of documents, equipment, records, and data, and they may involve the questioning of personnel or individuals regarding the alleged infringement. 指反垄断或其他监管机构对办公室或住宅进行的未经宣布的检查,以寻找违反反垄断法的证据。通常情况下,这会导致文件、设备、记录和数据等被扣押,并可能会对涉嫌侵权的人员或个人进行询问。综合上述释义可知,dawn raid 在反垄断领域指监管机构对涉嫌反垄断行为的经营场所进行的突击检查。

我国《反垄断法》第四十七条规定对执法机构的现场执法权做出了相关规定,具体规定为:反垄断执法机构调查涉嫌垄断行为,可以采取下列措施:(一)进入被调查的经营者的营业场所或者其他有关场所进行检查;(二)询问被调查的经营者、利害关系人或者其他有关单位或者个人,要求其说明有关情况;(三)查阅、复制被调查的经营者、利害关系人或者其他有关单位或者个人的有关单证、

---

① 参见 https://www.investopedia.com/terms/d/dawnraid.asp。
② 参见 https://uk.practicallaw.thomsonreuters.com/2-107-6173?transitionType=Default&contextData=(sc.Default)&firstPage=true。

协议、会计账簿、业务函电、电子数据等文件、资料；（四）查封、扣押相关证据；（五）查询经营者的银行账户。采取前款规定的措施，应当向反垄断执法机构主要负责人书面报告，并经批准。

通过对比 dawn raid 在反垄断语境中的源语释义以及我国《反垄断法》的相关规定发现，dawn raid 与我国反垄断执法机构的现场执法权的内涵基本相似。但从 dawn raid 的几种适用语境来看，进行该行为的主体虽然不同，但都在强调该行为的"突然性"。但我国《反垄断法》的规定中并没有突出这一特点。为了保证法律术语翻译的严谨性，应将其翻译为"（反垄断监管机构的）突击检查"。

death-knell doctrine

该术语来源于美国民事诉讼法，因在我国没有完全对应的制度，《元照英美法词典》中采用直译法将其译为"丧钟原则"。直译对等术语是创造新术语的一种形式，但译者要尽可能掌握第一手材料，正确理解源语术语的真正含义（张法连，2016）①。

根据《布莱克法律词典》，death-knell doctrine：A rule allowing an interlocutory appeal if precluding an appeal until final judgment would moot the issue on appeal and irreparably injure the appellant's rights。

根据上述定义并结合《元照英美法词典》的释义可知，这一原则规定：对法庭做出的中间命令（interlocutory order），如果上诉人需等到终局判决（final judgement）后才能提出上诉，将会导致案件争议点在上诉审判中变成无实际意义的问题（moot the issue）且会对上诉人的合法权利造成不可弥补的损害时，允许上诉人在终局判决前提出中间上诉（interlocutory appeal）。

《元照英美法词典》中将该术语译为"丧钟原则"。根据《汉语大词典》的解释，"丧钟"是指在西方风俗中，教堂在宣告本区教徒死亡或为死者举行宗教仪式时敲钟叫作敲丧钟，因此用敲丧钟来借指死亡或灭亡。该词在现代汉语中的使用多取"结束""死亡"等意思，含有消极意义。但由 death-knell doctrine 的源语定义可知，该原则是为了上诉人的合法权利免受损害而设立的终局判决前的上诉例外原则，对于上诉人而言具有积极意义。因此译为"丧钟"一词欠妥，不符合

---

① 张法连. 英美法律术语汉译策略探究[J]. 中国翻译，2016(02)：100-104.

汉语使用者的认知习惯。

为了深入理解源语的含义,还需进一步了解美国联邦法院上诉法院终局判决规则与制定 death-knell doctrine 的目的与价值追求。终局判决规则(final judgement rule)是美国联邦上诉程序中颇为重要的一项诉讼规则①。为了防止终局判决规则在适用中所产生的偏颇,其例外开始出现,包括司法例外(judicial exception)和制定法上的例外,制定法规定的例外又可以称为制定法上的中间上诉(statutory interlocutory appeal)。death-knell doctrine 可以看作是支持在终局判决之前许可申请人对法院做出的拒绝认证决定提出即时上诉的原则,interlocutory appeal 对应的就是中间上诉制度。虽然两个词内涵与外延相近,但由于 interlocutory appeal 已经固定翻译为中间上诉制度,为了将两个词相区分,保持规范性和统一性,尽量采取其他翻译,不使用"中间上诉"这一措辞。

从《布莱克法律词典》的详细定义中可以看出,death-knell doctrine 的提出与美国民事诉讼中对集团诉讼的证明程序有关。在民事诉讼过程中,初审法院有权针对集团诉讼②案件做出认证或者拒绝认证将一个特殊的诉讼按照集团诉讼对待的命令。如果初审法院通过审查,认为案件不符合集团诉讼的成立要件,将做出否定其为集团诉讼的裁定,并要求当事人另行提起独立的诉讼。但是此裁定若按照终局判决规则,需要在法院做出判决后才能上诉,可能对当事人的合法利益或诉讼权利造成损害,因此第二巡回法院为了处理此种决定的终局性和即时上诉的问题,从实用主义出发,提出了 death-knell doctrine 原则,许可申请人对法院做出的拒绝认证决定提出即时上诉。由此看出,death-knell doctrine 的原意是如果没有在终局判决前的即时上诉原则,当事人的权利保护就岌岌可危。

结合 death-knell doctrine 的定义,该原则许可的上诉行为发生在诉讼审理期间,不同于一般的发生在法院做出判决之后,因此在翻译时可以强调这一点,采用"审理期间"这一说法。同时,这种上诉行为是终局判决规则的例外情况,认

---

① 吴如巧.美国联邦上诉程序终局判决规则:内涵、例外与发展[J].人大法律评论,2013(02):225-238.
② 在集团诉讼中,每一集团成员的诉讼请求数额都比较小,其作为一个独立的诉讼,不符合诉讼经济的目标;而作为集团诉讼,所有集团成员的请求额加在一起,却有进行诉讼的必要性。拒绝某一成员的认证申请,无疑杜绝了其提起诉讼的道路。在这种情形下,不允许其提起即时上诉,则对其权力和利益的保护就敲响了"丧钟"。引自赵信会,逯其艳.美国民事上诉制度析论.东方论坛.青岛大学学报,2005(01):106-113.

为上诉的对象不具有终局性,因此可以即时判决前就提出上诉,因此在翻译中也可以引入"即时上诉",又与"中间上诉"相区分。

综上,death-knell doctrine 这一术语可以改译为"审理期间即时上诉原则"。

decision

decision 到底应该译为"裁定"还是"决定"?"判决"还是"裁判"? 这些中文表述虽然仅一字之差,但意思却大不相同。

《布莱克法律词典》给出的 decision 英文释义有:1. A judicial or agency determination after consideration of the facts and the law; esp., a ruling, order, or judgment pronounced by a court when considering or disposing of a case。结合《元照英美法词典》的解释可知,decision 指对事实问题和法律问题进行考虑或评议之后得出的结论,通常由法院做出,但也包括仲裁机关、行政机关或委员会等。2. 在议会法中指 the chair's ruling on a point of order,结合《英汉法律用语大辞典》(第 2 版)的解释可知,议员可对议长就议会规程所做的决定提出异议。

了解 decision 的英文释义后,我们可以进一步了解"裁定""决定""判决""裁判"在我国法律条款中的含义。

通常,法院在对案件进行审理之后要对当事人之间的实体争议、程序争议或者其他特定问题做出判定。

根据我国《民事诉讼法》和《刑事诉讼法》的相关规定可知:

"判决"专门用来解决实体问题,即定罪量刑问题。比如:我国刑事案件的判决,是人民法院经过法庭审理,根据已经查明的事实、证据和有关的法律规定,就被告人是否犯罪、犯了什么罪、是否应处以刑罚和处何种刑罚的问题所做的一种结论。判决只有人民法院可以做出。

"裁定"主要适用于解决程序性问题,比如诉讼期限的延展,中止审理,维持原判等;也解决少数实体性问题,比如减刑,假释等。裁定也只有人民法院才可以做出。

"决定"只适用于解决程序问题,其功能在于排除诉讼中的障碍,保证法院顺利审理案件。比如:对回避申请决定是否同意;对当事人、辩护人提出的通知新的证人到庭、调取新的物证、重新鉴定或者勘验的申请等。决定可以由人民法院、人民检察院、公安机关分别做出。

我们经常会看到"刑事裁判文书""民事裁判文书""行政裁判文书"这样的字眼,以我国《民事诉讼法》为例,其中提到审判人员的裁判行为,由此可知"裁判"是一个相对较为笼统的概念,法院的裁判包括了判决、裁定和决定,书面形式分别为判决书、裁定书、决定书。

综上可见,decision 的英文释义与"裁定""决定""判决"的含义并不能重合,相较而言,翻译为"裁判"更为合适一些。

declaratory judgment

declaratory judgment,declaratory decree 或 declaration 在《布莱克法律词典》中的英文释义为:A binding adjudication that establishes the rights and other legal relations of the parties without providing for or ordering enforcement.

根据源语的英文释义并结合《元照英美法词典》的解释可知,declaratory judgment 是帮助原告确认其某项权利的一种"替代性"救济形式,该判决中法院仅确认当事人之间的权利及其他法律关系,而不必对其他任何事项进行裁决。不论当事人在此之后是否会据之请求给予救济,法院都可以做出此种判决。通常在当事人对自己的权利或其他事项存在疑问时,可以请求法院就此做出确认判决,如保险公司请求法院确认某种风险是否属于其保险单中规定的承保范围。该术语通常被译为"宣告判决"或"确认判决",至于宣告或确认的内容是什么,并不能让读者一目了然。

美国《联邦民事诉讼规则》(Federal Rules of Civil Procedure)第五十七条对 declaratory judgment 做出了规定,结合《英美法律术语辞典》对该术语补充的背景知识可知,此种判决涉及的诉讼通常起因于双方当事人对于法律关系认识不一致,因此发生争议(controversy)而至无法解决,此时便要求法院予以认定,以确定双方存在或不存在某种法律关系。由于涉及的诉讼中的法律事实问题无可争议或相对无可争议,一般都会适用简易程序(summary proceeding)。这类诉讼并不要求被告履行一定的民事义务,一旦法院做出判决,消除当事人之间的争议后,此案即告结束。

综上可知,declaratory judgment 中宣告和确认的是当事人之间的法律关系,不涉及诉讼中的法律事实问题,为了让读者更便捷地了解该术语的内涵,可以翻译为"确认法律关系之判决"。

deed of arrangement

根据 US Legal Forms 数据库提供的英文释义可知：A deed of arrangement refers to a written agreement between a debtor and his/her creditors, in the absence of a bankruptcy order that arranges the debtor's affairs either for the benefit of the creditors generally or, when the debtor is insolvent, for the benefit of at least three of the creditors. Generally, a deed of arrangement is regulated by statute. A deed of arrangement is an agreement between an insolvent debtor and consenting creditors as a more advantageous alternative to the debtor's bankruptcy. A deed of arrangement can be in the form of a composition, an assignment of the debtor's property to a trustee for the benefit of his creditors, or an agreement to wind up the debtor's business in such a way as to pay his/her debts.

这个术语通常被译为"和解协议"。和解协议是我国破产申请程序中的一部分。根据《中华人民共和国企业破产法》（以下简称《企业破产法》）第九章关于"和解"的规定可知,和解协议通常指债务人与债权人之间就债务清偿、避免破产清算所达成的书面契约。和解程序开始后,为达成和解协议,债务人须向债权人会议提交和解协议草案,供其审查讨论。债权人召开会议表决通过和解协议,交法院裁定是否认可。法院裁定认可后,发布公告,中止破产程序。和解协议自公告之日起具有法律效力。通常,和解协议包括对债务人减免清偿债务的数额,债务清偿期限,清偿方式,债务清偿的担保等内容。

将 deed of arrangement 与和解协议的内涵进行对比,我们可以看出两者的确有一些重合之处。总体上看,都是当企业进入破产程序之后,在债权人和债务人之间通过协商形成的避免破产清算的书面协议。但两者在以下几个方面也存在着明显的不同之处：

1. deed of arrangement 形成的前提是由于缺少破产令（bankruptcy order）[①]，在

[①] 破产令是一种指定破产管理人管理破产人或负债人的财产的法院决议,是为维护债权人权益或是在债务人无力清偿时为保障至少三个以上债权人的利益而产生。

法院的干预下而产生。而和解协议产生的前提是企业不能清偿到期债务,并且资产不足以清偿全部债务或者明显缺乏清偿能力时,由债务人向人民法院提出的书面申请;和解协议是债务人与债权人进行协商而产生的,在这个阶段中,尚且不需要法院进行干涉,只需要企业出现资不抵债等实际情况向法院申请破产后就可以订立。2. deed of arrangement 的形式明显不仅限于订立和解协议一种,还包括转让债务人财产以及停止债务人业务等方式。3. 由前述 deed of arrangement 的实现形式可以看出,无论是订立协议、将债务人财产向托管财产人进行转让,或是停止债务人业务以偿还其债务,其根本目的都在于在债务人无力偿还其债务时保障债权人的财产利益;而我国《企业破产法》中规定的和解程序的达成,是需要依靠债权人的让步实现的,是一种消极的解决债务危机的方式,债权人承诺将自己拥有的债权进行调整(结果往往是减少债权)为债务人创造复苏的机会。

由此可见,deed of arrangement 与中文"和解协议"的内涵并不完全相似,甚至说有很大的出入,我国的破产程序中"和解协议"仅是其中一个重要的环节,因此该术语译为"和解协议"并不准确。

事实上,deed of arrangement 是一个内涵丰富的概念,其中包含了破产程序中的许多方面,比如会涉及财产担保或转让,企业重整、债务清算等。总之,deed of arrangement 的最终目的是为了保障债权人利益,通过在债权人与债务人之间达成协议从而解决债务,因此该术语可以翻译为"债务和解协议书"。

defendant

该术语大家比较熟悉,会不假思索地理解为"被告",但实际上此种理解并不全面。《布莱克法律词典》给出的英文释义为:A person sued in a civil proceeding or accused in a criminal proceeding。由此可见,该术语在民事和刑事诉讼程序中都会出现,指在民事诉讼中被诉之人或刑事犯罪中被指控之人。

根据我国程序法的相关规定(《刑事诉讼法》《民事诉讼法》《行政诉讼法》),在刑事案件诉讼中,被公诉机关指控涉嫌犯罪的当事人称作"被告人"。但在民事、行政案件诉讼中被指控的当事人称作"被告"。

因此,defendant 对应的就是我国民事诉讼中的"被告"或刑事诉讼中的"被告人",在翻译时一定要注意看该术语是适用于民事诉讼还是刑事诉讼。

此外，我们还可以区分 defendant，respondent，accused，defender 和 libel(l)ee 几者的区别。它们都指向"诉讼中被诉一方"，respondant 用于上诉审（此时也称为 appellee）及申请获得特别命令或离婚、遗嘱验证等衡平法案件中，与其相对的原告（或上诉人）有 appellant，petitioner，applicant 等[①]；accused 专指刑事被告[②]，与之相对的原告有 plaintiff（刑事自诉人）或 prosecution（公诉方）；defender 则是苏格兰专门用语，与其相对的原告为 pursuer[③]；libel(l)ee 则专指海事或离婚案件的被告，与其相对的原告为 libel(l)ant[④]；对比之下，defendant 更像是通用语，可用于一般民事或刑事案件的初审中，与其相对的原告为 plaintiff。

defense

该术语内涵丰富，结合《布莱克法律词典》的英文释义以及《元照英美法词典》的解释，主要有以下含义：

1. A defendant's stated reason why the plaintiff or prosecutor has no valid case; esp., a defendant's answer, denial, or plea. 指民事诉讼中被告对原告起诉状中的主张和请求，或者刑事诉讼中被告人对控诉方的指控所做的否认、反驳，以及支持被告人反驳主张的理由、证据等。强调的是用于反驳原告或公诉人的理由，可译为"辩护根据"或"辩护理由"。

2. A defendant's method and strategy in opposing the plaintiff or the prosecution; a doctrine giving rise to such a method or strategy，比如：the lawyer advised her client to adopt a passive defense and to avoid taking the

---

[①] "The party against whom an appeal is taken. At common law, the defendant in an equity proceeding. "Cf. Bryan A. Garner, Black's Law Dictionary, 9th edition, at p. 1454, West Group (1999).

[②] "A person or persons arrested, indicted, or otherwise formally charged with a crime; the defendant(s) or prospective defendant(s) in a criminal case." Cf. James E. Clapp, Random House Webster's Dictionary of the Law, at p. 10, Random House (2000).

[③] "Scots law: a party defendant in a legal proceeding … opposed to pursuer." Cf. Philip Babcock Gove, Ph. D. and the Merriam—Webster Editorial Staff, Webster's Third New International Dictionary, at p. 591, G &C Merriam Co. (1976).

[④] "The party against whom a libel has been filed in admiralty or ecclesiastical court. "Cf. Bryan A. Garner, Black's Law Dictionary, 9th edition, at p. 928, West Group (1999).

witness stand，由此可见该语境下主要强调的是反驳原告或公诉人时的方法或策略，可以译为"抗辩"。

3. One or more defendants in a trial, as well as their counsel，指在庭审中对一个或多个被告人及其代理律师的称呼，可译为"辩护方"。

4. Commercial law. A basis for avoiding liability on a negotiable instrument，此为商法中的概念，指商业票据持有人免除票据责任或免除因票据而生的义务的权利，可译"票据抗辩权"。

5. Measures taken by a country or individual to protect against an attack; A country's military establishment; 这两层含义类似，指个人或国家对非法暴力行为的反击、防御、防卫，比如 self-defense，national defense。

综上，defense 的法律含义较为丰富，理解和使用时一定要辨别具体的使用语境，不可一概而论。

determination

该术语通常会被译为"裁定书"或"裁决书"，具体指什么还是要先了解其英文释义。

《布莱克法律词典》给出的英文释义有：

1. A final decision by a court or administrative agency，指法院或行政机关做出的 final decision。根据《布莱克法律词典》可知 final decision 与 final judgment 同义，指 a court's last action that settles the rights of the parties and disposes of all issues in controversy, except for the award of costs (and, sometimes, attorney's fees) and enforcement of the judgment，即法院在案件事实审理清楚后，对当事人的有关权利、责任、赔偿等问题做出处理，经此处理后所有争端已获解决，法院无须再作进一步审理的判决。根据《元照英美法词典》的释义可知，final decision 也指未对涉讼事实做出判断，终止案件或诉讼程序的裁定。结合前文分析 decision 的翻译时的讨论，determination 由法院做出且解决的是案件的实体性问题，应译为"法院终局判决书"；determination 由法院做出且解决的是案件的程序性问题，应译为"法院裁定书"；如果由行政机关做出，则应译为"行政裁决书"，而非"行政裁定书"。行政裁决由行政主体做出，而行政裁定是由人民法院针对行政程序问题做出的裁判。

2. The ending or expiration of an estate or interest in property, or of a right, power, or authority,指地产权、财产利益、权利、权力等的终止。

综上,翻译 determination 时一定要注意其使用的语境,而不是信口拈来,用"裁决书""裁定书""判决书"这样看似很像,但是含义千差万别的译法"蒙混过关"。

domicile

翻译 domicile 时往往容易与 habitual residence 混淆,有的辞典将两词都译为"住所"或"住处"。事实上,这两个术语具有不同的法律意义,译得不准确会对案件的管辖权产生严重影响。

根据《布莱克法律词典》,domicile 的英文解释为:1. The place at which a person has been physically present and that the person regards as home; a person's true, fixed, principal, and permanent home, to which that person intends to return and remain even though currently residing elsewhere. A person has a settled connection with his or her domicile for legal purposes, either because that place is home or because the law has so designated that place. Also termed permanent abode, habitancy. 指某人意图作为住所、在临时外出或暂居他处后打算返回的长期、固定的居住地;是一个人事实上永久居住的地方,或由法律推定永久居住的地方,或正式户口所在地,此意义下应翻译为"永久住所地"或"户籍地"。注意此处不能翻译为"永久居所","居所"的含义可与 residence 对等,指实际居住的一定处所,而"住所"则指实际居住的处所且意愿以之为固定的、永久的居住地。一人可以同时有两个或多个"居所",但只能有一个"住所"。

2. The residence of a person or corporation for legal purposes. Also termed legal residence, domicile by operation of law. 结合《元照英美法词典》的解释可知,该意义下的 domicile 指法律上作为某人或某公司等商业机构的法定住址,可翻译为"法定地址"。

维基百科上将 habitual residence 与 domicile 进行了比较:Habitual residence is less demanding than domicile and the focus is more on past experience rather than future intention. There is normally only one habitual residence where the individual usually resides and routinely returns to after visiting other places. It is the geographical place considered "home" for a reasonably significant period of time. 大意为，habitual residence 的重点是过去一段时间已经在某地居住了一段时间，是外出后仍然要回去的地方，与我们所说的普遍意义上的"家"的含义更为接近，为经常居住地。

我国《民事诉讼法》第二十二条规定：对公民提起的民事诉讼，由被告住所地人民法院管辖；被告住所地与经常居住地不一致的，由经常居住地人民法院管辖。而且根据《最高人民法院关于适用〈中华人民共和国民事诉讼法〉的解释》第四条规定，公民的经常居住地是指公民离开住所地至起诉时已连续居住一年以上的地方。

综上，domicile 应根据适用语境译为"永久住所地、户籍地"或"法定住址"，habitual residence 应译为"经常居住地"。

due diligence

查阅《布莱克法律词典》得知，due diligence 有两层含义：

其一，the diligence reasonably expected from, and ordinarily exercised by, a person who seeks to satisfy a legal requirement or to discharge an obligation. Also termed reasonable diligence, common diligence. 某人为满足法律要求或履行义务，在合理时间内为完成某一事项而做的努力。起初是作为海商法中的专有名词，最早出现于美国 1893 年《哈特法》(Ushartzr Act)，对其完整的诠释在 the Muncaster Castle 一案中，该定义已被大多数海运国家所接受，随着中国海商法的颁布被引入中国，它要求承运人面对特定情况时，应作为一名谨慎行事的船舶所有人，采取各种为特定情况所合理要求的措施。总之，due deligence 强调的是某人应尽他所应尽的职责。结合《英美法律术语辞典（英汉双解）》的解释，此术语可译为"应有的注意"或"应有的勤勉"或"恪尽职守"。

其二，a prospective buyer's or broker's investigation and analysis of a target company, a piece of property, or a newly issued security，该含义我们较为熟悉，即"尽职调查"，是指企业在并购时，买方企业对目标企业进行的经营现状调查，目的在于搜集用于估算目标价值的信息，或者收集信息并制作资料以期向股东说明此次并购决策的合理性，从而履行管理层的应尽义务。

due diligence 的第一层含义需与 due care 进行区分,根据《布莱克法律词典》得知,due care 与 reasonable care, ordinary care, adequate care, proper care 同义,具体释义为:as a test of liability for negligence, the degree of care that a prudent and competent person engaged in the same line of business or endeavor would exercise under similar circumstances。此外结合《英美法律术语辞典》的解释可知,due care 是侵权法上的概念,指某特定情况中要求某人应尽到正当、合适和充分的注意。这类似于我国《民法典》侵权责任编中规定的过错适用原则,即对一般侵权行为来说,只要行为人尽到了一个合理、谨慎的人应尽的注意义务,即使发生了损害,行为人也应该被免除责任。

effective vote 与 counted vote

这两个术语常被译为选举中的"有效票",该译文是否准确以及两者间有何区别?

根据《布莱克法律词典》,effective vote 指 a vote that counts toward a winning candidate, to the extent needed to win. A vote that goes to a winning candidate is "effective" to the extent needed to win, and "excess" beyond that point。例如,如果候选人需要 100 票,最终获得 150 票,则多出的 50 票是超额选票。每张选票为三分之二有效,三分之一超额。

counted vote 是议会法中的概念,指 a vote taken in a way that individually counts each voter,即以单独计算每个选民的方式进行的投票,比如举手表决、站立投票、唱名表决或书面选票。

《中华人民共和国全国人民代表大会和地方各级人民代表大会选举法》第四十四条规定:

每次选举所投的票数,多于投票人数的无效,等于或者少于投票人数的有效。

每一选票所选的人数,多于规定应选代表人数的作废,等于或者少于规定应选代表人数的有效。

由此可见,汉语中的"有效票"指的是在选举中符合规定的选票,与"无效票"相对。由 effective vote 的释义看来,它其实指在选举中获胜起到作用的那部分选票,笼统来说,也就是选举获胜所需票数,而与汉语中的"有效票"含义不同。

counted vote,从英文释义来看,则是指通过某种投票方式而获得的选票,也就是计票法,这与汉语中的"有效票"的含义相差甚远。

综上,effective vote 应译为"选举获胜所需票数",counted vote 则可译为"计票法选票"。

election under the will

仅从字面上看,该词组很容易理解为"按照个人意愿自由选举",这与其本义相去甚远。

《布莱克法律词典》中,will 的释义为:the legal expression of an individual's wishes about the disposition of his or her property after death; esp., a document by which a person directs his or her estate to be distributed upon death,即遗嘱。

《英美法律术语辞典(英汉双解)》给出了该词组的英文释义:In those states which have statutes that give a widow a particular percentage of the late husband's estate (such as dower), the surviving wife may elect to take that percentage instead of any lesser amount (or assets with unacceptable conditions such as an estate which will be cancelled if she remarries) left to her under his will.结合相关背景知识可知,该术语体现的是继承法中的一项原则。在美国,大多数州都出台法规规定遗孀应继承已故丈夫遗产的百分比。根据 election under the will 原则,已故男子的遗孀可以选择违背遗嘱,即她可以选择接受依法可继承的已故配偶遗产的特定份额,而不是接受已故配偶遗嘱中留给她的指定份额。

所以,此处 election 并非"选举",而是"选择"。因此,该术语可译为"遗孀遗产继承选择"原则。

entrapment

该术语的译文五花八门,比如:圈套、诱捕、坑害、诱骗;侦查圈套;诱惑侦查;诱人犯罪;官诱民犯;警察圈套、设圈套诱人犯罪、执法人员诱人犯罪等。这些翻译哪一个才是最准确的呢?这需要结合术语的源语释义以及中英文所处的不同法律体系的内容进行分析。

《布莱克法律词典》中，entrapment 的定义是：1. A law-enforcement officer's or government agent's inducement of a person to commit a crime, by means of fraud or undue persuasion, in an attempt to later bring a criminal prosecution against that person. 2. The affirmative defense of having been so induced. To establish entrapment (in most states), the defendant must show that he or she would not have committed the crime but for the fraud or undue persuasion.

由此可以看出，entrapment 主要指执法人员或其代理人为了获得对某人提起刑事诉讼的证据，而诱使他人实施某种犯罪的行为。在英美刑法中，entrapment 是被告人的一种合法抗辩理由，是 undercover operation or investigation 的界限所在。根据英美刑法和司法惯例，如果被告人认为警察的侦查行为构成 police entrapment，可以此为由进行合法抗辩。如果查明警察的行为构成 entrapment，可采用排除非法证据、终止诉讼、宣判被告无罪、减轻刑罚处罚或追究侦查人员刑事责任等方式进行救济。

英美国家的学者、法官对 entrapment 这种行为存有很大分歧。总体来看，entrapment 并不是一种侦查行为，而是一种非法行为。entrapment 这一术语无论是在普通英语辞典还是在法律英语辞典中都具有消极意义，从一些权威学者或者经典判例中也可以窥见对该行为的否定态度。在英美法系国家，对一些特别重要的特殊侦查措施，常常会制定一些单行法律法规（如美国的《FBI 秘密侦查行动准则》和英国的《秘密行动实践法》），其目的都是为了使 undercover operations（秘密行动）或 undercover investigation（秘密侦查）更加规范。但英美国家并未在法律文件中将 entrapment 单独列为一种侦查行为，从侧面证明了这一手段并非正当的侦查行为。

因此，前文中所提到的 entrapment 的译文中包含"侦查"字眼的均不太准确。了解源语释义后，很多人会联想到"钓鱼执法"现象，维基百科中"钓鱼执法"的英文翻译也是 entrapment。在我国，钓鱼执法指行政执法者在经济利益的驱使下，采用一种非正常手段诱惑守法公民"违法"，从而进行经济处罚的一种行为，如利用控制的卖淫女引诱某人嫖妓，从而进行治安处罚或罚款；或假扮乘客将非营运车辆引诱至"执法伏击区"，然后对驾驶人进行罚款，以至于上海出现"防钓鱼车"，车主在车窗上贴上"防止钓鱼，拒绝搭乘"的字条。钓鱼执法在我国一直存在合法性与合理性的争议。相较而言，entrapment 的主体既可以是警察也可以是执法人员代表,所以两者有着明显的区别,如果简单地将 entrapment 译为"钓鱼执法"会使英美读者感到困惑或误解。

综上,结合 entrapment 的行为主体以及其非正当侦查行为的特征,可将其译为"执法圈套",或者采用"警察圈套";或者可以将"诱人犯罪;诱捕"修改为"执法人员非法诱捕",以增强翻译的准确严谨之特点。

equal-access rule

从字面意思上看,equal-access rule 意思为"同等机会规则",那么这是怎样的"同等机会"呢?

查阅《布莱克法律词典》可知,刑事诉讼中被告可援引这一规则作为抗辩理由,具体指:the doctrine that contraband found on a defendant's premises will not support a conviction if other persons have had the same access to the premises as the defendant. 结合《元照英美法词典》的解释,依据该规则,如果其他人也有同等机会与被告人进入同样的地方(土地或房屋),仅发现在被告人所占有地上有违禁物品并不足以对其定罪。被告如果想成功援引这一规则作为抗辩理由,要有证据能够肯定地证明其他人有同等的机会进入该土地,诸如"侵入他人土地者(trespassers)可能进入该土地"这样的推测性证据不会起到抗辩效果。

因此,如果简单将该术语译为"同等机会原则"的话,容易产生歧义,不能使读者想到这是刑事诉讼中被告可援引该规则作为抗辩事由,结合其源语释义及其功能,可译为"(刑)平等进入抗辩原则"。

equitable distribution

该术语常被译为"公平分配"。在没有探究其在源语中的含义时,"公平分配"这一译法看起来是很正确的,但其实不然。

从《布莱克法律词典》对该术语给出的释义得知,该术语是美国《家事法》中的概念,也称 equitable division,assignment of property,具体指:the division of marital property by a court in a divorce proceeding, under statutory guidelines that provide for a fair, but not necessarily equal, allocation of the property between the spouses. With equitable distribution, when a marriage ends in divorce, property acquired during the marriage is divided equitably between the spouses regardless of who holds title to the property. The courts consider many factors in awarding property, including a spouse's monetary contributions, nonmonetary assistance to a spouse's career or earning potential, the efforts of each spouse during the marriage, and the length of the marriage. The court may take into account the relative earning capacity of the spouses and the fault of either spouse.

根据其源语释义来看，equitable distribution 是美国《家事法》中用于规定夫妻在离婚时分配夫妻共同财产的一种方法，即对婚姻关系存续期间丈夫和妻子或任何一方所合法取得的财产进行公平分割（不一定是平均分配），不管这些财产是由他们共同所有还是个人所有。根据这种方式，法院分配夫妻两人离婚时所得财产的比例时会考虑诸多因素，比如：夫妻双方各自的工资水平、夫妻双方的身体状况、被抚养儿童的特殊需要、双方各自对家庭的贡献等；对离婚负有过错责任的一方所分得的财产会少于另一方，这也符合公平原则。美国 47 个州都适用该方法对离婚夫妇的财产进行分割，加利福尼亚州、路易斯安那州和新墨西哥州等适用"平等划分"（equal division）方法。

"公平分配"这一词语在我国有着特定的含义，即个人对所获报酬的公平分配，主要表现为个人消费品分配的相对公平，社会成员之间的收入差距不能过于悬殊，其目的是为了促进效率的发挥①（彭剑君、陈珏宇，2010:479）。由此可见，这一定义与婚姻完全没有关系，将 equitable distribution 译为"公平分配"显然不妥。

综上，结合 equitable distribution 的源语释义，可将其译为"公平分配婚姻财产"。

estoppel

该术语的翻译版本较多，比如"不得自驳、不得反言"；"禁止翻供"；"不容反悔"；"表意、表见、不许改悔（或反复）"；禁止反言、禁止翻供、不可反悔；不容否认、再诉禁止等。

《布莱克法律词典》对 estoppel 的释义有：

---

① 彭剑君,陈珏宇. 马克思主义公平分配观与和谐社会建设[J]. 武汉大学学报（哲学社会科学版）,2010(03):475-480.

1. A bar that prevents one from asserting a claim or right that contradicts what one has said or done before or what has been legally established as true，即禁止在此后的法律程序中提出与之前言行相反的主张或权利主张。结合《元照英美法词典》的解释可知有三种具体情况：因立有契据而不容否认（estoppel by deed）、因已记录在案而不容否认（estoppel by record）和因既有行为而不容否认（estoppel in pais），其中，前两种又称为普通法上的不容否认（legal estoppel），后一种称为衡平法上的不容否认（equitable estoppel）。

2. A bar that prevents the relitigation of issues，即既判事项不容否认，禁止对同一当事人之间相同或不同争点再次争讼，比如 collateral estoppel，direct estoppel，estoppel by judgement 这几个术语均含此意。

3. An affirmative defense alleging good-faith reliance on a misleading representation and an injury or detrimental change in position resulting from that reliance，此为一种积极抗辩，可主张因对他人的误导性陈述存在善意信赖而遭受损害从而可提出抗辩。

通过源语释义我们可以发现，这三种含义中蕴含的法律精神具有相似性。普通法中 estoppel 原则（doctrine of estoppel）认为，当事人不得反驳自己既定的立场，即使原先立场与事实真相不符。这是因为另一方当事人从上述定义中可以看出，若一方当事人变换立场，言行前后不一，则可能会对另一方当事人造成损害。estoppel 就是为了防止此类情况的发生。由此可以看出，estoppel 背后的原因是为了防止不公正或欺诈行为[①]。意义在于不允许当事人通过违背其先前做出的允诺的行为而造成对另一方当事人权益的损害，一言以蔽之，当事人必须言行一致[②]。英美法强调 My word is my bond，estoppel 原则（doctrine of estoppel）是英美法中维持契约公正性的主要工具[③]。

此外，还需注意以下两点：

1. estoppel 可在诉讼中作为抗辩（defense）的理由，要让其生效，必须满足：一方当事人的言语或行动足以让另一方当事人据此行事；另一方当事人有依据

---

① 吴煜晨. 民事诉讼中的禁反言规则研究[D]. 2004.
② 张文彬. 论普通法上的禁止反言原则[J]. 长江大学学报（社会科学版），2001(04)：48-54.
③ 王霞. 论英美法中弃权和禁止反言原则在保险法上的适用[D]. 对外经济贸易大学，2000.

一方当事人的言语或行动行事的行为；另一方当事人的权益因此受到了损害。

2. estoppel 作为体现英美法契约精神的一项重要原则，它统领许多细分的情况，例如：estoppel by deed，promissory estoppel，collateral estoppel，equitable estoppel，estoppel by representation，estoppel by conduct，estoppel by acquiescence 等。以上每一个术语中 estoppel 的作用也不尽相同。

综上所述，estoppel 作为一个统称，其译名应该能够适用于所有情况，而不是有所侧重和偏颇。相对而言，"禁止反言"能够包含上述几种含义，但也可根据具体语境进一步进行细化。比如适用于合同中时，可译为"允诺禁止反言"，从而突出"承诺不可反悔"此种契约精神对合同成立的重要性。

European Council

the European Council，the Council of Europe 和 the Council of the European Union 是同一机构吗？

这三个欧洲机构名称常被译为"欧洲理事会"或"欧盟理事会"，这其实非常不严谨，三者并不指代同一机构，不可一概而论。

根据 the Council of Europe 官网上的信息可知：the Council of Europe is an international organisation focused on protecting human rights, democracy, rule of law in Europe and promoting European culture. The organisation is distinct from the 28-nation European Union (EU)…

根据欧盟官网提供的信息可知：the European Council, charged with defining the EU's overall political direction and priorities, is the institution of the European Union (EU) that comprises the heads of state or government of the member states, along with the President of the European Council and the President of the European Commission。

同样根据欧盟官网提供的信息可知：the Council of the European Union is the institution representing the member states' governments. Also known informally as the EU Council, it is where national ministers from each EU country meet to adopt laws and coordinate policies. It is part of the essentially bicameral EU legislature (the other legislative body being the European Parliament) and represents the executive governments of the EU's member states.

由此可见，三个机构的差别甚远，the European Council 和 the Council of the European Union 均属于欧盟，而 the Council of Europe 则与欧盟相互独立。the European Council 是欧盟的主要决策机构，主要是由欧盟成员国政府首脑和欧盟委员会主席以及该理事会主席组成的；the Council of the European Union 是一个由来自欧盟成员国各国政府部长所组成的理事会，也是欧盟的主要决策机构之一。欧盟部长理事会主要任务是协调欧洲共同体各个国家间事务，制定欧盟法律和法规；the Council of Europe 则与欧盟相互独立，它包括更多的欧洲国家，致力于在欧洲范围内维护人权，民主以及法治。

由于名称相似，这三个机构常常为人所混淆。经查阅，这三个机构的译名参差不齐，无确切的译名，甚至三者被译为相同的名称，比如《英汉大词典》（陆谷孙主编，2007）将 the European Council 译为"欧洲理事会；欧盟首脑会议"；《牛津英美文化词典》（商务印书馆，2007）也将 the Council of Europe 译为"欧洲理事会"；在"中国知网"中，the Council of Europe 被译为"欧洲理事会"或"欧洲委员会"，the European Council 被译为"欧盟理事会"，the Council of European Union 也被译为"欧盟理事会"。而根据三个机构的组成和作用，首先来区分同属欧盟的 European Council 和 the Council of European Union。两个机构的组成不同在于 European Council 是由欧盟成员国政府首脑、欧委会主席和该理事会主席组成，而 the Council of European Union 是由来自欧盟成员国各国政府部长所组成的，据此，可将 European Council 译为"欧盟首脑会议"，the Council of European Union 译为"欧盟理事会"或"欧盟部长理事会"。而与欧盟互相独立的机构 the Council of Europe 则可译为"欧洲理事会"。

execution

根据《布莱克法律词典》，execution 的释义如下：

1. The act of carrying out or putting into effect (as a court order or a securities transaction)，指执行或实施，比如 execution of the court's decree, execution of the stop-loss order。

2. Validation of a written instrument, such as a contract or will, by fulfilling the necessary legal requirements，即通过满足必要的法律要求（如履行签名，盖章，交付等法律所要求的手续），使一些书面文件（如合同或遗嘱）生效。

比如 delivery of the goods completed the contract's execution 表示货物交付即表示执行合同。

3. Judicial enforcement of a money judgment, usu. by seizing and selling the judgment debtor's property, 指对涉及金钱的判决进行司法执行, 通常通过扣押和出售既定债务人的财产实现, 苏格兰法也称 diligence。值得注意的是, 如果判决中原告的债务人是外国债务人, 则执行有困难。

4. A court order directing a sheriff or other officer to enforce a judgment, usu. by seizing and selling the judgment debtor's property, 指一种法庭命令(court order), 也称 writ of execution, judgment execution, general execution, 指示行政司法官(sheriff)或其他官员通过扣押和出售既定债务人的财产从而执行判决, 比如 the court issued the execution authorizing seizure of the car(法院发布了授权扣押汽车的执行令)。

由上述源语释义可见, execution 基本具有"实施, 执行, 通过特定行为使生效"等含义, 可结合语境进行翻译。

false arrest

《布莱克法律词典》对该术语的解释较为简单, 指 an arrest made without proper legal authority, 即非经合适的法律机构执行的 arrest(刑事领域为"逮捕", 民事领域为"拘禁"), 强调执行主体不恰当。

康奈尔法学院 LII 在线数据库平台给出了更为详细的解释[①]:

The restraint or detention by one person of another without lawful justification (probable cause, a valid arrest warrant, or consent) under an asserted legal authority to enforce the process of the law…it refers to private as well as governmental detentions and does not require any malice or bad faith on the offender's part to make them guilty of the offense.

据此, 有几个要点值得注意:1. 无合法理由, 比如合理根据(probable cause), 无有效逮捕证(arrest warrant), 无当事人合意;2. 行为主体是法律规定的主体(an asserted legal authority);3. 以执行法律程序为目的;4. 行为主体可

---

① https://www.law.cornell.edu/wex/false_arrest, 最后访问时间 2021 年 12 月 7 日。

以是个人也可以是单位,个人通常为警察;5.不要求实施该行为的人有任何恶意或不诚实的行为从而促使其犯罪,即无主观意图但只需实施此种行为仍然会被判有罪。6.该术语中的"false"指的是此种限制行为的非法性。

根据康奈尔法学院LII在线数据库平台对false arrest的解释①可知:false arrest也称false imprisonment,都是轻罪。美国一些司法管辖区区分了false arrest和false imprisonment:对false arrest的指控要求逮捕方声称拥有进行逮捕的法律权力;而false imprisonment重在强调非法限制他人自由这种行为,无论是否有逮捕权利。通过该数据库对false imprisonment的解释②也可知:它是刑法和侵权法中规定的应受惩罚的行为。根据侵权法,该行为属故意侵权(intentional tort)。任何人对另一人实施限制行为,将该人限制在特定区域(bounded area)内,即构成false imprisonment。

同时,我们也可以进一步了解《布莱克法律词典》false imprisonment的释义:a restraint of a person in a bounded area without justification or consent. False imprisonment is a common-law misdemeanor and a tort. It applies to private as well as governmental detention. 结合《元照英美法词典》的解释可知,false imprisonment指非法剥夺他人的人身自由的行为。凡未经依法授权或无法律根据,以暴力或以暴力相威胁,强制他人违反自己的意愿留在某处或到某处去,即构成false imprisonment,而不论拘禁的地点或拘禁时间的长短。在普通法上属刑事上的轻罪行为及民事侵权行为。恶意虽非构成非法拘禁的必要条件,但可加重行为人的赔偿责任。False imprisonment的行为主体可以是个人可以是单位。

《元照英美法词典》将false arrest译为"非法拘捕",false imprisonment译为"非法拘禁"。由前文可知"false"强调的是此行为的非法性,所以我们需要对"拘捕"和"拘禁"进行区分。我国《刑法》第二百三十八条明确规定了"非法拘禁罪"③,

---

① https://www.law.cornell.edu/wex/false_arrest,最后访问时间2021年12月7日。
② https://www.law.cornell.edu/wex/false_imprisonment,最后访问时间2021年12月7日。
③ 我国《刑法》第二百三十八条规定:非法拘禁他人或者以其他方法非法剥夺他人人身自由的,处三年以下有期徒刑、拘役、管制或者剥夺政治权利。具有殴打、侮辱情节的,从重处罚。犯前款罪,致人重伤的,处三年以上十年以下有期徒刑;致人死亡的,处十年以上有期徒刑。使用暴力致人伤残、死亡的,依照本法第二百三十四条、第二百三十二条的规定定罪处罚。为索取债务非法扣押、拘禁他人的,依照前两款的规定处罚。国家机关工作人员利用职权犯前三款罪的,依照前三款的规定从重处罚。

但非法拘禁行为①,只有达到相当严重的程度,才构成犯罪。我国《民法典》第一千零一十一条也规定了:以非法拘禁等方式剥夺、限制他人的行动自由,或者非法搜查他人身体的,受害人有权依法请求行为人承担民事责任。由此可见,我国法律中规定的非法拘禁行为与 false imprisonment 同为非法剥夺他人自由的行为,且行为主体可以是个人或单位。因此 false imprisonment 可翻译为"非法拘禁"。但是,我国法律法规中未找到"拘捕"这样的表述,但"拘捕"其实是"拘留和逮捕"的简称。依据《中华人民共和国刑事诉讼法》(以下简称《刑事诉讼法》)的规定,拘留和逮捕,属于两种不同的强制措施。拘留是指公安机关在紧急情况下,对该逮捕的现行犯或重大嫌疑分子,直接采用的临时限制其人身自由的强制措施。逮捕是指人民法院、人民检察院和公安机关,为防止被告人逃避或阻碍侦查、审判继续犯罪,对被告采取的全面限制其人身自由并予以羁押的一种方法,它是强制措施中最严厉的一种。根据前文对 false arrest 的释义可知,它指 restraint or detention,即拘留和逮捕,因此将其翻译为"非法拘捕"较为合理。

false statement

false statement 通常被译为"虚假陈述"或"虚假表示"。此外,该术语与 misrepresentation 因为意义相近而常常被混淆适用,但实际上二者是有区别的。

《布莱克法律词典》对 false statement 的定义是:1. An untrue statement knowingly made with the intent to mislead,即故意误导的不真实陈述;2. Any one of three distinct federal offenses:(1) falsifying or concealing a material fact by trick, scheme, or device;(2) making a false, fictitious, or fraudulent representation; and (3) making or using a false document or writing,即三种不同的联邦罪行中的任何一种:(1)运用诡计,计谋或者设备伪造或隐瞒事实;(2)做出虚假,虚构或者欺骗性的表述;(3)制作或使用虚假文件或文书。而对于

---

① 比如我国《民事诉讼法》第一百零六条规定:采取对妨害民事诉讼的强制措施必须由人民法院决定。任何单位和个人采取非法拘禁他人或者非法私自扣押他人财产追索债务的,应当依法追究刑事责任,或者予以拘留、罚款。《刑事诉讼法》第十九条规定:人民检察院在对诉讼活动实行法律监督中发现的司法工作人员利用职权实施的非法拘禁、刑讯逼供、非法搜查等侵犯公民权利、损害司法公正的犯罪,可以由人民检察院立案侦查。

misrepresentation 的定义是：1. The act or an instance of making a false or misleading assertion about something, usu. with the intent to deceive. The word denotes not just written or spoken words but also any other conduct that amounts to a false assertion. 2. The assertion so made; an incorrect, unfair, or false statement; an assertion that does not accord with the facts. —Also termed false representation. 即(1)出于欺骗的意图做出虚假或误导性声明的行为或实例，这个词不仅指书面或口头的话，也指任何虚假的断言。(2)做出断言；做出不正确的、不公平的或错误的陈述；做出与事实不符的断言。也称为虚假表示。

综上，false statement 更多表示虚假的，不真实的陈述，重在"陈述"；而 misrepresentation 更多表示错误的，虚假的断言和表示，重在"表示"；因此，若要译 false statement，应该译为"虚假陈述"；而 misrepresentation 译为"虚假表示"比较妥当。

family allowance

family allowance 也是一个译者经常望文生"译"的法律术语，容易按字面意思翻译为"家庭津贴"。但查阅《布莱克法律词典》可知，它指 a portion of a decedent's estate set aside by statute for a surviving spouse, children, or parents, regardless of any testamentary disposition or competing claims。Every state has a statute authorizing the probate court to award an amount for the temporary maintenance and support of the surviving spouse (and often for dependent children). The allowance may be limited for a fixed period (18 months under the Uniform Probate Code) or may continue until all contests are resolved, and a decree of distribution is entered. 这说明了 family allowance 是指在遗产管理过程中，依法律规定为保障生存配偶、子女或父母的生活而从死者遗产中拨付的一部分财产，无论其是否有遗嘱处分权(testamentary disposition)或竞合求偿权(competing claims)。在美国，每个州都有一项法令授权遗嘱认证法院裁定一笔用作尚存配偶(通常用于受抚养子女)的临时赡养费和赡养费。该费用可以限定在固定期限内(根据《统一遗嘱认证法》规定为 18 个月)，也可以在所有争议得到解决并签署分配令之前继续发放。

此外，根据《元照英美法词典》的解释也可进一步得知，family allowance 也可为抚养双方当事人的子女而在离婚或分居判决中所规定的补助金,通常判决向其妻子和/或子女一次性支付。

因此,以上两种情况中对 family allowance 一词翻译为"家庭津贴"与其本意有所出入,会让读者误以为这笔津贴是政府拨付给某个家庭的,但实际上该费用与政府并无关系。因此结合该术语的使用情景,即分配给遗孀和子女的遗产或离婚后双方当事人一方为抚养子女而支付的补偿金,family allowance 应译为"家属扶养补助"或"子女抚养补助"。

而在英国法中,family allowance 的内涵则与"家庭津贴"或"家庭补助"更为接近。根据《新牛津英语词典》中对 family allowance 的定义:regular payment by the state to the parents of a child up to a certain age in the UK 可知,其已被列为 child benefit 一词的同义词,或者说 family allowance 是 child benefit 的前身。自 1945 年英国议会通过《家庭津贴法案》(The Family Allowances Act 1945),英国政府自 1946 年起向有两个或两个以上子女的家庭拨付的补助金,该补助依子女人数(长子或长女除外)按月由财政部提供的基金中支付,并为整个家庭所受益。在此类子女到达离校年龄之前或未满 18 岁且处于全日制在校阶段之前,可一直享受该补助。后于 1975 年被儿童津贴 child benefit 所取代。所以在背景涉及英国法的文本中出现 family allowance 一词,应首选翻译为"家庭津贴"。

final judgment

该术语常被误译为"终审判决"。根据《布莱克法律词典》可知,该术语的同义词比较多,有 final appealable judgment,final decision,final decree,definitive judgment,determinative judgment,final appealable order,意思是:a court's last action that settles the rights of the parties and disposes of all issues in controversy, except for the award of costs (and, sometimes, attorney's fees) and enforcement of the judgment,指法院的最后一项诉讼,解决双方的权利并处理争议中的所有问题,但不包括对费用的裁决(有时还有律师费)和判决执行。

此外,根据《布莱克法律词典》对 final-judgment rule 的解释可知:a party may appeal only from a district court's final decision that ends the litigation on the merits. Under this rule, a party must raise all claims of error in a single appeal,即初审法院对案件的实体(merits)进行审理后,当事人可就此判决进行上诉。

但在汉语法律语境中,比如我国《民事诉讼法》第十条规定:人民法院审理民事案件,依照法律规定实行合议、回避、公开审判和两审终审制度。第一百八十四条规定:第二审人民法院的判决、裁定,是终审的判决、裁定。由此可见,"终审判决"是法院对案件的最后一级判决。我国实行两审终审制,中级人民法院、高级人民法院和最高人民法院的第二审就是终审。最高人民法院的第一审也是终审。终审判决是不可以上诉的。

综上,final judgment 可以 appealable,很显然译为"终审判决"是误译,而应译为"最后判决"或者"判决",judgment of last resort 才对应"终审判决"①。

foreign

foreign 一词在法律文本中多含"涉外"之意,例如 foreign policy 是外交政策,foreign affairs 是涉外事务,foreign trade 是对外贸易等。但"涉外律师事务所"应如何翻译?通过查阅资料发现 foreign law firms 或 foreign lawyer office 这样的译文很常见。然而按照 WTO 法律文件的标准译法,在中国设立的外国律师事务所才称为 foreign law firms。而国内的涉外律师事务所应译为 foreign affairs lawyer office 或者 foreign-related law firms。同样的道理,foreign enterprises 是"外国企业",而非涉外企业;foreign securities institutions 是"外国证券机构",而非涉外证券机构;foreign award of arbitration 是"外国仲裁裁决"而非涉外仲裁裁决。

foreign judgment

foreign 除了熟知的"外国的;属于,关于,涉及另一个国家"之意,还表示"属于,关于,涉及另一个司法管辖区"。对于术语 foreign judgment,《布莱克法律词典》的定义是:A decree, judgment, or order of a court in a state, country, or judicial system different from that where the judgment or its effect is at issue. 根据该英文释义可知,此处的 foreign 并不是"外国的"意思,而是指另一个司法

---

① 张法连. 英美法律术语汉译策略探究[J]. 中国翻译. 2016(02):100-104.

管辖区,因此如果译为"外国的裁决"就是明显的望文生义,词不达意。

结合《元照英美法词典》的解释可知 foreign judgment 指外国法院做出的判决;在美国也指外州法院的判决。按照美国联邦宪法第四条第一款规定的精神,对外州法院做出的民事判决,其效力视同本州法院的判决。有些州采纳《统一外州判决执行法》(Uniform Enforcement of Foreign Judgments Act)。对有管辖权的外国法院经合法程序做出的最终民事判决,本国法院在审理同一案件时,原则上可作为决定性的证据,法院的各项认定都倾向于支持该项外国判决。但若该项判决系以欺诈手段获得,或有悖于公正和理性,则法院不予认可。对外国法院判决的承认和执行,一般按照互惠原则办理。英国在 1933 年制定有《外国判决(互惠执行)法》[Foreign Judgments (Reciprocal Enforcement) Act]。

综上,该术语可参照《英美法律术语辞典(英汉双解)》的译文"异州(或异国)互惠执行判决"。

forward merger

《元照英美法词典》对 forward 的解释有:向前;向将来;提前地;超前地;在前面的;在先的;发往目的地;发送;传送;传输;(由普通承运人)运输货物;(不按承运人的线路)直达某地的运输。与 forward 相关的词有 forward contract(远期合同),forwarding agent(货运代理人),forwarding fee(转运费)等,但是把这些意思套用到 forward merger 中都不太合适,首先应了解该词组的英文释义。该词的英文解释为:A merger in which the target company merges with and into the buyer, the buyer assumes all of the target company's assets, rights and liabilities and the target company ceases to exist as a separate entity (Practical Law, RESOURCE ID 8—382—3406),或者解释为:a forward merger is a merger in which the target merges into the buyer, and the target shareholders exchange their stock for the agreed-upon purchase price(See American Institute of Certi ed Public Accountants, Inc. New York, NY 10036--8775)。两种解释的汉语意思皆为:收购方将目标公司并入收购方中,收购方承担目标公司的资产、权利和债务,目标公司不再作为一个独立的实体存在。由此可知 forward merger 是公司合并的一种方式。

我国《公司法》第一百七十二条规定:公司合并可以采取吸收合并或者新设

合并。一个公司吸收其他公司为吸收合并，被吸收的公司解散。两个以上公司合并设立一个新的公司为新设合并，合并各方解散。

通常，吸收合并可分为三种形式：第一种，母公司作为吸收合并的主体并成为存续公司，上市公司注销；第二种，上市公司作为吸收合并的主体并成为存续公司，集团公司注销；第三种，非上市公司之间的吸收合并。

在检索 forward merger 这个词的含义时，频繁出现 forward subsidiary merger 这个词的翻译，而该词是有确切的汉语解释的，即"正向子公司合并"。同时，在《企业兼并之相关智慧财产管理策略与法律规制研究——以兼并美国高科技公司时专利查核评估探维》一书中也提出"公司亦可选择先成立一子公司为主体公司，出面与目标公司合并。方式上可以选择由子公司吸收合并目标公司之正向子公司合并（forward subsidiary merger）或由目标公司吸收合并子公司之反向子公司合并（reverse subsidiary merger）"（See Reed & Lajoux, Supra Note 38, pp. 262－263, 340, and Gaughan, Supra Note 10, p. 13.），可见该文中也将 forward subsidiary merger 译为"正向子公司合并"。

无论是从内容还是形式上来看，forward subsidiary merger 与 forward merger 都存在某种关联[①]。forward merger 与 forward subsidiary merger 的相同之处为：两者都是一个公司兼并目标公司，兼并后，目标公司的法人地位、财产、股权全都消失，归于实施兼并的公司；不同之处在于 forward subsidiary merger 中，出于某种考量，实施兼并的公司会先设立一个子公司，再由这个子公司来兼并目标公司，兼并后的目标公司无论是法人地位还是财产股权全都消失。

综上，forward merger 应表示母公司作为吸收合并的主体；forward subsidiary merger 应表示子公司之间的吸收合并，所以 forward merger 一词的翻译应该为"正向合并"。

---

① 从 Matt Farber 一篇名为 Forward Mergers & Triangular Mergers: The Differences 的演讲稿中也可以印证"forward subsidiary merger"与"forward merger"的关系，其讲稿内容为：In a forward merger, the target merges with and into the buyer, eliminating the target's existence. The buyer consequently assumes the target's rights and liabilities by operation of law. By contrast, a forward triangular (subsidiary) merger (also known as an indirect merger) is a transaction that requires a third entity, a merger subsidiary, or a shell company. This subsidiary company is capitalized with the consideration for purchasing the target company. Similar to a forward merger, the target merges with and into the merger subsidiary, with the subsidiary assuming all the target's assets and liabilities.

friend of the court

friend of the court 与前文中提到的 amicus curiae 一样，人们常译为"法庭之友"。根据《布莱克法律词典》的定义，这个法律术语其实有两重含义：1. AMICUS CURIAE. 2. In some jurisdictions, an official who investigates and advises the court in domestic-relations cases involving minors. The friend of the court may also help enforce court orders in those cases.

第一层含义中的 AMICUS CURIAE 是拉丁语词汇，具体解释可以参见前文，此处不再赘述。

第二层含义中 friend of the court 是指在一些司法管辖区中，遇到涉及未成年人的家庭关系案件时，未成年人法律援助办公室会派其工作人员调查案件以及向法院提交意见书，往往还会帮助法院执行在这些案件中给出的指令。但这层含义并未在大部分词典中得以体现，仅在较为权威的《布莱克法律词典》中给出了解释，所以译者在遇到这个法律术语时应首先判断其适用的案件背景，如果与第二层含义中给出的情形相同，涉及未成年人，此时就应结合此处的第二层含义进行翻译，综合此处源语的释义及 friend of the court 扮演的角色，可译为"未成年人案件法官顾问"。

有些法律英语术语的含义并非一成不变，平时应注意积累此类具有多重含义的术语，在翻译时要具体问题具体分析，多查证多联系多思考，尽量保证译文的准确性与严谨性。

fruit

fruit 一词如果出现在法律文件或文书中，显然不能套用普通英语中的"水果；果实"之意进行翻译。

《布莱克法律词典》对该术语的定义有两层：其一，the produce or product of something (as of land or property)，该含义下指"产物"；其二，income or goods derived or produced from property without a diminution of the property's inherent value，根据含义可以理解为法律意义上的孳息，指不损害原物的价值，从原物形成或产生的收入或产品。

法律意义上的孳息分为两类，即 civil fruit 和 legal fruit。《布莱克法律词典》对 civil fruit 的定义是 revenue derived from a thing by operation of law or by reason of a juridical act, such as lease or interest payments, or certain corporate distributions,根据含义可以理解为法定孳息。我国对于法定孳息的定义是因法律关系所获得的收益,如出租人根据租赁合同收取的租金、贷款人根据贷款合同取得的利息等,与该辞典的定义相近,因而可以采用 civil fruit 对应法定孳息。因此把法定孳息译为 legal fruit 或者 statutory fruit 都是不准确的,legal 多表示法律上的、合法的,statutory 多表示依照法令的、成文的、制定的,都不太能准确地表示"法定的"这层意义。《布莱克法律词典》对 natural fruit 的定义为:a product of the land or of animals. Examples are crops and eggs,根据含义可以理解为天然孳息。我国对于天然孳息的定义是指因物的自然属性而获得的收益,与原物分离前,是原物的一部分,如果树结的果实、从羊身上剪下的羊毛等,与辞典的英文定义相近,因而可以采用 natural fruit 对应天然孳息。

fundamental law

看到 fundamental 这个词,可能会理解为"根本的"或者"重要的",从而将 fundamental law 译为"根本法"或者"原则法",这些译法都只译出了字面含义,并未理解到其真正含义。

《布莱克法律词典》对这个词的定义是:The organic law that establishes the governing principles of a country or state; esp. Constitutional Law. Also termed organic law; ground-law,指建立一个国家统治原则的法律。

由此可见,译为"根本法"或者"原则法"都没有反映出该词的内涵。在我国,说到根本法指的就是宪法,宪法是我国的根本法律,是一切法律、法规的母法,其他一切法律法规都是宪法的子法;而提到我国的组织法,则指的是专门规定某类国家机关的组成和活动原则的法律,包括《中华人民共和国全国人民代表大会组织法》《中华人民共和国国务院组织法》等。基本法则包括各个级别的部门法等。因而根本法和组织法在定义上是有根本区别的。而该词的源语定义指的是建立统治原则的法律,更多地指的是国家的组织形式和统治原则。

综上,译为"根本法"是夸大了该词的内涵,译为"原则法"是缩小了该词的外延,都是不妥当的译法。译为"组织法"或者"基本法"相对合适,不仅反映出了源语的具体含义,而且目标语能够相对准确地对应该含义。

futures

许多人看到 futures 会自然而然地联想到是 future 的复数形式,实际上 futures 一词在法律语境下具有特殊含义。

《布莱克法律词典》对 futures 的定义有三层:1. Standardized assets (such as commodities, stocks, or foreign currencies) bought or sold for future acceptance or delivery. Also termed financial futures,第一层意义可以理解为为将来承兑或交付而买卖的标准资产(如商品、股票或外币),亦称金融期货。2. futures contract:An agreement to buy or sell a standardized asset (such as a commodity, stock, or foreign currency) at a fixed price at a future time, usu. during a particular time of a month. Futures contracts are traded on exchanges such as the Chicago Board of Trade or the Chicago Mercantile Exchange. Often shortened to futures. Also termed futures agreement; time-bargain,指在固定时间内以固定价格买卖标准资产的协议。3. Future claimants, esp. those who would become members of a class of persons injured by a defendant and thus included in a class action,即一类专门的索赔人。

综上,futures 的法律含义是"期货"。在见到类似 futures 这种极易望文生义的术语时,不能凭借个人的经验和所谓的常识来解决问题,要明确其所处的具体语境,找到其源语解释,才能最终确定其表达的准确含义。

futures contract

由《布莱克法律词典》对 futures 的第二层定义可知,futures contract 通常简写为 futures,也称为 futures agreement;time-bargain,具体指:An agreement to buy or sell a standardized asset (such as a commodity, stock, or foreign currency) at a fixed price at a future time, usu. during a particular time of a month. Futures contracts are traded on exchanges such as the Chicago Board of Trade or the Chicago Mercantile Exchange. 其译文"期货合同"已被普遍使用,《元照英美法词典》中也进一步解释了其含义:(1)买卖双方约定在将来某一时间交割的商品或证券或外汇等,合同价格随市场价格而定。

(2)买卖双方达成的按约定价格购买约定数量的期货的合同,其价格由双方在期货交易所以公开竞价方式确定。期货合同对商品品级、交货方式、保证金等条件均有统一规定,买卖双方只在交易中确定价格、交货期与合同数量。期货交易一般不导致实际交割,因为卖方在交货期之前可以转手或购买同样数量的合同对原合同进行对冲。期货交易者分为两大类:其一,为规避价格风险而利用期货作套期保值业务的商人;其二,利用期货市场的价格变动赚取价差的投机者。

此外,要注意区分 futures contract 与 forward contract。《布莱克法律词典》对 forward contract 的定义为:An agreement to buy or sell a particular nonstandardized asset (usu. currencies) at a fixed price on a future date. 此外,词典中也提到与 futures contract 不同的是,forward contract 不是在 formal exchange 中缔结的,通常被译为"远期合同"。远期合同是 20 世纪 80 年代初兴起的一种保值工具,它是一种交易双方约定在未来的某一确定时间,以确定的价格买卖一定数量的某种金融资产的合约。合同中要规定交易的标的物、有效期和交割时的执行价格等项内容。

远期合同与期货合同相同点在于,都是在确定的将来时刻按确定的价格购买或出售某项资产的协议。不同之处在于:1. 期货是标准化的合约,标的物的品质、数量、交割日期等均是标准化的,交易地点是在交易所采用集中交易的方式进行,发生违约的风险非常低,甚至几乎没有。期货合同的流通性更好,因为吸引了投机者的加入。2. 远期合同是合同双方当事人根据需要商定标的物、品质、数量、价格、到期日等。交易通常只在场外交易,由于合约非标准化,所以流通量不如期货,如果其中一方违约,另一方则会因此而承受违约风险。

garnishee

《布莱克法律词典》对该术语的定义是:A person or institution (such as a bank) that is indebted to or is bailee for another whose property has been subjected to garnishment. Also termed garnishee-defendant (as opposed to the "principal defendant," i.e., the primary debtor). 结合《元照英美法词典》的解释可知,garnishee 是指占有属于被告的金钱或财产的人,或对被告负有债务的人,此项金钱、财产或债务由法院扣押或冻结。《元照英美法词典》将其翻译为"案外债务人"。"案外"所指的范围广,且并没有明确地指出该债务人是否与被告有关系。而 garnishee 与被告是有债务关系的,所以这个关系应该在译文中体现出来才更准确,读者也更容易理解。

根据康奈尔法学院LII在线数据库平台对garnishee的解释①：在扣押程序中，如果法院为原告债权人做出裁决，被告债务人在第三方（the third party）控制下的资产将被扣押。第三方在这里被称为garnishee，原告是garnishor。最常见的garnishee是债务人的雇主，或债务人有账户的银行。

综上，"第三债务人"这个译法更为合适。"第三"，在这里指第三方，通常指两个相互联系的主体之外的某个客体，可以和两个主体有联系，也可是独立的。"第三债务人"意为对执行案件中的被执行人负有到期应履行给付义务的第三人，可与主要负债人明确分开，但又表明了其与被告的联系，不会造成意义模糊或者有歧义。

general demurrer

根据《布莱克法律词典》的定义，general demurrer 与 general exception 同义，即：An objection pointing out a substantive defect in an opponent's pleading, such as the insufficiency of the claim or the court's lack of subject-matter jurisdiction; an objection to a pleading for want of substance，指以起诉状中存在某种实质性缺陷为根据而提出的抗辩，如权利主张不充分或法院缺乏对诉讼标的的管辖权等。

《布莱克法律词典》对 demurrer 的定义是：A pleading stating that although the facts alleged in a complaint may be true, they are insufficient for the plaintiff to state a claim for relief and for the defendant to frame an answer. In most jurisdictions, such a pleading is now termed a motion to dismiss, but demurrer is still used in a few states, including California, Nebraska, and Pennsylvania. 结合《元照英美法词典》对该术语的解释可知，demurrer 指一种抗

---

① In a garnishment proceeding, if the court rules for the plaintiff-creditor, the defendant-debtor's asset under a third-party's control will be garnished. The third party here is called a garnishee, and the plaintiff is a garnishor. The most common garnishees are employer of the debtor, or a bank in which the debtor has an account. When the garnishee receives a court judgment of garnishment (often called the writ of garnishment), the garnishee should stop the debtor's access to the fund under the garnishee's control. The garnishee essentially acts as an officer for the court, and the garnishee can be held liable if it transfers the debtor's funds or assets upon the debtor's request. 参见 https://www.law.cornell.edu/wex/garnishee，最后访问时间2022年1月10日。

辩形式,尽管诉讼一方当事人承认对方主张的事实是真实的,但认为它在法律上却不足以支持其救济请求,或认为其诉状表面上仍存在某些缺陷,使得本方在法律上无义务继续推进诉讼,从而提出抗辩。现美国联邦民事诉讼及刑事诉讼中均已不再使用这种抗辩形式,但在加利福尼亚、内布拉斯加州和宾夕法尼亚等少数州仍有保留。《元照英美法词典》将其翻译为"诉求不充分抗辩;法律抗辩"。general 做形容词有"一般的,综合的"的含义。

general demurrer 可译为"一般抗辩"。《元照英美法词典》将其译为"一般诉求不充分抗辩",在字面含义的基础上根据术语解释做了一些补充,清晰表明该术语是说因诉求不充分有缺陷而进行的法律抗辩。有一些网站将该术语误译为"总的抗辩"。该术语强调的是因为对方诉求不充分而进行的抗辩。"总的抗辩"并不能清楚解释这个术语的含义。

golden parachute

根据《布莱克法律词典》对 golden parachute 的定义,该术语是公司法常用术语,具体指:an employment-contract provision that grants an upper-level executive lucrative severance benefits,including long-term salary guarantees or bonuses——if control of the company changes hands（as by a merger）。由此可知,该术语用以指公司管理层变动时保护原高层管理人员利益的解职协议。如果公司的控制权易手(如通过合并),可通过 golden parachute 这种雇佣合同协议,为离开原公司或退出管理层的高层管理人员和某些董事提供优厚的津贴和其他福利,包括长期工资保障或奖金。

parachute,降落伞,又称保险伞,是使人或物体减速、稳定的一种气动力减速器。golden,指富裕的,高额的。许多词典和网站按照字面意思将其直译为"黄金降落伞",借用 golden 和 parachute 的比喻意义。从《布莱克法律词典》的定义可以看出,在劳动合同中给予高层管理人员丰厚的离职金额,是为了让高层管理人员在公司控制权发生转移时有一个缓冲,不使其直接进入离职无来源的状态。这一笔收益可以使得高层安全退职,同时因为有这一项保障也可以使得高层管理者在工作期间安心、高效工作。也有一些地方将其称为"降落伞计划",这种说法也十分形象,但并不准确。因为现在,除了 golden parachute,还有 penson parachute 和 tin parachute。同时还有一种译法"优厚退职金",将术语背后的含义译出,虽然不如"黄金降落伞"生动形象,但是读者不需要有背景知识即可看懂,也是一种很好的译法。

good cause

根据《布莱克法律词典》,该术语的同义词有 good cause shown, just cause, lawful cause, sufficient cause。其英文释义为:A legally sufficient reason. Good cause is often the burden placed on a litigant (usu. by court rule or order) to show why a request should be granted or an action excused. The term is often used in employment-termination cases. 即该术语表示"合法的充分的理由"。通常,法院会裁定诉讼当事人承担责任以表明为什么应批准请求或免除诉讼,需有 good cause 支撑诉讼当事人的请求。该术语通常用在终止劳动关系的案件中。

《元照英美法词典》将此术语解释为"实质性的、充分的、法律上的理由或依据",译为"充足理由"。"充足"有足够,充分的含义,所以这个译法与《布莱克法律词典》的解释相符,即诉讼当事人举证应充分。然而"充足"一般多指数量上多,或是广度上全面,它只满足了对理由的一个要求,但是根据词典的说明可以看出理由仅是充足的是不够的。使请求被批准,免除诉讼的理由不仅应在数量上是充足的,更应该是从事实上合法合理的。所以"充足理由"这一译法并没有完全包含 good cause 的含义。

综上,good cause 更侧重于强调举证的合法性,所以译为"正当理由"更合适准确。"正当"一词通常是指人的行为合理和合法。在法律上,正当可以解释为一个人的行为、愿望等符合政策、行为规范及法律的要求,这更符合术语的含义。

graded offense

《布莱克法律词典》对 graded offense 的定义是:a crime that is divided into various degrees of severity with corresponding levels of punishment, such as murder (first-degree and second-degree) or assault (simple and aggravated),即根据犯罪事实的不同严重程度对犯罪行为处以相应程度的惩罚,例如谋杀罪分一级谋杀和二级谋杀,或伤害罪分轻伤和故意伤害。

《元照英美法词典》对该术语给出的译文是"分等级犯罪"。graded 一词有

"分级的"含义,按字面意思来看,即是分级的犯罪。但从上述英文解释可以看出,graded offense 不是分等级的犯罪,而是根据犯罪严重程度不同,处以相应级别的刑罚。与其说是分等级犯罪,更贴切的是分等级处罚,即量刑。量刑即刑罚裁量。裁量,裁剪并计量,意为度量,衡量,甄别。在我国法律用语中,量刑是指法院根据行为人所犯罪行及刑事责任的轻重,在定罪的基础上,依法决定对罪犯是否判处刑罚、判处何种刑罚、所判刑罚是否立即执行、所进行的刑事审判活动。

量刑的含义与 graded offense 的英文释义相吻合,所以该术语译为"量刑"更为准确。

ground lease 与 ground rent

ground lease 与 ground rent 两个术语中,虽然 lease 与 rent 都可以译成"租赁""租借",这两个术语的含义却不尽相同。

《布莱克法律词典》对 ground lease 的英文释义为:A long-term (usu. 99-year) lease of land only. Such a lease typically involves commercial property, and any improvements built by the lessee usually revert to the lessor. 意同 ground-rent lease,land lease。由此可知,ground lease 仅限长期(通常 99 年)土地租赁,这种租赁通常涉及商业地产,承租人进行的任何改造通常归出租人所有。通常在 ground lease 协议中,土地所有者所有权与土地使用者使用权在一定时期内相分离,土地使用者在使用土地期间向土地所有者支付租金,期满后,土地使用者归还土地。而且 ground lease 中租赁的土地上无建筑物,是对未开发土地的租赁,在英国专指 the first lease on a freehold building(对完全保有的房地产的首次出租)。因此,ground lease 译为"光地租赁"更能凸显其内涵。

根据《布莱克法律词典》,ground rent 的英文释义是:1. Rent paid by a tenant under a long-term lease for the use of undeveloped land, usu. for the construction of a commercial building. Also termed redeemable ground rent. 2. A heritable interest, in rental income from land, reserved by a grantor who conveys the land in fee simple. This type of ground rent is found primarily in Maryland and Pennsylvania. Also termed (in Scots law) irredeemable ground rent; ground annual. 据此可知 ground rent 的两层含义是：1. 承租人为在土地上建造建筑物（通常为商业建筑）而向土地所有人支付的租金。结合《元照英美法词典》的解释可知，这种租赁合同往往是长期的（如 99 年），并且可以续订。城市中的办公楼、酒店或类似的大规模建筑物通常采用这种土地租赁。2. 非限定继承土地的转让人对所转让的土地，为自己及继承人保留的永久性租金，其性质为永佃权的佃租。这种地租主要存在于马里兰州和宾夕法尼亚州。

总之，ground rent 就是土地所有者凭借土地所有权而得到的收入，也就是土地使用者为了取得土地使用权而向土地所有者交纳的费用，应译为"地租"。

halfway house

《布莱克法律词典》对该术语的定义是：A transitional housing facility designed to rehabilitate people who have recently left a prison or medical-care facility, or who otherwise need help in adjusting to a normal life. Also termed residential community treatment center，由此可知，halfway house 是旨在为刚离开医院或监狱者重返社会提供适应性训练的松散型组织机构。比如为协助精神病患、吸毒者或即将出狱的犯人等重新适应社会而建立的庇护所、戒护所、职训中心等。halfway house 是美国等国外社区提供的一种过渡性社区矫正设置。

按照字面意思，将其译为"中途之家"或"中途住所"，令人不知所云。可译为"过渡性社区矫正中心"或"重返社会训练中心"，从而凸显其职能。

hell-or-high water clause

hell-or-high water 来自于短语 come hell or high water，意思为无论遇到什么困难，即使赴汤蹈火也要不惜一切完成某项任务。若仅按照字面意思，则会译为"赴汤蹈火条款"，但是此译文并不能让读者理解该术语在法律语境下的含义。

根据《布莱克法律词典》，该术语指：A clause in a personal property lease requiring the lessee to continue to make full rent payments to the lessor even if the thing leased is unsuitable, defective, or destroyed. 结合维基百科对该术语

的解释①可知,该术语指个人财产租赁合同中的一项条款,即使租赁物不适用、有缺陷或已损坏,仍要求承租人继续向出租人支付全部租金。例如,在国际并购中,由于海外并购项目的不确定因素较多,而这些不确定因素自然会带来较大的风险,其中政府审批就是一大不确定因素,因此,为了避免由于政府审批问题导致交易放弃,卖方根据情况会在并购协议中加入 hell-or-high water 条款,要求买方有绝对义务采取所有必要的行动来获得政府监管部门的审批,这些必要的行动不仅包括全盘接受政府部门提出的任何要求,甚至还包括在政府部门提起的诉讼中始终对政府部门的任何主张做出应对和辩护②。从中可以看出,hell-or-high water 条款具有极高的严苛性,要求买方须"有绝对义务采取所有必要的行动"来获得政府监管部门的审批,否则将视为违约并承担责任。

综上,根据该术语的英文释义以及国际并购协议的实例可以看出,hell-or-high water 条款是为保证交易能够进行到底,从而对合同中的买方提出的极具严苛性的条款,要求买方无论付出多大的成本与代价,具有绝对的责任并尽一切措施保证条款内容的实现,否则将视为违约并将承担责任,所以,hell-or-high water clause 可以译为"(买受方)绝对责任条款"。

high crime

high crime 常被翻译成"严重犯罪"。《布莱克法律词典》给出的英文释义是:A crime that is very serious, though not necessarily a felony. Under the U.S. Constitution, a government officer's commission of a "high crime" is, along with treason and bribery, grounds for removal from office。由此可知,high crime 指一种非常严重的罪行,但并不一定是重罪(felony)。根据美国宪法,政府官员如犯有该罪行,同叛国罪和贿赂罪一样,都将被免职。结合《元照英美法

---

① A hell or high water clause is a clause in a contract, usually a lease, which provides that the payments must continue irrespective of any difficulties which the paying party may encounter, usually in relation to the operation of the leased asset. The clause usually forms part of a parent company guarantee that is intended to limit the applicability of the doctrines of impossibility or frustration of purpose. The term for the clause comes from a colloquial expression that a task must be accomplished "come hell or high water", that is, regardless of any difficulty. 参见 https://en.jinzhao.wiki/wiki/Hell_or_high_water_clause。

② http://www.managershare.com/post/312104

词典》的解释可知,high crime 指违背公共道德的不名誉罪,尤指参议院认为构成总统、副总统或其他文职官员不适合担任行政职务,应受到弹劾的适当理由的犯罪。

汉语"严重犯罪"指犯罪的程度,表示此类犯罪行为主观恶意明显、社会危害严重、群众反映强烈,比如危害国家安全犯罪、危害公共安全犯罪、黑社会性质组织犯罪和个人极端暴力犯罪、腐败、金融诈骗、人口贩运、海盗,以及支持恐怖主义活动等。再比如《最高人民法院发布五起毒品犯罪及吸毒诱发的严重犯罪典型案例》的官方英文译名为 Five Model Cases Involving Drug-Related Crimes and Serious Crimes Induced by Drug Abuse Issued by the Supreme People's Court,这里的严重犯罪译为 Serious Crimes。又如:《最高人民检察院关于办理核准追诉案件若干问题的规定》中"依法打击严重犯罪"译成,cracking down on serious crimes according to the law。由此可见,中文"严重犯罪"与 high crime 的含义相差甚远。

综上所述,high crime 与"严重犯罪"信息不对等。而 high crime 又区别于刑法术语中严格意义上的重罪。因此,建议细化 high crime 的范围,根据源语含义译为"一级重罪"。

highway by user

highway by user 常被翻译成"使用者公路"。此译法仅实现了语言转换的过程,但并未实现法律机制中的交际目的,未实现法律功能的对等,源语和译文在各自的法律语境中所起的作用和效果并不对等。

highway by user 的英文定义是:After long time uninterrupted use, the highway gets legitimate rights for further use of users,指经长期不间断使用而获得使用权利的公路。中文里并没有"使用者公路"的法律概念,会被人平白理解为任何人可以使用的公路,汉语"使用者公路"并不能精确表达出源语的真正涵义。根据源语含义建议 highway by user 翻译成"合法续用公路"。

holistic marketing

holistic marketing 常被翻译为"整体营销"。实际上,holistic marketing 是指 an integrated marketing approach that focuses on bringing together all aspects of marketing and uniting the various marketing strategies. This often involves taking a holistic view of all internal processes, including the structure of various company departments, manufacturing processes, and other products created by a company, but it can often include evaluating the competition as well. Holistic marketing generally requires a broader view of the situation that factors in details as well as the long-term goals of a company①。由此可见 holistic marketing 指营销时将企业作为一个整体来考虑，是一种整合营销方法。其重点是整合营销的各个方面，并将各种营销策略结合起来。这通常涉及将所有内部流程视为整体，包括公司各部门的结构、制造流程和公司创建的其他产品，也可能包括对竞争对手的评估。holistic marketing 通常需要从更广的角度来看待具体情况以及公司的长期目标。

中文"整体营销"实际对应的英文是 total marketing，这是市场营销学界权威菲利普·科特勒 1992 年提出的跨世纪的营销新观念，指公司营销活动应该囊括内外部环境的所有重要行为者，其中包括供应商、分销商、最终顾客、职员、财务公司、政府、同盟者、竞争者、传媒和一般大众，前四者构成微观环境，后六者体现宏观环境。

进一步查阅资料发现，中文"全方位营销"对应的英文恰好是 holistic marketing，指在营销方面，除了传统的销售渠道之外，还要突破空间和地域的限制，建立一种多层次的、立体的营销方式，如内外销联动、网络营销、公司团购、跨区域销售等②。由此可见中文的"全方位营销"概念是指营销应贯穿于"事情的各个方面"（涉及整合营销、关系营销、内部营销和绩效营销四个方面）而且要有广阔的统一的视野，这与 holistic marketing 的内涵一致。

hornbook

《布莱克法律词典》对 hornbook 的定义是：A textbook containing the rudimentary principles of an area of law，指包含法律领域基本原则的教科书。

---

① 参见 https://www.wise-geek.com/what-is-holistic-marketing.htm。
② 参见 https://wiki.mbalib.com/wiki/%E5%85%A8%E6%96%B9%E4%BD%8D%E8%90%A5%E9%94%80。

在美国法律教育中，hornbooks 为法学院学生撰写，内容包括了法学院课程通常涵盖的科目，总结并解释了特定领域的法律，通常是法学院学生的入门读物。它们不同于案例书(casebook)，案例书是案例(或部分案例)的集合，选择这些案例来帮助说明和激发关于法律问题的讨论。

所以，可将 hornbook 译为"法律专题概论"。

hotchpot

《布莱克法律词典》对 hotchpot 的英文解释为：The blending of items of property to ensure equality of division, as practiced either in cases of divorce or in cases in which advancements of an intestate's property must be made up to the estate by a contribution or by an accounting①. Also termed hotchpotch; hotchpot rule. 由此可知，hotchpot 的大致意思为：在离婚案件或者是未立遗嘱人的财产分割案件中，为确保公平，将财产混合之后再进行分配。在现代法中，主要针对遗产分配中的预赠，即预早遗赠，即获得预赠财产的子女应将财产与无遗嘱死亡人的遗产进行遗产的平等分割，后由其与该无遗嘱死亡人的其他子女共同进行遗产的平等分割。

hotchpot 常被译为"财产混同"，看似符合其英文释义，但还需了解一下"财产混同"的中文含义是否与其英文释义等同。查询后发现，中文"财产混同"的含义为：指债务人将自己的财产与他人的财产混合，从而模糊其作为产权人的属性，使承担债务的财产形式减少，避免该财产被直接执行。财产混同一方面表现为公司与股东财产的同一或不分，如公司与股东使用同一办公设施、公司财产无记录或记录不实，公司账簿与股东账簿不分或一体化；另一方面也可表现在公司与股东利益的一体化上，及公司与股东的收益之间没有区别，公司的盈利可以随意转化为公司成员的个人财产，或转化另一个公司的财产，而产生的负债则为公司的负债。

---

① 《布莱克法律词典》(Black's Law Dictionary, 9th Edition, p. 807)提供了更详细的解释：In some states … a child who has received his advancement in real or personal eatate, may elect to throw the amount of the advancement into the common stock, and take his share of the estate descended, or his distributive share of the personal estate, as the case may be; and this is said to be being the advancement into hotchpot, and it is a proceeding which resembles the collation bonorum in the civil law.

由此可见,将 hotchpot 译为"财产混同"是不严谨的,hotchpot 与"财产混同"并不属于同一部门法,指代范围更是大相径庭,同时在中国法律中,亦未发现与此完全功能对等的词,可考虑将之译为"财产合算分配"。

house law

house law 常被译为"家法",这是望文生义、"想当然"的翻译。应通过了解其英文释义准确解读其内涵,从而给出恰当的译文。

《布莱克法律词典》对 house law 的英文释义是:A regulatory code promulgated by the head of a royal or noble family, or of a prominent private family, governing intrafamily relationships and acts concerning events such as marriage, disposition of property, and inheritance. Such a code had no legal authority but was enforced within the family by personal and economic sanctions.结合维基百科的释义①可知,house law 在 19 世纪盛行于欧洲君主制的国家中,是早期一种特殊类型的、具有规范性的法典。是一种由王室、贵族或显赫家族的家长或首脑颁布的管理法规,用于管理和调整家庭内部关系以及处理涉及婚姻、财产处置和继承等事件有关的事务。这种法典通常没有法律权威,但可通过王室或家族内部的人身和经济制裁得以在家庭内部实施。

在汉语法律语境中,"家法"指在封建社会,封建家长统治本家或本族人的一套法度。不仅对自家人,而且对家丁丫鬟一类的仆人也同样适用。汉语中的"家法"应当翻译成:domestic discipline (exercised by the head of a feudal household)。如,家法伺候,翻译成 inflict punishment on a servant or somebody。

综上,house law 指早期一种特殊的法典,由王室、贵族或其他显赫家族的首脑颁布,用以调整婚姻、继承、财产处理的内部事务。汉语"家法"与 house law 的含义差之千里,可根据源语含义将 house law 翻译为"贵族家庭法"。

---

① House law or House laws (Hausgesetze) are rules that govern a royal family or dynasty in matters of eligibility for succession to a throne, membership in a dynasty, exercise of a regency, or entitlement to dynastic rank, titles and styles. Prevalent in European monarchies during the nineteenth century, few countries have house laws any longer, so that they are, as a category of law, of more historical than current significance. If applied today, house laws are mostly upheld by members of royal and princely families as a matter of tradition.参见 https://en.jinzhao.wiki/wiki/House_law。

incapacity of physician

《布莱克法律词典》对 incapacity 的定义是：1. Lack of physical or mental capabilities. 2. Lack of ability to have certain legal consequences attach to one's actions. For example, a five-year-old has an incapacity to make a binding contract. 3. Disability. 所以，incapacity 指缺乏法律能力、身体能力等，缺乏为某事或处理某事的能力、权力的状态，具体所指应依语境而定。

查阅《牛津高阶英汉双解词典》(第 8 版)可知，physician refers to a doctor, especially one who is a specialist in general medicine and not surgery。即"医师；(尤指)内科医生"。

《元照英美法词典》将 incapacity of physician 译为"身体能力的不充分"，并解释说，此为能力明显不充分(manifest incapacity)的一种。按照《元照英美法词典》的解释，manifest incapacity 指明显缺乏理解能力或作为能力，因此对其已证实的作为或不作为无须其他证明。由前文 physician 的释义可知，physician 并不含"身体"之意，所以"身体能力的不充分"此译法欠妥。

通过查阅资料可知，incapacity of physician 通常出现于医师的雇佣合同①中，规定：Upon the inability or incapacity of Physician to legally be employed, or continue to be employed, in the United States to provide the Services as required hereunder, regardless of reason or cause. 由此可见，在实践中它强调的是医师缺乏作为医师提供服务(service)的能力。

综上，该术语可译为"医师缺乏称职能力"。

inchoate offense 与 inchoate crime

根据《布莱克法律词典》的解释，inchoate offence 与 inchoate crime 为同义词，其定义是：A step toward the commission of another crime, the step in itself being serious enough to merit punishment. The three inchoate offenses are attempt, conspiracy, and solicitation. 意为犯下另一罪行而做出的行为，该行为本身严重到应得以惩罚，比如：犯罪未遂(attempt)、犯罪共谋(conspiracy)

---

① https://www.wyomed.org/wp-content/uploads/2017/06/Template-Physician-Employment-Agmt-140601.pdf

和犯罪教唆(solicitation)①。《元照英美法词典》将其译为"不完整罪";《英汉双解法律词典》中给出的译文是"未完成之罪"或"犯罪未遂"。(陈庆柏,1998:273)②;也有人将其与 preliminary crime 混为一谈,认为 inchoate crime 应译为"初步犯罪"。

我国刑法分则对具体犯罪的规定,是以既遂为标本的。但是现实中并非一切犯罪都能达到既遂。有的可能在为犯罪作准备的阶段就被迫停止;有的可能在着手实行犯罪的阶段被停止;还有的可能由于犯罪分子自动中止犯罪,使之在犯罪的预备阶段或者实行阶段停止下来。这样,就在犯罪过程中,出现了犯罪的预备、未遂和中止等各种不同的停止状态。相对于犯罪既遂而言,这些犯罪可以称为未完成罪,即犯罪的未完成形态。因此,未完成罪是指在犯罪过程中,由于主观与客观原因,停顿在不同犯罪阶段的各种未完成的犯罪形态。结合上述英文释义,将 inchoate crime/offense 翻译为"未完成罪"或者"不完整罪"并不准确(未完成罪应为 unaccomplished crimes;不完整罪应为 incomplete crime)。

根据其英文解释可以看出,inchoate offence 与 inchoate crime 是为了犯另一种罪而做出某行为的一个过程,从释义中的 another crime 而不是 a crime 可以看出 inchoate crime/offense 本身就是一个犯罪,而此犯罪是另一个犯罪其中的一个环节。美国《示范刑法典》中规定了三种 inchoate crime/offense,即:attempt,conspiracy 和 solicitation,这三种 inchoate crime/offense 只需要有初始

---

① 《布莱克法律词典》(Black's Law Dictionary, 9th Edition, p. 1187): The term is sometimes criticized. These preliminary crimes have sometimes been erroneously described as 'inchoate' offences. This is misleading because the word 'inchoate' connotes something which is not yet completed, and it is therefore not accurately used to denote something which is itself complete, even though it be a link in a chain of events leading to some object which is not yet attained. The offence of incitement is fully performed even though the person incited immediately repudiates the suggested deed, a conspiracy is committed although the conspirators have not yet moved to execute their purposed crime, and the performance of a criminal attempt must always have been reached before the end is gained. In all these instances it is the ultimate crime which is inchoate and not the preliminary crime, the position indeed being just the same as in the example imagined above of a man who stole a revolver and committed other crimes in order to effect his purpose of murder. There the murder was inchoate, but the larceny and other crimes (including the attempt) were completed. J. w. Cecil Turner, Kenny's Outlines of Criminal Law 77 (16th ed. 1952).

② 陈庆柏等.英汉双解法律词典(第 2 版)[Z].北京:世界图书出版公司,1998.

犯罪行为，而无论其是否造成实质性的犯罪结果，其本身都是一个完整的犯罪。这和我国的刑法有很大的差别，比如故意杀人罪，在我国杀人未遂是归在故意杀人罪的范畴的，对杀人未遂比照既遂从轻处罚。但在英美法系中，杀人未遂本身就构成一个犯罪，即：attempted murder，是 criminal attempt，属于 inchoate crime 的范畴，译为"企图谋杀罪"。

将 inchoate crime 翻译为初步犯罪也是错误的（初步犯罪应为：preliminary crimes）。因为《布莱克法律词典》中也进一步解释说，inchoate connotes something which is not yet completed, and it is therefore not accurately used to denote something which is itself complete, even though it be a link in a chain of events leading to some object which is not yet attained。如果你企图犯罪，这本身就是一种犯罪。例如，如果你试图抢劫某人而没有得到任何东西，这仍然是一种犯罪，即企图抢劫罪。又如：一个人为了实现谋杀目的而偷走手枪并且犯了其他的一些罪，这里不管有没有将人杀死、完成谋杀，盗窃和其他罪行已经完成。如果最终没有完成谋杀，那么这个未完成的谋杀就是 inchoate crime/offense，而盗窃和其他罪行是为了完成谋杀所做的初步犯罪行为，即 preliminary crime。

根据以上分析可知，将 inchoate crime/offense 译为"未完成罪""不完整罪"或"初步犯罪"都是不正确的，通过剖析其概念，将 inchoate crime/offense 翻译为"早期犯罪"（指可导致其他犯罪行为的发生，而且其自身也是犯罪的行为）更为合适。"早期"是指某个过程的最初阶段，也就意味着"早期"本身既是一个单独阶段，也是可以导致某一过程的必经阶段，那么，"早期犯罪"指本身既是一个单独的犯罪，也是可以导致某一犯罪的必经阶段。

insider trading

《布莱克法律词典》给出的 insider trading 的定义是：The use of material, nonpublic information in trading the shares of a company by a corporate insider or other person who owes a fiduciary duty to the company. This is the classic definition. The Supreme Court has also approved a broader definition, known as the "misappropriation theory": the deceitful acquisition and misuse of information that properly belongs to persons to whom one owes a duty. Thus, under the misappropriation theory, it is insider trading for a lawyer to trade in the stock of XYZ Corp. After learning that a client of the lawyer's firm is planning a takeover of XYZ. But under the classic definition, that is not insider trading because the lawyer owed no duty to XYZ itself. Also termed insider dealing the illegal practice of trading on the stock exchange to one's own advantage through having access, because of personal or business relationship, to confidential information.

由上述英文释义和示例可知，insider trading 的传统定义是：公司内部人士或与该公司有信托关系的其他人基于公司内部信息或预先获取的信息（advance information）等重要的非公开信息而进行的股票交易行为。最高人民法院已经采纳更为宽泛的定义，称为"不当理论"（misappropriation theory），即欺诈性获取和滥用属于应承担保密义务者的信息。

在美国，对于与证券发行、销售或者购买相关的任何欺诈性行为，联邦证券法均予完全禁止。此类禁止性规定是许多惩罚性行为，包括针对欺诈性内部交易所采取的惩罚措施的行使依据。任何人在其掌握某项尚未公开的实质性信息时，违反对该信息的保密义务，或者违反因其掌握该信息而不得进行相关交易的义务，从事相关的内部证券交易，均属非法[①]。

综上，常见的"内部交易"这一译文容易使读者产生误解，误以为是内部人士之间进行交易，分析上述定义得知实际是基于不应公开的内部信息而进行的交易，翻译为"内幕交易"更符合其定义。

instantaneous seisin

《布莱克法律词典》对 seisin 的定义是：1. Hist. Completion of the ceremony of feudal investiture, by which the tenant was admitted into freehold. 2. Possession of a freehold estate in land; ownership. 3. Louisiana law. The right that the law accords universal successors to own and possess a person's estate directly and immediately upon that person's death. 结合《元照英美法词典》对 seisin 的解释可知，seisin 用来指对动产或某种权利的占有。seisin 不同于

---

① 张法连. 英美法律术语辞典（英汉双解）[Z]. 上海：上海外语教育出版社，2014.

possession 和 occupation,它主要是基于一种分封关系而产生,在这种关系下,一旦某人占有了某块地产(be seised of such land),他便拥有近乎所有权的权利。而 possession 在法律意义上仅用来指租约地和其他动产的占有,occupation 则指实际上的占有、占用(actual possession)。seisin 的成立须以具备某种占有的意图为要件,这种意图要求占有人主张一种完全保有地产的权益(freehold interest)。因此,如果某人进入土地时拥有某项权利,则法律不再要求进一步的证据而仅依此权利推定其占有意图;相反如果他进入土地时没有权利依据,则他必须显示出要获得占有的意图。

虽然法律词典中未查询到 instantaneous seisin 的定义,但英美国家的一些判例对此有所解释:Under the doctrine of instantaneous seisin, when a deed and a purchase money deed of trust are executed, delivered, and recorded as part of the same transaction, the deed of trust attaches at the instant the vendee acquires title and constitutes a lien superior to all others. E. g., [Smith Builders Supply, Inc. v. Rivenbark, 231 N. C. 213, 56 S. E. 2d 431 (1949)]①.

《元照英美法词典》也给出了该术语的译文和解释:实时占有;该学说意指瞬间的暂时占有,即同样的一个行为将地产转移给一个人而又立即将其从该人处转移。此种占有并非"停留"在该个人处,即该个人不得为其自己而利用、受益,即时占有允许在有关土地上设置诸如遗孀地产权、宅基地、技工留置权或卖方留置权等权利。

综上,instantaneous seisin 突出的是当满足一定条件时便立即产生对某不动产的所有权,但当某条件发生时马上便失去该所有权。因此,可译为"瞬间占有"。

intrinsic fraud

intrinsic fraud 这个术语很容易令人望文生义,将其汉译为"内部欺诈",该译文与其真正含义差之千里。

《布莱克法律词典》给出的定义是:Deception that pertains to an issue involved in an original action. Examples include the use of fabricated evidence,

---

① https://law.justia.com/cases/north-carolina/court-of-appeals/1991/9017sc1094—1.html a false return of service, perjured testimony, and false receipts or other commercial documents.

维基百科中对该术语的英文解释为:Intrinsic fraud is an intentionally false representation that goes to the heart of what a given lawsuit is about, in other words, whether fraud was used to procure the transaction. (If the transaction was fraudulent, it probably does not have the legal status of a contract)①.

根据以上英文释义,并结合《元照英美法词典》对该术语的解释可知,intrinsic fraud 是一种故意虚假陈述的欺诈行为,涉及诉讼的核心,换句话说,即欺诈是否被用于促成合同交易,如果交易是欺诈性的,则合同不成立。此种欺诈可以是伪证、使用错误的或伪造的文件或对证据加以隐瞒或作虚伪的陈述。

通过查阅资料了解到,该术语实际上是英美侵权行为法中的术语。欺诈人在进行意思表示时,明知其陈述不实而仍进行表示的一种主观心理状态。在中国,欺诈是指以使人发生错误认识为目的的故意行为,也就是说欺诈本身就包含"故意的意思"。在中国法律体系中,有一个概念与该术语所表达的含义非常接近,那就是"虚假陈述"。虚假陈述是指案件当事人为了获得非法利益,故意陈述虚假案件事实,或者故意虚假否认、虚假自认,严重影响民事诉讼的行为,有时这种行为可以构成欺诈。

因此,可以将 intrinsic fraud 翻译为"故意欺诈,虚假陈述欺诈"。

introduced evidence

introduced evidence 在法律词典中找不到英文释义,从语法上来理解其实是将动词 introduce 形容词化,将其作为 evidence 的定语。所以首先可以理解一下 introduce 在法律语境下的含义。

通过查阅《牛津高阶英汉双解词典》(第 8 版)可知,introduce 其中一个含义为:to make sth. available for use, discussion, etc. for the first time。比如:The new law was introduced in 2007。此语境下的汉语意思为:推行;实施;采用。

---

① https://en.wikipedia.org/wiki/Intrinsic_fraud

《布莱克法律词典》对 introduce into evidence 做出了英文解释：To have (a fact or object) admitted into the trial record, allowing it to be considered by the jury or the court in reaching a decision，由此可推断 introduce 的含义是 have fact or object admitted，即将（事实或客体）记入审判记录（也就是使法庭认可该类事实），使陪审团或法庭在做出裁决时能加以考虑。

《元照英美法词典》将该 introduced evidence 译为"（庭审中）当事人提出的并已被法庭采纳的证据"。结合前述分析，该译文意思准确，但有些许冗杂，并且民事诉讼中举证责任遵循"谁主张，谁举证"原则，本来就应该是当事人负有举证责任，所以可精简为"当庭采纳的举证"。

invented consideration

根据《布莱克法律词典》，invented consideration 指 fictional consideration created by a court to prevent the invalidation of a contract that lacks consideration，即法庭为避免合同因无对价无效而提出的一种虚构对价（fictional consideration）。《元照英美法词典》将其翻译为"虚构的对价"。

对价（consideration）又称做约因，指当事人一方在获得某种利益时，必须付对方相应的代价，其原本是英美合同法中的重要概念，是一方为换取另一方做某事的承诺，而向另一方支付的金钱代价或得到该种承诺的承诺，从法律上看是一种等价有偿的允诺关系。对价必须合法，已经存在的义务和法律义务不能作为对价。

在我国，有无对价并非合同成立的必要条件，"对价"是从英美法中引进的概念，我国法律中也明确存在"对价"一词。《中华人民共和国票据法》第十条第二款规定：票据的取得，必须给付对价，即应当给付票据双方当事人认可的相对应的代价。由此可见如果一方当事人提供不符合双方认可的对价，不仅构成民法中的违约责任，在票据法中也被认为是无对价，只有在事后追认同意的，才构成对价。

但汉语"虚构"指凌空构作；凭空捏造；虚幻之实化体现。可见"虚构"具有一定的贬义意义，其实法庭提出 invented consideration 是避免合同因无对价而失效，从而保障合同双方的交易能够顺利进行，不是为了欺骗民众或者编造，而是创设了一种虚拟但是有一定根据的东西以促成法律判定过程，达到一个积极正面的结果。因此可翻译为"创设性对价",从而凸显原合同中本不存在对价,但法庭为了避免合同无效而创设了对价。

involuntary association

《布莱克法律词典》对 involuntary 的定义是:Not resulting from a free and unrestrained choice; not subject to control by the will。康奈尔法学院 LII 在线数据库平台对 involuntary 的解释①是:In reference to law, involuntary is used to indicate a lack of control or intent。由此可见,involuntary 强调的是"非自愿;不是出于本人意愿"。

《布莱克法律词典》中 association 的定义有:1. The process of mentally collecting ideas, memories, or sensations. 2. A gathering of people for a common purpose; the persons so joined. 3. An unincorporated organization that is not a legal entity separate from the persons who compose it. If an association has sufficient corporate attributes, such as centralized management, continuity of existence, and limited liability, it may be classified and taxed as a corporation. 其中第三层含义中指出 association 意同 voluntary association,指由个人组成的非法人型实体,但并不具备公司(corporation)属性,例如集中管理、存在的连续性和有限责任。结合《元照英美法词典》的解释也可知:该实体的组成是出于社会、政治、道德、宗教、慈善动机,或为了促进公共、科技、教育目标,或者为了便利工商业而不是为了贸易或直接的盈利,其成员是自由选择加入的。如果其成员资格的取得有法律或专业上的要求,这种组织便不能称为 voluntary association。由此可见,voluntary association 强调的是成员"自愿"且"不受法律或专业上的限制"。

《元照英美法词典》将其译为"非任意加入的社团",并解释道:这种社团是如"律师协会"等专业人士的社团,不仅赋予其成员某种社会地位,还赋予其成员某种有价值的权利。由此可推断,involuntary association 不同于 voluntary association,不是仅靠个人意愿即可参与,需要有一定专业或者资质。"非任意加入的社团"此译法符合字面意思,但没有传达出其本质含义,可译为"专业性

---

① https://www.law.cornell.edu/wex/involuntary

社团"。

jactitation of marriage

jactitation of marriage 这一法律术语,现有的翻译有"诈婚罪""冒充配偶罪""冒称配偶罪"等,但这些译文都存在不妥之处。

《布莱克法律词典》给出的定义有两层[①]:1. False and actionable boasting or claiming that one is married to another. 2. An action against a person who falsely boasts of being married to the complaint. 以上两层含义有相通之处,结合《元照英美法词典》的解释可知,这是英国教会法中的一个概念,指诈称为他人之夫或妻,从而令他们二人的婚姻关系获得承认,其中一方可以据此提起诉讼获得司法救济。但自从1766年婚姻法改革之后,法定婚姻形式已有相当确定性,可避免个人单凭诈称已婚而致使他人受损,因此相关的司法救济已很少被采用。

我国没有"诈婚罪"这一罪名,但有"诈骗罪"这一罪名。根据我国《刑法》第二百六十六条规定,诈骗罪是指以非法占有为目的,用虚构事实或者隐瞒真相的方法,骗取数额较大的公私财物的行为。此外,在我国日常生活中,"诈婚"一词通常指的是以非法占有为目的,以结婚为借口,骗取他人财产;如果数额较大的话,会构成诈骗罪。通过这个分析,可以发现"诈婚罪"这一翻译,与 jactitation of marriage 的定义明显不同,因此这个翻译犯了"望文生译"的错误。

"冒充配偶罪"这一译文乍一看似乎符合 jactitation of marriage 的定义,但两者仍然不同。"冒充"一词指以假充真,为了骗过别人,以假的东西代替真的事物或人;也指当中含有欺骗和欺诈成分。所以,"冒充配偶"的前提是对方存在"配偶",而 jactitation of marriage 的定义中,并没有说到只有有配偶的人才能主张这个诉讼权利。因此,"冒充配偶罪"这一译文无形中缩小了主张 jactitation of marriage 的权利主体范围,因此这个翻译也有欠妥当。

---

① 《布莱克法律词典》在这一法律术语之下还引用了另一定义:"Jactitation of marriage is a cause of action which arises when a person falsely alleges that he or she is married to the petitioner, and the remedy sought is perpetual injunction against the respondent to cease making such allegations. The cause is now uncommon in English municipal law and almost unknown in the conflict of laws." R. H. Graveson, Conflict of Laws 349 (7th ed. 1974)

"冒称配偶罪"这个译文中的"冒称"一词,比"冒充"的程度似乎更小,"称"这一词也能够对应术语定义中的 false and actionable boasting or claiming,因此和前两种翻译相比更为合适。但法律翻译中最常见的是使用源语法律制度已有的术语直译对等词①。"冒称配偶罪"中的"配偶"一词和 jactitation of marriage 中的 marriage 还是有些区别,"配偶"这一词是译者对 marriage 一词的延伸,源语释义中指的是婚姻关系而非配偶。

综上,为了突出该术语定义中的 false and actionable boasting or claiming,可将该术语译为"造谣存在婚姻关系"。"造谣"一词的基本含义是,为达到某种目的而编造虚假消息,迷惑群众,强调"说"的动作;而"存在婚姻关系"是指"造谣"的内容。

jail breaking

通过查阅维基百科得知:Jailbreak or jail breaking refers to a prison escape②. 而维基百科对 prison escape 的解释为:A prison escape (or prison break) is the act of an inmate leaving prison through unofficial or illegal ways. Normally, when this occurs, an effort is made on the part of authorities to recapture them and return them to their original detainers. Escaping from prison is also a criminal offense in some countries, e. g. United States and Russia, and it is highly likely to result in time being added to the inmate's sentence, as well as the inmate being placed under increased security③. 由此可知,jail breaking 指囚犯通过非官方或非法方式离开监狱的行为,在美国和俄罗斯等国该行为是一种刑事犯罪行为,囚犯被追回后,原本的刑期会延长,监狱也会使用各种安全设施,采取更严格的监管方式。

通过对该术语释义的了解,容易联想到我国法律语境中的"越狱"。通过我国《刑法》第三百一十六条、三百一十七条、三百一十八条得知,与"越狱"相关的

---

① 张法连.英美法律术语汉译策略探究[J].中国翻译,2016(02):100-104.
② 参见 https://en.wikipedia.org/wiki/Jailbreak_(disambiguation)。
③ Aggravating factors include whether or not violence was used. Many prisons use security features such as motion sensors, CCTV, barred windows, high walls, barbed wire (or razor wire in some countries) and electric fencing to prevent escapes. 参见 https://en.wikipedia.org/wiki/Prison_escape。

罪行一共有 3 种：逃脱罪；组织越狱罪；暴动越狱罪、聚众持械劫狱罪[①]。

《元照英美法词典》中将 jail breaking 译为"突破监所罪"，对其的解释为：使用暴力从监所逃脱的行为。只要用暴力制服监所看守即满足"暴力"条件，而从敞开的门出去或仅仅停留在计划逃脱的预谋阶段，都不构成此罪。

综上，"越狱""越狱行为"并非规范的法言法语，结合该术语的英文释义以及对应我国法律中的相关规定，可以将 jail breaking 译为"逃脱罪"或"暴动越狱罪"。由于源语释义中并未指定罪犯的越狱行为是否通过暴力手段，所以具体译法应根据案件内容决定。

jail credit

《布莱克法律词典》对 jail credit 的定义是：Time spent by a criminal defendant in confinement while awaiting trial. This time is usually deducted from the defendant's final sentence (if convicted). Also termed jail-credit time. 由此可知，该术语指刑事被告人等待审判期被羁押的时间。如果该被告人最终被定罪，则此段羁押时长可从终审判决的刑期中扣除，用以折抵刑期。

我国《刑事诉讼法》第七十六条规定了指定居所监视居住的期限应当折抵刑期。被判处管制的，监视居住一日折抵刑期一日；被判处拘役、有期徒刑的，监视居住二日折抵刑期一日。

《元照英美法词典》将该术语译为"刑期折抵"，但此译文强调 jail credit 是一种行为，而源语很明显指的是一段时间。综上，结合该术语的英文释义，对应我国法律中的相关规定，将 jail credit 译为"可折抵的刑期"更为合适。

jeopardy

《布莱克法律词典》对该术语的定义是：The risk of conviction and punishment that a criminal defendant faces at trial. Jeopardy attaches in a jury trial when the jury is empaneled，and in a bench trial when the first witness is

---

① (1)逃脱罪：依法被关押的罪犯、被告人、犯罪嫌疑人脱逃的，处五年以下有期徒刑或者拘役。(2)组织越狱罪：组织越狱的首要分子和积极参加者，处五年以上有期徒刑；其他参加的，处五年以下有期徒刑或者拘役。(3)暴动越狱罪、聚众持械劫狱罪：暴动越狱或者聚众持械劫狱的首要分子和积极参加的，处十年以上有期徒刑或者无期徒刑；情节特别严重，处死刑；其他参加的，处三年以上十年以下有期徒刑。

sworn. Also termed legal jeopardy. 由此可知该术语指的是刑事被告在审判中面临的被定罪或被处罚的危险。

《元照英美法词典》中将 jeopardy 译为"危险",并附解释:指在审判过程中刑事被告人面临的被定罪和判刑的危险。通常在陪审团审判的情况下,从组成陪审团起,在由法官审判的情况下,从第一个证人宣誓时起,被告人即开始面临这种危险。此译文过于简单,未将两种危险的情形指出,不够准确。

综上,法律翻译过程中如果在目标语语境中找不到对应的术语,可以谨慎地进行创造。结合该术语的释义,可将其译为"(刑事被告所处的)被定罪或被处罚的危险",具体译法根据案件的相关语境适用。

Jewell instruction

由于该术语的名称源于美国的一起案例:United States v. Jewell,532 F. 2d 697 (9th Cir. 1976),所以通常直译为"朱厄尔指令",即以当事人的名字作为名称。但读者通过该译文并不能得知其所指的含义,必须通过原文释义来理解这个词的含义。

通过查询《布莱克法律词典》得知该术语指一种刑事诉讼程序,即 A court's instruction to the jury that the defendant can be found to have the requisite criminal mental state despite being deliberately ignorant of some of the facts surrounding the crime,也被称作法庭对陪审团的指示。简单来说,它指的是法庭对陪审团的一种引导,即尽管被告故意隐瞒有关犯罪的一些事实,但仍能被发现其具有必要的犯罪心理状态(requisite criminal mental state)。此外,词典中举了一个例子[①]便于读者理解该术语的含义。假如一个被告人宣称他不知道自己携带的包里的东西是毒品,但在那种情况下,任何一个正常人都能根据所处环

---

① "The goods must not be swept away by the violence of the waves, for then the loss falls entirely upon the merchant or his insurer, but they must be intentionally sacrificed by the mind and agency of man, for the safety of the ship and the residue of the cargo. The jettison must be made for sufficient cause, and not from groundless timidity. It must be made in a case of extremity, when the ship is in danger of perishing by the fury of a storm, or is laboring upon rocks or shallows, or is closely pursued by pirates or enemies; and then if the ship and the residue of the cargo be saved by means of the sacrifice, nothing can be more reasonable than that the property saved should bear its proportion of the loss," 3 James Kent, Commentaries on American Law * 232—233 (George Comstock ed., 11th ed. 1866)

境察觉到包里的东西有很大可能是不合法的。如这个被告人是从一个有名的毒品贩子那里接过来的包并且闻到了里面大麻的味道。那么,法庭会提示陪审团有权推断这个被告人的犯罪意识充足,他在刻意回避一些关键的犯罪事实。所以该术语也被称作 deliberate-indifference instruction,通常被翻译为"故意无视指令"。

鉴于法律术语翻译中经常存在一些约定俗成的译文,虽然不能很好地通过译文展现其含义,但由于此类译文传播范围广泛,大众已接受此类译文,比如 Miranda warning 翻译为"米兰达警告",该术语和 jewell instruction 一样都是经判例确立的规则,读者已经接受此类直译法,而后再通过其判例了解该术语的释义。综合上述英文释义以及示例,可以保留 jewell instruction 的直译译文,同时为了方便读者理解其含义,可以翻译为"朱厄尔指令"(法庭引导陪审团发现关键犯罪事实及犯罪意图)。

joint petition

该术语很容易根据其字面意思译为"联合请愿""请愿联署"等。事实上,此类译文将法律术语与政治性用语混同,从而忽略了 joint petition 在法律语境中适用的主体的特定性。

从美国联邦法院官网查询到 joint petition 的定义为: One bankruptcy petition filed by a husband and wife together①. 根据该定义我们可以看出,joint petition 的适用主体为夫妻,是夫妻的共同行为。如果将它与日常生活中的 joint petition 混同,就会导致其法律意义的含糊不清,故应当在汉译中强调其主体的特殊性。同时,在许多情境中将这一术语译成"夫妻联合申请",比如绿卡申办过程中。然而,这一用法在法律语境中并不合适,于是我们可以根据定义中的 bankruptcy 来对这一术语进行进一步的限定。从定义中的 bankruptcy 一词我们可以得知这一术语来源于特定的情形。在英美法律体系中,"夫妻联合申报"作为一种独立个人所得税纳税单位的方式而存在,其具体意义是指将夫妻的所得综合起来进行联合申报纳税,世界上有许多国家实行夫妻联合申报,如美国、

---

① 参见 uscourts. gov/educational-resources/educational-activities/bankruptcy-basics-glossary # content-for-j。

英国、西班牙、新加坡、瑞士等①。而由于联合申报需要很高的征管水平，中国目前尚未实施这一税收制度。因此，joint petition 在"征税"语境中应当被译为"夫妻联合申报"。

另外，joint petition 这一术语同样适用于离婚情形中。比如，从美国某律师事务所官网对该术语的解释②中可以得知，joint petition 作为 dissolution of marriage 的一种申请方式而存在。在这一语境中，joint petition 同样可以被译为"夫妻联合申报"，但它是夫妻申请离婚时的一种表现形式，与上文中的适用情景并不相同。

journeys accounts

《布莱克法律词典》对该术语的定义是：The number of days (usually 15) after the abatement of a writ within which a new writ could be obtained. This number was based on how many days it took for the plaintiff to travel (for journey) to the court. 由此可知该术语指旧令状被撤销时起至法院签发新令状的期限（通常为 15 天）。因其属于英国法律中比较古老的概念，所以在源语中难以查到相关材料，在译入语中也难以找到相关对应的法律术语。

《元照英美法词典》将其译为"（英格兰古法）在途时间"，指一项令状被撤销后到另一新的令状签发大概所需的最短期间。在旧时，一项令状非因原告的过错而被撤销（abated）后，原告有权在尽可能短的合理期限内取得一项新的令状，

---

① 美国通过婚姻关系把个人分为两类——已婚个人和未婚个人，已婚个人可以合并他们的所得和扣除项目只进行一次申报（联合申报），也可以各自单独申报。未婚的纳税人分成单身和户主两类，这样就产生了四类申报身份：已婚、联合申报；已婚、单独申报；单身申报；户主申报。联合申报，就是把已婚夫妻的综合所得分成两半，并按照对单身个人相同的税率对每一半征税。这样，与同一所得水平上的单身个人相比，联合申报的已婚夫妻就可以少缴税，减轻他们的税收负担，实现按综合能力征税。参见陈文龙. 夫妻联合申报——个人所得税纳税单位的另一种选择[J]. 科技经济市场，2007（03）：258-259。

② 对 joint petition 的解释：We file joint petition annulments when either or both parties were intoxicated at the time of this marriage or when one or both of the parties were already married to someone else at the time of this marriage. Both parties must sign the joint petition and the decree. Once the joint petition and decree have been signed and notarized, the joint petition is filed with the Court and the decree submitted for the signature of the judge assigned to your case. Once the judge signs the Decree of Annulment, the clerk files it and your annulment becomes final. 参见 https://nevadaannulment.org/joint-petition-annulment/。

该期限依其到达法院所需的时间来计算,通常为 15 日。

综上所述,《元照英美法词典》提供的译文"在途时间"概念过于宽泛,可以用来指很多事物。所以,在译入语中没有对等概念的情况下,可以结合其源语释义,进行大胆谨慎的创造,可将其译为"(原告申请法院新令状的)合理期限"。

judicial opinion

根据《布莱克法律词典》,judicial opinion 通常简称 opinion,具体指:A court's written statement explaining its decision in a given case, usu. including the statement of facts, points of law, rationale, and dicta. 由此得知它指的是法院给出的针对已判决的案件的书面陈述或声明。

《元照英美法词典》将其翻译为"法官意见",此外还有"法官判决意见""司法见解"等译法。"司法见解"并未指明 written 这一特征,而且"见解"并不是规范的法言法语;"法官判决意见"中"法官"二字显得片面,因为在英美国家陪审团也可以对案件的结果做出裁断;而《元照英美法词典》中的译法"法官意见"既未突出"书面"这一性质,又因"法官"二字略有不妥。

综上,将 judicial opinion 译为"司法意见书""司法判决意见书"更为合适。

jus tertii

从词源上来讲,jus tertii 来自拉丁语。根据《布莱克法律词典》,该术语有两层含义:1. The right of a third party. 2. The doctrine that, particularly in constitutional law courts do not decide what they do not need to decide.

从其字面上来看,jus tertii 是第三人的权利。该权利是侵权法上的一种辩护主张,它主张反对侵权占有或非法占有。这是对第三方权利的承认,即维护第三方的权利比索赔人的权利更重要。具体到法律关系中,受到争议或索赔的影响,租客或受托人或其他拥有财产的人的所有权属于那个人而不是该人的房东或委托人。再者,这也是一种宪法上的权利,是对第三权利人在财产权利得不到救济时的一种保护。

此外,该术语也被应用于合同关系中①。jus tertii 是作为第三方权益而存在于诉讼中的,它与诉讼的原被告所主张的权益不同,是独立存在并被主张的。在我国的相关法律中,与之相对应的就是在民事诉讼程序中有独立请求权第三人所主张的权利。有独立请求权第三人即对当事人争议的诉讼标的,认为自己有独立请求权,以独立实体权利人的身份并提出诉讼请求而参加诉讼的人。

我国《民事诉讼法》第五十六条第一款规定:对当事人双方的诉讼标的,第三人认为有独立请求权的,有权提起诉讼。在我国,有独立请求权的第三人参加诉讼的条件:(1)他人之间的诉讼正在受诉法院进行;(2)对他人之间的诉讼标的有独立请求权;(3)以起诉的方式参加诉讼,并以本诉双方当事人为被告。有独立请求权的第三人在诉讼中地位同于原告,他既反对本诉原告,也反对本诉被告,是以本诉的原、被告双方为被告提出了一个新的诉讼,应当享有原告的诉讼权利,承担原告的诉讼义务。

据此,根据 jus tertii 的词源、适用主体与适用语境,该法律术语最适宜的翻译为"第三方权利"。

key-man insurance

该术语易被按字面意思翻译为"关键人物保险",但在汉译法律术语时,首先应当了解其在法律语境下的英文释义。

根据《布莱克法律词典》,key-man insurance 与 key-employee life insurance, key-employee insurance, key-person insurance, key-executive insurance 同义,指 life insurance taken out by a company on an essential or valuable employee, with the company as beneficiary。由此可知 key-man insurance 指的是公司为在商业活动中有核心地位、具有重要价值的人投保办理人身保险,公司整体作为受益人。

通过查阅相关资料亦可知,key-man insurance 有绝对的适用范围,即在商业中;而且有绝对的对象范围,即有重要价值、关键意义的公司内部人员且人员

---

① A third party beneficiary, in the law of contracts, is a person who may have the right to sue on a contract, despite not having originally been an active party to the contract. This right, known as a jus tertii, arises where the third party is the intended beneficiary of the contract, as opposed to a mere incidental beneficiary.

具有广泛性①；其保险内容，是在商业规划环境下使用人寿保险②；其背后的法律意义正是为了保护公司的利益。

在中国的商业环境中会使用"要员"一词。"要员"，指担任非常重要工作的人（如在商业组织中）。同时香港特别行政区政府税务局的官网上也做出了这样的规定③："要员保险"在法律上未有定义，但一般会有以下特点：由雇主购买一份保单，为该雇员因死亡、疾病或受伤而引致的营商利润损失投保。受益人为该雇主。假设是一份人寿保险单，便属于定期人寿保险，在保险期内可提供雇员的寿险保障，并无其他利益。保险期不长于该雇员对雇主的有用期限。购买这项保险的目的，是在要员因死亡、疾病或受伤而不能工作时，对雇主的营业收入可能引致的损失做出补偿。

结合上述规定可以看出，中文法律含义"要员保险"与美国法律中的key-man insurance 所蕴含的法律含义是相同的，所表示的范围也是相似的。因此，

---

① 在 Preliminary Expert Witness Report of Harold "Trey" Fireman III In the matter of GROUNDMETRICS, INC. v. LINCOLN NATIONAL CORPORATION 一文中，作者也强调"Key person insurance, also called key man insurance, is not a type of life insurance but rather a use of life insurance in a business planning context. A business will often have an employee with unique skills and/or industry knowledge vital to the success of that business. The business typically relies on this 'key person' to generate a majority of their profits and would likely suffer a financial loss of that individual were to die. In summary, when a business owns a life insurance policy on an important or 'key' employee that arrangement is referred to as key person insurance."在这份专家证人报告中，又向我们解释了key-man insurance 不是一种普通的人寿保险，而是在商业规划环境下使用人寿保险，而被保人是企业的商业发展有至关重要的人员，因为该类人员为公司创收了大部分的利润，一旦这些人死亡，就会给公司致命一击，所以公司要作为投保人，投保这类人员，在发生意外时对营业收入可能引致的损失得到补偿，在一定程度上也是保护了公司的利益。还有"The key person may be an executive, principal shareholder, a senior scientist, or a particularly effective salesperson"，由此可以看出，key man 的范围其实不只是局限于公司的管理人员或者是掌权人员，凡事对公司的商业发展起到了重大意义作用人，都可能受到公司的投保。

② The UNITED STATES LIFE INSURANCE COMPANY IN THE CITH OF NEW YORK v. LOGUS MANUFACTURES CORP., and George S. Hack Irrevocable Trust 一案中描述到："Under Florid law, a life policy insuring the life of a closely held corporation's president was a 'key man' policy" and "'key man' policies differ from typical life insurance policies in one important respect, specifically, the consent of the corporation is typically required for any change in beneficiary, absent any arrangement to the contrary approved by the corporation's directors or trustees."投保在公司主席身上的人寿保险就是"key man policy"（policy 在这里是保单的意思），这种人寿保险和一般的保险不同，重点在于该保单的受益人进行变更时需要得到公司的同意，而公司董事或是信托人做出任何与其决定相反的安排都是无效的。从这可以看出，"key man policy"在最大程地保护公司整体利益，防止公司在利益受威胁时受到少数人的支配，减缓公司受到致命打击的可能性。

③ 参见 https://www.ird.gov.hk/chs/faq/keyman.htm。

key-man insurance 汉译为"要员保险"更为合适。

Knock-and-announce Rule

若从字面直译 Knock-and-announce Rule 的话,可能会译为"敲门并宣告原则""敲门并宣布原则"或"敲门并声明原则"。术语中 knock 一词的翻译无可争议,即"敲门",而对于 announce 的译法则有较大分歧,那么在 Knock-and-announce Rule 这一原则中,对 announce 究竟应该做何理解与释义呢?

根据《布莱克法律词典》,Knock-and-announce Rule 属于刑事诉讼程序领域的概念,也称为 Knock-and-notice Rule,其释义为:The requirement that the police knock at the door and announce their identity, authority, and purpose before entering a residence to execute an arrest or search warrant,即根据该原则,警察在进入住所执行逮捕或搜查时,必须敲门并表明他们的合法身份、职权和进入住所的目的。该规则起源于 17 世纪英格兰的一个判例。该判例确认郡长为执行国王的传票而要强行进入私宅之前,应当先说明其目的,并要求户主将门打开。这一古老的法律原则也被现代法律所吸收,被纳入美国宪法第四修正案,即"人民的人身、住宅、文件和财产不受无理搜查和扣押的权利,不得侵犯。除依照合理根据,以宣誓或代誓宣言保证,并具体说明搜查地点和扣押的人或物,不得发出搜查和扣押状"。这条原则目前也被编纂入美国法典,对第四修正案中提到的搜查进行规制①。由此可知,Knock-and-announce Rule 作为一项刑事搜查程序原则,其根本目的在于保护公民免受公权力不合理搜查的侵扰。

在我国,关于搜查程序,《刑事诉讼法》第一百三十八条规定:进行搜查,必须向被搜查人出示搜查证。在执行逮捕、拘留的时候,遇有紧急情况,不另用搜查证也可以进行搜查。因此在汉语法律语境中,刑事搜查程序一般遵循搜查证出示原则,这是搜查的一般原则。搜查证是侦查人员依法进行搜查时的法律凭证。

---

① 在美国法典(U.S. Code)第 18 卷罪行和刑事诉讼程序第 3109 条入室搜查写明:"The officer may break open any outer or inner door or window of a house, or any part of a house, or anything therein, to execute a search warrant, if, after notice of his authority and purpose, he is refused admittance or when necessary to liberate himself or a person aiding him in the execution of the warrant."警察需要敲门,表明其合法身份、搜查权和目的(announce their identity, authority, and purpose),并在他们进入之前等待一段合理的时间(wait a reasonable period of time before they enter)。只有在当事人确认警察合法身份后仍拒绝搜查时,警察才会强行进入。

出示搜查证是为了证明执行搜查人员的身份和履行搜查职责,防止非法搜查,保证公民的人身权利、财产权利和住宅不受侵犯。

那么搜查证出示原则是否与 Knock-and-announce Rule 法律内涵相同呢?搜查证出示原则也强调证明搜查人员的身份和搜查职责,与 Knock-and-announce Rule 要求表明其合法身份、搜查权和目的(announce their identity, authority, and purpose)有着相似之处。但是两者的内涵存在差别。搜查证出示原则强调的是搜查人员在进行搜查时向被搜查人出示搜查证的行为,但并未对这种出示行为的时间和顺序进行限定。出示行为既可发生在搜查前,也可在搜查过程中,甚至有可能直至搜查结束才出示。因此,我国的搜查证出示原则其实并未对出示与搜查程序的先后顺序进行严格限制。而美国的 Knock-and-announce Rule 则不同,这一原则明显强调的是程序的先后顺序,要求敲门和亮明身份必须先于入门搜查(before entering a residence),仅在极其特殊的情况下才有颠倒顺序的例外。

综上,Knock-and-announce Rule 在中国法语境中无法找到合适的对等术语,因此在正确理解该术语含义的基础上进行合理创造是必要的。结合 Knock-and-announce Rule 的目的,即让住户在警察破门而入前就知晓警察的到来与警察进入住所的目的,所以 announce 翻译为"告知"更为合适,即告诉某人,使其知晓某件事情。因此,术语 Knock-and-announce Rule 汉译为"敲门告知原则"最为合理恰当。

knockoff

根据《布莱克法律词典》,knockoff 是知识产权领域的术语,其定义是: An unauthorized counterfeit and usu. inferior copy of another's product, esp. one protected by patent, trademark, trade dress, or copyright, usu. passed off at a substantially lower price than the original. 由此可知,该术语指未经授权生产假冒伪劣商品的行为,通常抄袭复制受专利、商标、商业外观或版权保护的产品,而且以超低价格进行售卖。

由此,根据其释义可以将 knockoff 翻译为"廉价仿制品",使读者可以明确了解该法律词汇的含义。此外,"山寨"这个词在中国使用的也非常普遍,比如"山寨机""山寨明星""山寨食品"等层出不穷,并且这些山寨产品价格十分低廉,许多都抄袭大牌的设计、图案，或者与大牌产品的名称相似，比如，奥利奥的山寨品"粤利粤"，其包装纸颜色与正品一模一样，名称字形相似，不仔细看很容易买错。因此也可以将 knockoff 翻译为"山寨产品"，此译更加简洁，在普通民众中的接受度也更高；译文"廉价仿制品"相比更为规范和符合法律语言庄重、正式的特点。

knowingly

knowingly 多译为"故意地，蓄意地"，此译与 purposely 的译文相同，但实际上这两个词存在细微差别。

根据《美国示范刑法典》(the Model Penal Code)，knowingly 的英文释义为：An individual is deemed to have acted knowingly in regard to a material element of an offense when: in the event that such element involves the nature of his or her conduct or the circumstances attendant thereto, he or she is aware that the conduct is of such nature or that those circumstances exist; if the element relates to a result of the person's conduct, he or she is conscious of the fact that it is substantially certain that the conduct will precipitate such a result. 即如果一个人在付诸一项行动时，明确知道该行动将造成的后果，或者对当时情景和环境可能造成的各种影响，那么这个人就被认定为是 knowingly。purposely 的英文解释为 According to plan, deliberately or with an express purpose in mind. 强调的是按计划，心中有明确的目的，蓄意地做某事。

具体举例来说，假设 A 要谋杀 B，打算在 B 将要乘坐的飞机上安置炸弹，届时将炸弹引爆。A 听说 C 也将乘坐这班飞机，但还是决定按计划进行，引爆飞机，导致 B 和 C 全部死亡。在这个例子中，A 对 B 就是 purposely，而 A 对 C 就是 knowingly。这便是 knowingly 和 purposely 的区别，所以 knowingly 翻译为"明知地"更为合适，purposely 应翻译为"蓄意地"。

labes realis

labes realis 是一个拉丁文法律术语，其字面意思是"真实的故障"。《布莱克法律词典》给出的释义是：A real defect that attaches to the thing.《元照英美法词典》给出的译文和解释是：实质瑕疵，指影响财产所有权的固有的瑕疵或污点，例如该财产是赃物。即使财产转移给第三人,该瑕疵的影响仍存在。大多数人在查阅词典后对该术语的含义仍然是一头雾水,因为中国的法律体系里并没有"实质瑕疵"这个术语。即使看到这个译文,读者也不能立刻明白 labes realis 的具体含义,当然也不能正确运用和学习。那么显然,该术语的现存译文尚有值得商榷之处,还需进一步了解其深层含义和实际运用。

在英美法系的买卖合同中,为了保护善意买受人的合理信赖、维护交易安全方,设立了权利瑕疵担保制度。该制度起源于罗马法,现已被英美法系、大陆法系和国际公约所承认。英美法系对于权利瑕疵担保的立法实践以判例为主,再加上数量不多的成文法。由于货物买卖的核心法律关系是所有权的移转,只有卖方对合同标的物具有所有权,且所有权上不存在瑕疵,无任何负担,任何第三人不可正当地对其主张权利,买方才能和平地占有、使用货物或自由转售而不受干扰,因此卖方必须承担权利担保,负有担保买方安宁地占有标的物而不受第三人干扰的义务[①]。

除了对买受人的权利保障,美国《统一商法典》还体现了对买卖双方权益的平衡。其 312—318 款规定中除了权利担保的内容,也有对于担保排除的规定。在美国的商事法律中,卖方对其所提交的货物必须承担权利担保和品质担保的义务,但是卖方可以通过具体明确的语言和实际情况取消其权利担保,可以清晰而醒目的、能够引起买方注意的、以书面形式取消担保的条款来否定所有不包括在书面合同中的口头明示担保,并以此对抗对其口头担保虚假的指控;可以通过买方检查货物或拒绝检查货物,通过交易过程、行业惯例和当事人的言语取消其默示担保的责任[②]。由此看来,美国的权利担保并非强制性规定,可根据买卖双方意见自治以适用。

综上所述,labes realis 在英美法系中具有的特征应当包括:买卖合同中卖方义务规定应当避免其出现;是合同标的物上第三人能正当主张的权利,此权利应为所有权;并非强制排除,双方当事人可以根据双方意见自治许可其存在。

整体来看,labes realis 翻译为"实质瑕疵"并无不妥,只是这样译一来与买卖

---

① 熊云武.《合同法》中的权利瑕疵担保制度研究[J]. 科教文汇,2007(08):127—129.
② 吴志忠. 美国《统一商法典》("货物买卖"篇)评析[J]. 中南财经政法大学学报,2004(05):123—129.

合同法律语言差异较大，读者乍看很难理解什么是实质瑕疵，合同也可以有瑕疵，行为、权利、物品都可以成为"实质瑕疵"的主体；二来与中文用语习惯不同，容易引起歧义；如果用"实质瑕疵"，未必是指所有权方面的瑕疵，物的效用或交易价值灭失解释为"实质"也说得通，毕竟实质并非专指所有权。根据 labes realis 在英美法系语境中的特征，"所有权瑕疵"或许是更恰当的译法。"所有权"即表示主体是物，且是能被占有、使用和处分的物。"所有权"的使用既缩小了"瑕疵"的范围，又能使人立即联想到民商法。其次，这与英美法系中的使用背景最大限度地吻合。而且"所有权瑕疵"与我国法律术语相通。《人民司法》上曾刊载一文《对不动产的强制执行——以所有权瑕疵为问题》；《人民法院报》上也曾刊载《有权占有可对抗瑕疵所有权人之排除妨害请求权》一文，文中含义与这里的释义完全重合。这证明"所有权瑕疵"在我国法律语言中有一定认知度和接受度，是符合我国法律用语习惯的。

land charges

该术语常被误译为"土地费"，这完全没有准确再现术语的含义。该术语英文释义是：Third party rights affecting unregistered land that require to be registered in the Land Charges Register in order to bind purchasers for value of that land. Included in the categories of land charges are restrictive covenants, equitable easements, estate contracts, mortgages not protected by the deposit of title deeds and the right of a deserted spouse to remain in the matrimonial home. Additionally, local authorities in England and Wales are required to keep a Register of Local Land Charges in which are to be entered details of local authority charges, planning charges and the like, which, when registered, bind successive owners of the land. Local land charges affect registered as well as unregistered land[①].

由上述释义并结合《元照英美法词典》的解释可知：land charges 是指英格兰法上影响到土地的某些权利或权利主张，它们通常都属于不能通过对财产的勘

---

① land charge. (n. d.) *Collins Dictionary of Law*. (2006). Retrieved February 22 2022 from https://legal-dictionary.thefreedictionary.com/land＋charge

察或通过正常的所有权调查即能发现的那些类别的权利或权利主张,如租金、年金,或应由土地所有人偿付的与土地相关的费用。根据《元照英美法词典》给出的解释,land charges 共分六级:地租,或因有人按 Land Charges Act① 在土地上开支了金钱,现根据任何制定法之条文提出申请要求索取该项金钱因而责令土地承担的钱款;非根据任何人之申请而设定的此类之土地负担;普通抵押、有限制的或法定的土地所有人的负担、一般的衡平法上的负担以及地产合同;为遗产税、限制性合同和衡平法上有效的地役权而设定的负担;某些年金;作为婚姻住所的土地上的负担。综上所述,land charges 可译为"土地负担"。

law review

《布莱克法律词典》对 law review 的定义是:1. A journal containing scholarly articles, essays, and other commentary on legal topics by professors, judges, law students, and practitioners. Law reviews are usu. published at law schools and edited by law students (law reviews are often grossly overburdened with substantive footnotes). 2. The law-student staff and editorial board of such a journal (she made law review). Also termed law journal.

结合《元照英美法词典》对该词条的解释可以得知:law review 是刊载有关法律的最新进展、司法判决以及立法等方面学理评论与专题文章的期刊出版物,一般由法学院高年级优秀学生主编,作者大部分为法学教授、法官、律师以及法律学生。最早的法律评论出现在 1875 年,即 Albany Law School Journal。当时的目的是为了使学生增进对法律学术的认识。大部分法学院还不止出版一种学生主编的 law review,除了有一般性的、针对时下一切议题的 law review,许多法学院还出版针对某一具体领域法律的 law review。law review 中的文章都是对法律的学理讨论,经常包含法律能作如何改进的建议。美国现今的 law review 不仅议题广泛,而且数量繁多,它们实际上已变成法律研究的重要渠道。值得指出的是,学生主编的 law review 在决定法学院教师的学术升迁、地位与影响方面

---

① The Land Charges Act 1972 is a UK Act of Parliament that updates the system for registering charges on unregistered land in England and Wales. It repealed and updated parts of the Land Charges Act 1925 and other legislation affecting real property. 参见 https://en.wikipedia.org/wiki/Land_Charges_Act_1972.

发挥关键性作用,这与其他学科采用同仁主编传统形成鲜明对比;而且能够参与编辑 law review 也被法学院的师生视为最高荣誉。

该术语通常被译为"法律评论",但分析其英文释义和其功能可知,它实质上指的是刊载有关法律的最新进展、司法判决以及立法等方面学理评论与专题文章的期刊出版物,所以在译文中加入"期刊"二字能够让读者更直观地领会其含义,否则易让读者误解为其仅仅是评论类的文章。

lawful age

该术语被直译或者误译为"合法年龄",这是一种不恰当的译法。

根据《布莱克法律词典》,lawful age 有两层含义:1. 与 age of majority 同义,指:The age, usu. defined by statute as 18 years, at which a person attains full legal rights, esp. civil and political rights such as the right to vote. The age of majority must be the same for men and women. In almost all states today, the age of majority is 18, but the age at which a person may legally purchase and consume alcohol is 21. 该层含义下,lawful age 指根据法律规定,一个人在 18 岁可获得全部法律权利,尤其是公民权利和政治权利,如投票权。但为特定行为(如饮酒、开车等)的 lawful age 在各州有所不同。由此可见,该含义下的 lawful age 主要划分的是一个人是否能够享有一些法律规定的基本权利。2. 与 age of capacity 同义,指:The age, usu. defined by statute as 18 years, at which a person is legally capable of agreeing to a contract, maintaining a lawsuit, or the like. A person may be authorized to make certain critical personal decisions at an earlier age than the general age of capacity, such as the decision whether to bear a child, to donate blood, to obtain treatment for sexually transmitted diseases, to marry, or to write a will. The age of capacity to write a will is typically not 18, but 14. 该层含义下,lawful age 指根据法律规定,一个人在 18 岁即可签订合同、参与诉讼、决定是否生育、献血、获得性病治疗、结婚或立遗嘱等。由此可见,此含义下的 lawful age 重在强调一个人是否能够独立进行一些会产生法律效力的行为。

在我国,"合法年龄"这一说法是不确切的,代替它的是"法定年龄",即在法律意义上将成年人与未成年人之间划清界限。当未成年人满足了法律规定的年龄,其不再被法律条文认定为是儿童,法律将终止父母或监护人监护未成年人的责任,而法律意义上的成年人将承担起法律规定的责任和义务。

综上所述,lawful age 可以译为"法定行为能力年龄""法定成年年龄"。

legal person

legal person 到底应翻译成"法人""法定代表人"还是"法定代理人"? 首先还是应了解其英文释义。

根据《布莱克法律词典》,legal person 与 fictitious person, juristic person, juridical person, artificial person, moral person 具有相同含义,具体指:An entity, such as a corporation, created by law and given certain legal rights and duties of a human being; a being, real or imaginary, who for the purpose of legal reasoning is treated more or less as a human being. An entity is a person for purposes of the Due Process and Equal Protection Clauses but is not a citizen for purposes of the Privileges and Immunities Clauses in Article IV § 2 and in the Fourteenth Amendment,由此可知,legal person 是依法设立的实体(如公司),并被赋予一定的法律权利和义务;它可以是真实的人也可以是虚构的人。

康奈尔法学院 LII 在线数据库平台给出了更为详细的解释①:Legal person refers to a human or non-human entity that is treated as a person for limited legal purposes. Typically, a legal persons can sue and be sued, own property, and enter into contracts. 由此可知,legal person 可以起诉也可以被诉,可以拥有财产,亦可以签订合同。

汉语中的"法人"是民事权利主体之一,与自然人(natural person)相对,指按照法定程序设立,有一定的组织机构和独立的财产,并能以自己的名义享有民事权利,承担民事义务的社会组织。可指企业、事业、社团等各种性质的法人机构。法人虽然是组织,但是拥有某些自然人具有的行为能力,例如签订合同以及起诉或被起诉的能力。在某些法律文件中(例如合同、协议或招股说明书等),会明确"人"(person 或 persons)包含法人和自然人。法人和自然人的一个区别是

---

① 参见 https://www.law.cornell.edu/wex/legal_person。

自然人具有刑事责任能力、可以为自己的犯罪行为承担刑事责任,而法人只有民事行为能力、不能承担刑事责任。我国《民法典》中的"法人"一词的英译便是 legal person(s)。

而"法定代表人"是依法代表法人行使民事权利以及履行民事行为义务的主要责任人。我国《民法典》第六十一条规定:依照法律或者法人章程的规定,代表法人从事民事活动的负责人,为法人的法定代表人。所以法定代表人必须是法人组织的负责人,能够代表法人行使职权。法定代表人可以由厂长、经理担任,也可以由董事长、理事长担任,这主要看法律或章程如何规定。

本来,"法人"和"法定代表人"这两个概念界限是很清楚的。但是,在有些行文不严谨的中文稿件中,可能自然而然地把"法人"当成"法定代表人"的简称来使用。也就是说,文章里写的是"法人",但是作者心目中的概念其实是"法定代表人"。只要仔细留意,这个坑倒不难躲过:如果实际所指是个实体,那么使用"法人"就是没问题的;如果所指看起来是位自然人(比如称某企业的法人是谁),即便用词是"法人",所对应的概念其实就是"法定代表人"。而法定代表人的英文是 legal representative①。

"法定代理人"则较容易与前两者区分开,指由法律规定的代理人,法定代理人依法为被代理人处理民事法律行为。比如《民法典》第二十三条规定:无民事行为能力人、限制民事行为能力人的监护人是其法定代理人。

legal fiction 与 legal presumption

根据《布莱克法律词典》,legal fiction 一词在源语中的定义为:An assumption that something is true though it may be untrue, made esp. in judicial reasoning to alter how a legal rule operates; specifically, a device by which a legal rule or institution is diverted from its original purpose to accomplish indirectly some other object. The constructive trust is an example of a legal fiction—Also termed fiction of law; fictio juris. 其中 judicial

---

① One who represents or stands in the place of another under authority recognized by law esp. with respect to the other's property or interests; as a personal representative; an agent having legal status, esp. one acting under a power of attorney. One who represents another by operation of law, most often as a guardian, but may be an executor, an administrator, a trustee, a receiver, etc.

reasoning 是指法律推理,即从一定的前提中,以法律和法学中的理或理由为基础,按照一定的推论规则或规律,为法律适用提供正当性证明的逻辑思维活动。constructive trust 是指推定信托,指法律根据当事人的某些行为以及衡平原则而推定产生的信托关系,以阻止不法行为人从其不法获得的财产上不当得利。如违反他人意愿或滥用其信任,以实际或推定的欺诈、胁迫或各种违法、不公正、阴谋、隐瞒手段获得在公平和诚信情况下本不应该获得并享有的权利。法律推定此类行为违反信托关系。推定信托就是 legal fiction 的一个例子。legal fiction 在源语中的意思就是法庭对事实做出的假设,以此作为裁决某一法律问题的基础,即假设某一事实是真实的,即使它可能并不真实。该词主要是用在司法推理过程中,以改变某一法律规则的适用。该术语在普通法体系中普遍使用,尤其是在英国。这也验证了一种表达即 Fictions arise from the law, and not law from fictions。

根据上面的释义,我们很可能想到另一个法律术语 legal presumption,那么我们该如何区分 legal fiction 和与之相近的另外一个词组 legal presumption 呢? 通过查找源语,我们发现 legal presumption 是指 A presumption may be defined to be an inference as to the existence of one fact from the existence of some other fact founded upon a previous experience of their connection(William P. Richardson, The Law of Evidence at 25),指当特定的事实已经证实,且无相反的证据提出时,要求法庭做出的法律上的假定,即裁决推定的事实成立。法律推定允许反驳。例如无罪推定即是一项法律推定,除非能排除合理怀疑地证明被告人有罪才可予以推翻,因此 legal presumption 可以译为"法律推定"。举例来说,presumption of paternity 是否可以翻译成为"生父推定"呢? 该词出自家庭法,在源语中①的解释认为:可以推定一个孩子的父亲是(1)在孩子孕育或出生的时候和孩子的母亲存在婚姻关系的男人,即便婚姻关系可能是无效的;或者(2)在孩子出生后与孩子母亲拥有婚姻关系,并且同意将自己的名字写在出生证明上

---

① 《布莱克法律词典》(Black's Law Dictionary, 9th Edition, p.1334)对 Presumption of Paternity 的定义是:*Family law*. The presumption that the father of a child is the man who (1)is married to the child's mother when the child was conceived or born (even though the marriage may have been invalid), (2) married the mother after the child's birth and agreed either to have his name on the birth certificate or to support the child, or (3) welcomed the child into his home and later held out the child as his own. Also termed *paternity presumption*; *presumption of legitimacy*; *legitimacy presumption*.

或者抚养孩子;或(3)欢迎孩子到自己家,并且像亲生孩子一样对待。而"生父推定"在《元照英美法词典》中的解释是:除非证明丈夫没有与妻子发生性交,否则推定婚内所生子女是丈夫的子女。可见汉语中的释义和源语的意思是基本对等的,因此可以将 presumption of paternity 译为"生父推定"。该术语就是 legal presumption 在应用过程中的一个实例。然而,legal fiction 在承认"童贞生子"的法律中的解释则是未婚所生的孩子应认定为并不具有基因的、生物的和心理上的父亲。因此 legal fiction 可以译为"法律拟制"和"法律假设",而 legal presumption 则更加强调"法律推定"的含义。

legitimate child

该术语被译为"婚生子女",但这并不能全面再现原文的含义。《布莱克法律词典》对 legitimate child 的定义是 1. At common law, a child conceived or born in lawful wedlock. 2. Modernly, a child conceived or born in lawful wedlock, or legitimated either by the parents' later marriage or by a declaration or judgment of legitimization. 由此可知,该术语指:1. 合法婚姻中怀孕或出生的孩子;2. 因其父母随后结婚或通过其他准正方法而取得婚生子女地位的非婚生子女。

"婚生子女"在我国法律语境中指婚姻关系存续期间妻子所生育的子女,即因婚姻关系受胎所生的子女。其父母为具有夫妻身份的合法配偶。这与上述释义的第一层含义相吻合,该含义下 legitimated child 完全可以译为"婚生子女"。而第二层含义所指的非婚生子女的准正,是指已出生的非婚生子女因生父母结婚或司法宣告而取得婚生子女地位的制度。即非婚生子女因其生父与生母在其出生后结婚,而被婚生化,使非婚生子女取得婚生子女的身份,被赋予与婚生子女相同的地位,所以此含义下的 legitimated child 应译为"通过准正而取得婚生子女地位的非婚生子女",而不能简单翻译为"非婚生子女"。

Lemon Law

根据其字面意思,该术语通常被直译为"柠檬法",但其背后的法律含义还需通过了解其英文释义得知。《布莱克法律词典》Lemon Law 的释义为:1. A statute designed to protect a consumer who buys a substandard automobile, usu. by requiring the manufacturer or dealer either to replace the vehicle or to refund the full purchase price. Almost all states have lemon laws in effect. Also termed *lemon protection*. 2. By extension, a statute designed to protect a consumer who buys any product of inferior quality. Also termed (in sense 2) quality-of-products legislation. 根据定义，Lemon Law 是美国一种消费者保护法，主要保障汽车买主的权益。它是美国的一种州法律，旨在为汽车买主以及其他产品的消费者在所购买的商品质量不达标准的时候提供救济，消费者可以要求赔偿损失或更换产品。如果没有 Lemon Law,汽车制造商或经销商有时候会要求消费者反复到店修理汽车，或者花费较长的时间修理汽车，导致消费者使用上的不方便。所以通过 Lemon Law 可以将汽车质量的否决权交给汽车消费者，把质量不好的损失留给汽车公司。

我国虽然没有"柠檬法"这种称呼，但是却存在消费者权益保护法。中国的消费者权益保护法是维护全体公民消费权益的法律规范的总称，是为了保护消费者的合法权益，维护社会经济秩序稳定，促进社会主义市场经济健康发展而制定的一部法律，虽然没有更加细致地划分对不同商品的保护，包括汽车市场，但是却可以切实在消费者权益保护法中找到与 Lemon Law 类似对等的表达。一种是对"柠檬法"进行解释，如翻译成"（给在规定时间内发现新车故障的买主以赔偿的）柠檬法"，另一种是翻译成"次品补偿法"或"伪劣商品赔偿法"也未尝不可，两种汉译都可以在法律背景下使得交流双方达到有效沟通的目的。

libel

该词常被误译为"诽谤；诽谤罪"，但其实这是一种以偏概全的译法。根据《布莱克法律词典》,libel 的定义有：1. A defamatory statement expressed in a fixed medium, esp. writing but also a picture, sign, or electronic broadcast. Libel is classified as both a crime and a tort but is no longer prosecuted as a crime. Also termed defamatory libel. 2. The act of making such a statement; publication of defamatory matter by written or printed words, by its embodiment in physical form or by any other form of communication that has the potentially harmful qualities characteristic of written or printed words. 由此可知,libel 指通过文字、图片等书面形式对他人进行的诽谤。

一般 defamation，slander 和 libel 这三个词容易被混淆。而根据《布莱克法律词典》可知：defamation 指：1. The act of harming the reputation of another by making a false statement to a third person. If the alleged defamation involves a matter of public concern, the plaintiff's constitutionally required to prove both the statement's falsity and the defendant's fault. 2. A false written or oral statement that damages another's reputation. 根据其释义可知 defamation 对应"诽谤，诽谤罪"，是一个统称。根据我国《刑法》第二百四十六条的规定，诽谤罪指故意捏造并散布虚构的事实，足以贬损他人人格，破坏他人名誉，情节严重的行为。诽谤一般有两种形式，一种是口头上的诽谤，一种是书面上的诽谤。由于书面形式的诽谤容易被更大范围人接触，所以其严重程度明显高于口头诽谤。《布莱克法律词典》对 slander 的定义是：A defamatory assertion expressed in a transitory form, esp. speech. 对应"口头诽谤，言词诽谤；对……进行言词诽谤"。而 libel 则对应"书面诽谤；书面诽谤（某人）"。

综上所述，libel 应译为"书面诽谤；书面诽谤（某人）"，这样比较贴切，也不会与其他词语混淆。

life imprisonment

Lexisnexis Law English-Chinese Dictionary 对该词条的定义是：Imprisonment for the term of a person's natural life. The most severe sentence that may be passed. The general criteria for imposing a life term are (1) the offence itself must be grave enough to require a very long sentence; (2) either the nature of the offences or the defendant's history indicates that he is a person of unstable character likely to commit such offences in the future; (3) if such offences were again committed, the consequences to others would be specially injurious, as in the case of crimes of violence or sexual offences[①]. The primary consideration is the interests of society[②]. Where a judge is

---

① R v Pang Chun Wai [1993] 1 HKC 233, [1994] 1 HKCLR 137 (CA); Criminal Procedure Ordinance (Cap 221) ss 67B, 67C.

② R v Ho Tung Shing & Ors [1994] 2 HKC 404 (CA)

considering a sentence of life imprisonment, he should inform counsel of that fact and counsel for the defendant should then be invited to make submissions on that proposed sentence. 由此可知，life imprisonment 指以某人的自然生命之长短为监禁刑期，是一种最严重的判刑，做出该判决的一般准则为：(1) 所犯罪行非常严重而致需要一个非常长的刑期；(2) 根据罪行的性质以及被告人的历史，显示该被告人性格不稳定，并很有可能在未来会再次犯同样的罪行；(3) 假如被告人再次犯同样罪行，这些罪行会对他人造成极大的伤害，比如暴力罪行或性犯罪。设置此类刑期主要是出于对社会利益的考量。通常该术语会被翻译为"终身监禁"或"无期徒刑"。

在中国的法律语境中，无期徒刑是对罪犯实行终身监禁的刑罚，但是在中国的实际执行中，被判处无期徒刑的罪犯在服刑期间如果确有悔改或者有立功表现的，可以被减为有期徒刑或者被假释，真正被终身监禁的只是极少数。比如我国《刑法》第七十八条规定：被判处管制、拘役、有期徒刑、无期徒刑的犯罪分子，在执行期间，如果认真遵守监规，接受教育改造，确有悔改表现的，或者有立功表现的，可以减刑。再比如我国《刑法》第八十一条规定：被判处无期徒刑的犯罪分子，实际执行十三年以上，如果认真遵守监规，接受教育改造，确有悔改表现，没有再犯罪的危险的，可以假释。如果有特殊情况，经最高人民法院核准，可以不受上述执行刑期的限制。其第二款规定：对累犯以及因故意杀人、强奸、抢劫、绑架、放火、爆炸、投放危险物质或者有组织的暴力性犯罪被判处十年以上有期徒刑、无期徒刑的犯罪分子，不得假释。

但根据 life imprisonment 的英文释义可知，监禁时长即等同于罪犯的自然寿命，即终身监禁。而在我国法律执行的实际情况中，无期徒刑在特定条件下，可减刑为有期徒刑或假释，也就是说，无期徒刑并非绝对意义上的终身监禁。所以，life imprisonment 并不能完全等同于国内的无期徒刑，翻译为"终身监禁"更为合适。

longevity pay

该术语常被误译为"按年资增加的工资"，但是这是一种以偏概全的译法。

其英文释义为：Longevity pay is a contractual agreement by which an employee receives compensation according to seniority… Typically, longevity pay is given to the top earning employees in a company. The payment is often looked upon as a means of giving due compensation to workers who have made a significant contribution to the firm. It is also sometimes meant to reward loyalty and encourage continuing employee satisfaction①. 根据其英文解释，longevity pay 是一种合同协议，员工根据资历获得报酬……，longevity pay 通常被视为对公司做出重大贡献的员工和高职位的员工给予应有补偿的一种手段。它也意味着对员工的一种奖励和激励。此外还了解到 the amount of annual longevity pay is usually a percentage of the employee's annual rate of pay on the employee's anniversary date. The annual rate of pay may not include bonuses, or pay for extra duties. The percentage is determined by the length of total service②，即按其年薪的一定比例(百分比按照服务的总年限确定)以每若干固定年数为期，另外增加的津贴和报酬。

"按年资增加的工资"这种译法并没有体现出 according to seniority 和 is given to the top earning employees in a company 的意思。

综上所述，longevity pay 应译为"高资历或高职位员工的工龄津贴"。

lump-sum agreement

根据《布莱克法律词典》可知该术语是国际法领域的概念，它在源语中的解释为：An agreement for one nation that caused injuries to another nation's citizens to make a single payment to the other nation to settle outstanding claims for those injuries. The recipient nation has the power to decide how the settlement funds should be distributed. This method of settling claims has become increasingly common since the mid-20th century as an alternative to submitting the claims to an international tribunal. 其中 single payment 释义为一次性支付，整笔支付。由上述释义可知，lump-sum agreement 指两国之间达成的一种协议，如一国对另外一国居民造成了一定损害，针对该损害，该国一次性支付一定金额的赔偿金、安抚款给受损害方。受援国有权决定结算资金的分配方式。自 20 世纪中期以来，两国间这种解决索赔的方法越来越普遍。

---

① 参见 www.wise-geek.com/what-is-longevity-pay.htm。
② 参见 https://definitions.uslegal.com/l/longevity-pay/。

该术语通常被翻译为"一次性付款",而在中国"一次性付款"是指一次性付清全费用(包括房产费、物业管理费、相关手续费)等等,并不能体现源语释义中"两国之间达成协议"的概念。因此直接将 lump-sum agreement 译为"一次性支付"可能会使得源语中两国之间的概念意义有所省略和减损,可以尝试添加一定的限制条件,翻译为"(由于一国对另一国居民造成损害而进行的)一次性支付协议",这样可使得源语的内涵更加准确地表述出来。

malfeasance

根据《布莱克法律词典》,malfeasance 指 A wrongful or unlawful act; esp. wrongdoing or misconduct by a public official,可知该术语指不法的或非法的行为;特别是公职人员的不当行为。维基百科对该词条给出了更详细的释义[①]: Malfeasance has been defined by appellate courts in other jurisdictions as a wrongful act which the actor has no legal right to do; as any wrongful conduct which affects, interrupts or interferes with the performance of official duty; as an act for which there is no authority or warrant of law; as an act which a person ought not to do; as an act which is wholly wrongful and unlawful; as that which an officer has no authority to do and is positively wrong or unlawful; and as the unjust performance of some act which the party performing it has no right, or has contracted not, to do. 即根据其他司法管辖区上诉法院给出的定义,malfeasance 指行为人没有合法权利的不法行为;影响、中断或干扰履行公务的任何不法行为;没有法律授权或保证的行为;一个人不应该做的行为;完全不法和非法的行为;指一名官员无权从事绝对错误或非法的活动;不公正的行为,履行义务的一方无权或约定无权这样做。由此可知 malfeasance 指广泛意义上的不法行为。

该术语通常被误译为"渎职罪"。但在我国,渎职罪是指国家机关工作人员利用职务上的便利或者徇私舞弊、滥用职权、玩忽职守,妨害国家机关的正常活动,损害公众对国家机关工作人员职务活动客观公正性的信赖,致使国家与人民利益遭受重大损失的行为。

---

① 参见 https://en.wikipedia.org/wiki/Malfeasance_in_office。

综上,中文渎职罪的主体是国家机关工作人员,而 malfeasance 也可以用于指公职人员的不当行为,但并没有仅限定在这一主体范围内。所以两者之间的主体不完全一致,将 malfeasance 直接翻译为"渎职罪"则缩小了其适用范围,不符合法律翻译"精准性"的要求,可将其翻译为"不法行为(也可指公务人员渎职行为)"。

material evidence

《布莱克法律词典》对 material evidence 的定义是:Evidence having some logical connection with the facts of consequence or the issues,由此可知 material evidence 指因其与重要事实或争议问题的逻辑联系而可能影响案件审理者对事实的认定的证据。可见 material evidence 对案件事实的认定具有重大影响作用。

该术语容易被误译为"物证",但物证是指以外部特征、物质属性、所处位置以及状态证明案件情况的实物或痕迹。如作案工具、现场遗留物、赃物、血迹、精斑、脚印等。这明显与 material evidence 的含义不符。

《元照英美法词典》将该术语翻译为"实质性证据",并补充道:对诉讼中未出示的证据,如果可以合理地认为,若该证据被提出,案件结果将可能不同,则可认为该证据为实质性证据。综合该术语的英文释义及其重要作用,译为"实质性证据"较为合理。

memorandum of alteration

该术语易被误译为"变更备忘录",从字面上看是没有问题的,但却忽略了其具体适用的专业领域。alteration 的英文释义是:An alteration is a variation made in the language or terms of a legal document that affects the rights and obligations of the parties to it. When this occurs, the alteration is material and the party who did not consent to the change can be released from his or her duties under the document by a court. 从中可以了解到这种变更是一种法律文件上的权利与义务的变更,具有法律意义。

根据《布莱克法律词典》对 memorandum of alteration 的定义可知,这是英国专利法上的一个概念,具体指:A patentee's disclaimer of certain rights—

such as rights to part of an invention that is not new and useful—to avoid losing the whole patent. Until the mid-19th century, if a single patent was granted for two inventions, one of which was not new and useful, the entire patent would be defective. 结合《元照英美法词典》对该术语的背景介绍可知：英国专利法早先规定,同一专利授予两项发明,如其中一项不具有新颖性或实用性,则整个专利无效。同一规则也适用于如果单个发明的实质性部分具有上述瑕疵,则该发明的专利无效。如果想要补救这一专利,专利法允许专利权人提出放弃部分专利或变更专利权利要求或说明书的声明,该声明即称为 memorandum of alteration。这一声明并不属于延伸专利权性质,该声明将成为专利证书或说明书的组成部分。

综上,将 memorandum of alteration 这一术语译为"专利权变更备忘录"更为准确。

modification order

仅从字面意思上看,该术语常被误译为"变更顺序""更改订单"或"变更令"等。了解该术语真实含义还需通过查证其英文释义。

法律英语中,order 有其专业含义。《布莱克法律词典》对 order 的定义是：1. A command, direction, or instruction. 这一层含义是普通英语中的含义,表示命令、指示、指令。2. A written direction or command delivered by a court or judge. 该层含义下,order 指法庭或法官做出的书面命令,也被称作 court order 或 judicial order。

根据《布莱克法律词典》可知,modification order 属于美国《家事法》中的概念,具体指：A post-divorce order that changes the terms of child support, custody, visitation, or alimony. A modification order may be agreed to by the parties or may be ordered by the court. The party wishing to modify an existing order must show a material change in circumstances from the time when the order sought to be modified was entered. 由此可见,该术语指离婚后变更子女抚养、监护、探视或赡养费条款的书面命令。modification order 可以由当事人同意,也可以由法院直接下发指令。

综上,可将该术语译为"(离婚后对子女的抚养、监护和探视或赡养费)变更令",从而突出其表示的意义与夫妻离婚后对孩子的抚养与监护以及家人的赡养等方面有关系。

moral evidence

该术语通常被误译为"道德证据""道义上的证据",但这并不能使读者理解其真实含义。

《布莱克法律词典》对该术语的定义是:Loosely, evidence that depends on a belief, rather than complete and absolute proof. Generally, moral evidence is testimonial. 根据该释义可以得知,证据通常都依赖于一种信念,完整和绝对的证据较难存在;一般来说,moral evidence 具有证明性。但该解释并不能使我们直观地了解到 moral evidence 的本质。根据 USLEGAL 网站提供的定义①可知:Moral evidence refers to that evidence which is not obtained either from intuition or demonstration. It consists of those convictions of the mind, which are produced by the use of the senses, the testimony of men, and analogy or induction, 即 moral evidence 指既不是通过直觉也不是通过实证获得的证据。它包括通过使用感官、人证、类比或归纳而产生的心灵信念。LawInsider 网站提供的释义②是:Moral evidence here means evidence from and about matters of fact. The contrast is with matters which can be demonstrated as deducible from logically necessary truths, 即来自或关于事实的证据。与之形成对比的是那些可以通过逻辑从必然真理中推断出来的事物。由此可以总结 moral evidence 的特点:1.具有证明力;2.是一种心灵信念(通过感官、人证、类比或归纳而产生);3.来自事实或关于事实。

《元照英美法律词典》将其翻译为"盖然性证据",指不能说明绝对的、必然的确定性,而只能表明具有高度可能性,并具有说服力(persuasive force)的证据。"盖然性证据"能够突出该证据具有一定证明力,相比"道德证据"更贴切一些。"道德证据"易对读者产生误导,毕竟证据应为客观存在,而道德则具有主观性,该译文容易使读者误判证据的客观性。

---

① https://definitions.uslegal.com/m/moral-evidence/
② https://www.lawinsider.com/dictionary/moral-evidence

municipal corporation

该术语常见的翻译有"市政公司""市自治团体""城市联合体"等。corporation 有多重意义:社团,公司;企业;法人;有限公司;(市、镇的)自治机构;(政治和经济的)组合。《布莱克法律词典》对 municipal corporation 的定义是:A city, town, or other local political entity formed by charter from the state and having the autonomous authority to administer the state's local affairs; esp., a public corporation created for political purposes and endowed with political powers to be exercised for the public good in the administration of local civil government. Also termed municipality. 由此可知该术语在宪法上指由市镇宪章授权成立的州以下的行政区划或公法人,如市(city)、县(county)、镇(town)或其他地方政府,有的国家还包括州级行政区划及政府,也称为 municipality。它拥有管理州地方事务的自治权,在地方政府的管理中为公共利益而行使权利。

《元照英美法律词典》给出的翻译是"市政法人",其给出的详细背景为:1. 在美国是指为了地方政府的管理,由州通常以特许状形式,将某一地区的居民联合起来而建立的既具有公司实体所具有的一般特性但又被赋予一定公权力的法律实体。联合而成的市、镇即属典型的市政法人,不过,依法律,其他的政府实体,如有权征税的灌溉区(water district)也可成为市政法人。州在创立市政法人时毋需经当地居民的同意,市政法人享有地方事务的立法权和管理权,经授权也可享有在该地区对州事务的管理权;2. 在英国则指通常由国王颁发特许状将英格兰或威尔士自治市(borough)的居民联合起来而构成的法人团体,它由市长、高级市政官和市民或公民组成。

综上,该术语译为"市政法人"是合适的,此处法人不是自然人,可以是公司、市政机构等。也可以译为"地方自治团体"或"地方公法人"从而突出其地方性和自治属性。

mutual insurance company

《布莱克法律词典》对 mutual insurance company 的定义为:An insurance company whose policyholders are both insurers and insureds because they pay premiums into a common fund, from which claims are paid; an insurer whose policyholders are its owners, as opposed to a stock insurance company owned by outside shareholders. 关于这个英文释义，结合《元照英美法词典》的解释，我们可以了解到：这是保险公司的组织形式之一，公司没有股东，公司成员既是保险人又是被保险人，其业务经营不以盈利为目的，而是为了保护保险单持有人（即公司成员）的利益。投保人按公司章程规定可作为法人的组成人员向公司缴纳保费。公司为赔偿保险单持有人的损失而支付保险赔偿金所需的资金，是由公司成员以保险费形式和以分摊形式向公司缴纳的。因此，该类保险公司实质上是公司成员之间相互保险的一种合作企业形式。

因此，依据其释义可将该术语译为"（公司成员）互助保险公司"。

necessary party

《布莱克法律词典》对该术语的定义是：A party who, being closely connected to a lawsuit, should be included in the case if feasible, but whose absence will not require dismissal of the proceedings. 由此可知 necessary party 指与诉讼有密切联系，应当参与到诉讼中的当事人，但是如果其缺席，也无需将诉讼驳回。康奈尔法学院 LII 在线数据库平台给出了更为详细的解释[①]：a person or entity whose interests will be affected by the outcome of a lawsuit, whose absence as a party in the suit prevents a judgment on all issues, but who cannot be joined in the lawsuit because that would deny jurisdiction to the particular court (such as shifting jurisdiction from a state to federal court)。由此可知，该术语所指的主体是"人或者实体"，在诉讼中其利益会受到审判结果的影响，该主体的缺席会妨碍法官对所有问题的判断，但是由于法院管辖权的原因，该主体无法参加诉讼。

该术语通常被按照字面意思翻译为"必要当事人"。我国法律对"必要当事人"的解释为：必要当事人（必要共同诉讼人），即当事人一方或双方为两人以上，诉讼标的是共同的，人民法院必需合并审理的诉讼。必要共同诉讼中的共同原告或共同被告就是共同诉讼人。《最高人民法院民事诉讼法司法解释理解与适用》第五十二条规定：当事人一方或者双方为二人以上，其诉讼标的是共同的，或

---

① https://www.law.cornell.edu/wex/necessary_party

者诉讼标的是同一种类、人民法院认为可以合并审理并经当事人同意的,为共同诉讼。

通过对比可以发现,英文中 necessary party 的含义主要指的是诉讼中重要的当事人,但是其不能参加诉讼的主要原因是管辖权的问题。而中文"必要当事人"主要是指当事人一方或双方为两人以上,且诉讼标的是共同的。此外,即便 necessary party 不能参与诉讼,诉讼也不会被驳回,此含义与中文"必要"之意不匹配。可见,necessary party 与"必要当事人"并不能画等号。

由于英美法律制度与我国法律制度的不同,在中文中我们无法找到对等的术语。在这种情况下,我们应该本着"准确严谨、清晰简明、前后一致、语言规范"的原则进行合理的创造,以满足读者对该术语的理解需求①。

通过以上的分析,该术语简单来说指由于管辖权问题无法参与诉讼的重要当事人,因此其比较合理的译文是"(因法院无管辖权不能参与诉讼的)重要当事人",首先明确其身份是诉讼中的当事人,其次明确其所处的特殊情况,即管辖案件的法院对其无管辖权。

necessity doctrine

该术语的源语解释为:The doctrine of necessity is a term used to describe the basis on which extra-constitutional actions by administrative authority, which are designed to restore order or attain power on the pretext of stability, are found to be constitutional even if such an action would normally be deemed to be in contravention to established norms or conventions. It also includes the ability of a private person to violate a law without punishment where the violation of law was necessary to prevent even worse harm. ②由此可知,行政当局为了恢复秩序或以稳定为借口获得权力的违宪行为能够适用该原则作为认定前述行为符合宪法的依据,即使这种行为通常会被视为违反既定规范或公约。它还包括既定条件下个人即便违反法律但不受法律惩罚,因为违反法律是防止

---

① 张法连. 英美法律术语汉译策略研究[J]. 中国翻译. 2016(02):100—104.
② 参见 https://en.wikipedia.org/wiki/Doctrine_of_necessity。

更严重伤害的必要条件①。

通过源语解释,我们可以看出该原则是基于一种超出法律管辖的行为,这种行为以国家为主体,目的是为了维持秩序,这种情况下该行为合宪;或以个人为主体,目的是避免更严重的伤害,这种情况下该行为不受法律惩罚。

该术语经常被翻译为"必要性原则",但在给我国法律中,必要性原则又称谦抑原则,是定罪的基本原则之一。所谓刑法的谦抑原则,是指用最少量的刑罚取得最大的刑罚效果。它是指立法机关只有在该规范确属必不可少——没有可以代替刑罚的其他适当方法存在的条件下,才能将某种违反法律秩序的行为设定成犯罪行为。

通过以上叙述可以看出源语对 necessity doctrine 的解释与我国刑法中的"必要性原则"完全不对等。结合该术语的英文释义可知,它比 necessity(紧急避险)的含义多了一层含义,即"国家为了维持秩序而不得已违宪的合宪行为",可以将 necessity doctrine 翻译为"国家或个人紧急避险原则"。

no-contest clause

《布莱克法律词典》对该术语的定义是:A provision designed to threaten one into action or inaction; esp., a testamentary provision that threatens to dispossess any beneficiary who challenges the terms of the will. Also termed in terrorem clause; nonconiest clause; terrorem clause; anticontest clause; forfeiture clause.

维基百科给出的释义是:A no-contest clause is a clause in a legal document, such as a contract or a will, that is designed to threaten someone, usually with litigation or criminal prosecution, into acting, refraining from action, or ceasing to act. The phrase is typically used to refer to a clause in a will that threatens to disinherit a beneficiary of the will if that beneficiary

---

① 该层含义与 necessity 的含义相同。《布莱克法律词典》(Black's Law Dictionary, 9th Edition, p.1158)对 necessity 的定义是:1. Criminal law. A justification defense for a person who acts in an emergency that he or she did not create and who commits a harm that is less severe than the harm that would have occurred but for the person's actions. 2. Torts. A privilege that may relieve a person from liability for trespass or conversion if that person, having no alternative, harms another's property in an effort to protect life or health. 该术语通常被翻译为"紧急避险"。

challenges the terms of the will in court. Many states in the United States hold a no-contest clause in a will to be unenforceable, so long as the person challenging the will has probable cause to do so[①].

通过上述英文释义我们可以看出，这是一个法律文件中包含的条款。比较典型的例子是在遗嘱或信托文件中为防止对遗嘱或信托提出争议或进行攻击而制定的条款，通过该条款迫使受益人不得将相关事宜诉诸法律，不得起诉等。也就是说该条款的主要目的是迫使某人作为或不作为，尤指约束受益人不得就遗嘱中所涉及的其他条款进行起诉。

《元照英美法词典》给出的翻译版本为"不争条款，即遗嘱中一项关于不得提出异议的条款。它规定某一项赠与或遗赠以受益人对该遗嘱不提出异议为条件。

我国保险业存在"不可争条款"，又称不可抗辩条款。其基本内容是：人寿保险合同生效满一定时期（一般为两年）之后，就成为无可争议的文件，保险人不能再以投保人在投保时违反最大诚信原则，没有履行告知义务等理由主张保险合同自始无效。在保险合同中列入不可抗争条款，是维护被保险人利益、限制保险人权利的一项措施。

由此可见，将 no-contest clause 翻译成"不争条款"很容易与保险相关的"不可争条款"混淆。因此，为了避免相似法律条款名称的混淆使用，no-contest clause 可以翻译成"不可争论条款"，既与保险中的"不可争条款"区分开，又突出该术语中"不可提出争议"的含义。

obiter dictum

根据《布莱克法律词典》对该术语的释义可知，obiter dictum 是拉丁语词汇，经常缩写为 dictum 或 obiter（相较少见）翻译成英文为 something said in passing，其具体含义为：A judicial comment made while delivering a judicial opinion, but one that is unnecessary to the decision in the case and therefore not precedential (although it may be considered persuasive). 由此可知，obiter dictum 是指法官在做出判决的过程中就某一与案件并不直接相关的法律问题所做的评论，它并非为本案判决所必要，因此不具有判例的拘束力（尽管它具有

---

① https://en.wikipedia.org/wiki/No-contest_clause

一定说服力)。

通常,obiter dictum虽然不具有判例的约束力,但也会被写入判决书中,从而为今后的案件审理起到指导作用。所以在司法实践中,法官在做出裁决时,有时会引用先前案件意见中obiter dictum一些段落。引用的段落可能会对支持或裁决后来案件起到一定作用,这具体取决于后者的法院实际裁决的内容以及法院如何处理引用段落中体现的原则。

综上,结合该术语的含义和特征,即由法官做出的不具有约束力,随附在意见书中的意见,应将其翻译为"(法官在意见书中做出的不受先例约束的)附带意见"。

omission

《布莱克法律词典》对omission的定义有四层:1. A failure to do something; esp., a neglect of duty (the complaint alleged that the driver had committed various negligent acts and omissions). 2. The act of leaving something out (the contractor's omission of the sales price rendered the contract void). 3. The state of having been left out or of not having been done (his omission from the roster caused no harm). 4. Something that is left out, left undone, or otherwise neglected (the many omissions from the list were unintentional). Formerly also termed omittance. 根据上述释义和示例,可以总结出omission的含义有:1. 做某事失败;尤其是玩忽职守;2. 遗漏某事的行为;3. 被排除在外或没有做某事的状态;4. 被遗漏、未完成或以其他方式被忽略的事物。

维基百科给出的定义是:An omission is a failure to act, which generally attracts different legal consequences from positive conduct. In the criminal law, an omission will constitute an actus reus and give rise to liability only when the law imposes a duty to act and the defendant is in breach of that duty. In tort law, similarly, liability will be imposed for an omission only exceptionally, when it can be established that the defendant was under a duty to act[①]. 即omission通常与积极行为(positive conduct)相较,两者产生不同的

---

① https://en.wikipedia.org/wiki/Omission_(law)

法律后果。在刑法中,只有当法律规定了行为义务,而被告违反了该义务时,才构成 omission,并产生责任。同样,在侵权法中,只有在可以确定被告有义务采取行动的情况下,才需为 omission 行为承担责任。

由上述定义可知,omission 在法律层面的意义可以概括为:忽视或未为一定行为,尤指未为法律、职责或特定环境要求从事的行为,一定条件下行为人须对此承担法律责任。因此,可以将该术语翻译为"疏忽(尤指道德或法律义务);遗漏"。

one day, one trial

《布莱克法律词典》对该术语的源语释义是:A system of summoning and using jurors whereby a person answers a jury summons and participates in the venire for one day only, unless the person is actually empaneled for a trial, in which event the juror's service lasts for the entire length of the trial. This system, which is used in several states, reduces the average term of service and expands the number of individual jurors called.

美国某政府网站对 one day, one trial 的解释是:Under the one day/one trial jury system, instead of being summoned to serve lengthy terms of 30 days or more, jurors not selected to hear a case on the day on which they are summoned are excused. Those chosen for a jury panel serve only for the duration of that one trial。

由此可知,one day, one trail 规定了公民担任陪审员的时间限制。在美国,每个公民有两项最重要的义务——纳税和当陪审员。每位公民都有可能收到法院函告,要求其在特定时间到法院参与陪审团的遴选程序,收到法院的函告后必须认真对待,否则可能会因蔑视法庭而被重罚。众所周知,一般情况下法院审理案件的周期较长,案件越复杂,周期越长。公民一旦被选中为正式陪审员则必须在案件审理周期内按时到庭出席。但根据 one day, one trail,公民在陪审员遴选阶段(voir dire),出席当天没有被点到名即算完成此周期内的陪审员义务;被点到后如果没有被选中也视为完成陪审员义务;选中后则只需参与完一个案件的审理则完成此次周期内的陪审员义务。下一个周期(各州规定不同)开始后公民有可能再次收到法院通知。这一制度在美国几个州都有使用,它缩短了陪审员的平均服务期限,也节约了成本,体现了美国的陪审团制度的极大改进。

有些人将其翻译为"一天或一审"或"一天及一审",这容易让读者混淆陪审员服务时长为"一天"或"一次审理",但实际上其服务时长有可能只有一天(未被选为正式陪审员时),也有可能必须参与完一整个案件的审理(被选为正式陪审员)。综上,one day, one trail 可翻译为"一天/一案陪审法"。

opinion evidence

《布莱克法律词典》对该术语的定义是:A witness's belief, thought, inference, or conclusion concerning a fact or facts. 维基百科给出了个更详细的解释:Opinion evidence refers to evidence of what the witness thinks, believes, or infers in regard to facts, as distinguished from personal knowledge of the facts themselves. In common law jurisdictions the general rule is that a witness is supposed to testify as to what was observed and not to give an opinion on what was observed[①]. 由此可知,opinion evidence 指证人就争议问题陈述的自己的观点、看法或推论,区别于证人就自己所了解的案件事实而做的客观性陈述。

英美国家将证人分为"普通证人"(layman witness)和"专家证人"(expert witness)。证据规则通常不允许普通证人以其对案件事实的意见或推论作证。原因有:1. 证人发表意见侵犯了审理事实者的职权;2. 证人发表意见有可能对案件的事实的认定产生误导;3. 普通证人缺乏发表意见所需要的专门性知识或者基本的技能训练与经验;4. 普通证人的 opinion evidence 对案件事实的认定没有价值[②]。但是有例外,如因具有相应的科学技术或其他专业知识而具备专家资格的专家证人的意见可以作为证据采信;普通证人的意见证词一般只有在符合法律规定的少数例外情况下才可予采信,如美国《联邦证据规则》(Federal Rules of Evidence)规定,对普通证人以意见或推论形式做出的证词只有在符合:合理建立在证人的感觉之上,和对清楚理解该证人的证词或确定争议中的事实有益时,才可被采纳。

综上所述,普通证人就争议问题做出的自己的观点、看法和推论这一类 opinion evidence 一般不可采,而专家证人基于其专业知识而出具的意见可采

---

① https://en.wikipedia.org/wiki/Opinion_evidence
② 参见张法连.英美法律术语辞典(英汉双解)[Z].上海:上海外语教育出版社,2014.

信。现存在译文"意见证据"容易将普通证人的意见证据和专家证人的意见证据混淆,建议将其翻译为"(普通证人)意见证据"以作区分。

O. R.（own recognizance）

O. R.（own recognizance）的译文有"具结释放""自我保释"。为了确保法律术语译文的准确性,首先应查阅该术语的源语释义。

康奈尔法学院 LII 在线数据库平台给出的解释[①]为:Own recognizance (O. R.), also called personal recognizance, means a release, without the requirement of a posting bail, based on a written promise by the defendant to appear in court when required to do so. 由此可知该术语指被告人出具书面承诺为自己担保且保证随时到庭,在不要求保释的情况下被释放,从而在监狱外等待审判的一种方式。法院往往会考虑以下因素[②]:指控的严重程度、被告的犯罪记录、被告与社区的联系、被告返回法庭的可能性以及被告对公共安全的威胁。然而,即使被告证明他们将出庭且不存在安全风险,他们也不能保证在自己担保的情况下获释。在自己担保的情况下获释后未能出庭将被处以罚款,并将导致额外指控。

通过上述释义可以发现 O. R. 与 bail（保释）之间存在着一定的区别。在美国,当一个人被逮捕关进监狱后,法官会对其情况进行审查,并在许多不同层面上对该人进行评估。一般来说,O. R. 只会发生在偷窃等轻罪行为中。而 bail（保释）以失去实质财务的可能性保证被告人出庭受审。可以是在法院存放现金、债券、易兑现的财产,还可以是由具有相应偿付能力的保证人来提供担保。另外还有职业保证人的担保和百分之十替代,其不要求被告交纳全额的保释金,只需要交纳保释金的一部分(多数州为全额保释金的百分之十)。因此,O. R. 翻

---

① https://www.law.cornell.edu/wex/own_recognizance_(or)。
② 根据康奈尔法学院 LII 在线数据库平台给出的解释:Courts may consider the following factors when determining whether release on own recognizance is appropriate: the severity of the charges, the defendant's criminal record, the defendant's ties to the community, the likelihood that the defendant will return to court, and the defendant's threat to public safety. However, even if a defendant demonstrates that they will appear in court and are not a safety risk, they are not guaranteed to be released on their own recognizance. Failure to appear after a release on own recognizance is punishable by a fine and will result in additional charges. 参见 https://www.law.cornell.edu/wex/own_recognizance_(or)。

译为"自我保释"并不恰当。

O. R. 的释义难免使人联想到中国的"取保候审",它指公安、人民检察院和人民法院在刑事诉讼过程中,对于被刑事追诉而又未被刑事羁押之人,责令其提出保证人或交纳保证金,并出具保证书,以防止其逃避侦查、起诉和审判,保证刑事诉讼程序顺利进行的一种非羁押性刑事强制措施。因此,在我国取保候审制度之中的"保",不仅有被保释之人的"保证",还应包括财产之担保或他人之担保。而其中的"审",除了法院的审判外,还包括公安和人民检察院的讯问。不过,O. R. 中被告人需要履行的义务是出庭,显然中国的取保候审制度中被告人需要履行的义务多于 O. R. 中所规定的义务,所以翻译为"取保候审"也不恰当。

根据我国《刑事诉讼法》的有关规定,人民法院、人民检察院和公安机关对被取保候审、被监视居住的犯罪嫌疑人、被告人违反该法规定情结较轻的,应责令其具结悔过。因此可见,中文中的"具结书"虽起到让犯罪嫌疑人认罪悔过的作用,但是它只是一种非刑罚处理方式之一,犯罪嫌疑人在上交具结书后并不能解除其拘留或羁押状态,所以将 O. R. 翻译为"具结释放"是不太准确的。

综上,结合 O. R. "自我担保以获得释放"的含义,可将其翻译为"自保释放"。

ordinance

《布莱克法律词典》对 ordinance 的定义是:An authoritative law or decree; esp., a municipal regulation. Municipal governments can pass ordinances on matters that the state government allows to be regulated at the local level. A municipal ordinance carries the state's authority and has the same effect within the municipality's limits as a state statute. Also termed bylaw; municipal ordinance. 由此可知 ordinance 指市政一级的立法机关通过的法规(州政府允许市政府在地方一级实行监管),因此也称为 municipal ordinance,它在市政范围内具有与州法令相同的效力。结合《元照英美法词典》的解释可知:该词主要用在美国英语中,等同于 municipal law;而英国英语中与其对应的词为 by-law。但在美国英语中,by-law 一般指公司章程(articles of incorporation)之外的内部规则。

在了解该术语的英文释义后,还需了解中国不同行政级别组织机构所制定的法律的名称以及效力问题。在我国,部门规章是指中央部门规章,地方性法律分为地方性法规和地方政府规章。中央部门规章一般高于地方性法律。我国实际情况基本是部门立法,所谓立法部门化。为了使法规迅速产生效力,通常都以部门规章形式出现,但仍属于全国性法律。而地方法规永远只局限于地方,所以部门规章效力大于地方性法规。我国《立法法》第七十二条规定:省、自治区、直辖市的人民代表大会及其常务委员会根据本行政区域的具体情况和实际需要,在不同宪法、法律、行政法规相抵触的前提下,可以制定地方性法规。

综上,"地方性法规"与 ordinance 的制定主体在各自的行政等级中具有相似地位,可将 ordinance 翻译为"地方性法规"。

outcome responsibility

根据《布莱克法律词典》,outcome responsibility 的英文释义是:The view that those who cause harm are responsible for it even in the absence of fault. 根据此释义及词典中补充的内容[①]可知:outcome responsibility 指导致损害的人即使没有过错也须为其负责任。outcome responsibility 是法律可以建立赔偿义务的基础。有问题的行为不仅不被社会所接受,并且还有理由将所遭受的损害视为对权利的侵犯,那么建立 outcome responsibility 是在情理之中的。

outcome responsibility 的译法有"结果义务"和"结果责任"。"结果义务"是指合同履行完毕应当以服务提供人完成并交付特定工作结果为标志,其核心是结果实现义务。因此"结果义务"所适用的语境是在服务合同内,是以合同过程为线索,以先合同义务、过程义务和结果义务为框架的服务合同义务群体系。综上,"结果责任"是更为合适的译法。

---

① "Outcome responsibility serves to foster a sense of identity because it does not stretch indefinitely into the future but enables each of us to claim for ourselves, or to share with a few others, outcomes of limited extent, whether successes or failures. Yet outcome responsibility for harm to another does not by itself create a duty to compensate. The form that our responsibility for an outcome should take remains an open question. An apology or telephone call will often be enough. But outcome responsibility is a basis on which the law can erect a duty to compensate if there is reason to do so. There will be some reason to do so if the conduct in question is socially undesirable and if there is also reason to treat the harm suffered as the infringement of a right." Tony Honore, *Responsibility and Fault* 77-78 (1999).

overrule

《布莱克法律词典》对 overrule 的定义是：1. To rule against; to reject (the judge overruled all of the defendant's objections). 2. (Of a court) to overturn or set aside (a precedent) by expressly deciding that it should no longer be controlling law (in Brown v. Board of Education, the Supreme Court overruled *Plessy v. Ferguson*). 康奈尔法学院 LII 在线数据库平台给出的解释为：Overrule is used in two circumstances：（1）when an attorney raises an objection to the admissibility of evidence at trial① and（2）when an appellate court issues its ruling②。

综合上述两种释义并结合《元照英美法词典》的相关解释可知 overrule 有三种适用情形：(1)律师在庭审过程中对证据的可采性提出异议；(2)在审判过程中，法官驳回律师提出的反对意见；(3)上诉法院推翻此前的判决。具体指在同一法律问题上，同一法院或上级法院做出的后一判决与前一判决相反时，就表示前一判决不再具有作为判例的效力。但该词不适用于同级法院或各独立法庭就相同问题做出相互冲突的判决的情况。在美国，同一法院系统内的上级法院有权推翻下级法院先前做出的判决，各法院也可以推翻自己先前的判决；而在英国，只有上级法院才可推翻下级法院先前的判决，除上议院自 1966 年以后有权

---

① In the first circumstance, in accordance with Rule 103 of the Federal Rules of Evidence or various state statutes such as Section 2104 of Oklahoma's evidence code, the trial judge will either overrule or sustain the objection. When the trial judge overrules the objection, the trial judge rejects the objection and admits the evidence. On the other hand, sustaining the objection means that the trial judge allows the objection and excludes the evidence. 该情形下，根据《联邦证据规则》第 103 条或俄克拉荷马州《证据法》第 2104 条等各州法规，初审法官将驳回或维持异议。当初审法官驳回异议时，初审法官驳回异议并承认证据。另一方面，支持异议意味着初审法官允许异议并排除证据。参见 https://www.law.cornell.edu/wex/overrule。

② In the second circumstance, when an appellate court overrules a case, the appellate court overturns a precedent. As a result, the precedent is no longer the controlling rule of law. For example, in the landmark case Brown v. Board of Education, the Supreme Court ruled that segregating children in public schools solely based on race violated the Fourteenth Amendment Equal Protection Clause. With this decision, the Supreme Court overruled its prior decision in Plessy v. Ferguson that separate but equal accommodations based on race did not violate the Fourteenth Amendment. Thereafter, Brown v. Board of Education, not Plessy v. Ferguson, became the controlling rule of law for issues on separate but equal accommodations based on race. 该情形下，上诉法院驳回案件时，上诉法院便推翻了先例。因此，先例不再具有效力。参见 https://www.law.cornell.edu/wex/overrule。

推翻自己先前的判决外,其他法院不能推翻自己先前的判决。

overrule 常见的译文有"驳回起诉"。在中国的法律语境中,驳回起诉是指人民法院收到原告的起诉书后,依法对其进行立案审查,发现原告没有起诉权利,依照法定程序裁定予以驳回。由此可见,驳回起诉虽与 overrule 的第三种适用情形相似——都适用于上诉阶段,但二者含义并不相同。"驳回起诉"是因原告没有起诉权利;而 overrule 是指上诉法院做出与初审法院相反的判决从而推翻之前的判决。

综上,翻译 overrule 需结合其适用语境,因此上述三种适用情形中 overrule 应分别翻译为:(1)反对;(2)驳回;拒绝;反对无效;(3)推翻。

personal property 与 **private property**

personal property 容易与 private property 混淆,但两者含义并不相同。

《布莱克法律词典》对 personal property 的定义是:1. Any movable or intangible thing that is subject to ownership and not classified as real property. 与 personalty,personal estate,movable estate,(in plural) things personal 同义。指除不动产外的拥有所有权的有形或无形物。2. 税收方面的含义:Property not used in a taxpayer's trade or business or held for income production or collection. 指不用于创收或征收收入的财产。康奈尔法学院 LII 在线数据库平台给出的解释①为:Any movable thing or intangible item of value that is capable of being owned by a person and not recognized as real property. 即任何动产或无形的有价物品,有所有权,但不被确认为不动产。与 chattel 同义。由此可知 personal property 主要指个人的动产财产。

《布莱克法律词典》对 private property 的定义是:Property—protected from public appropriation over which the owner has exclusive and absolute rights. 即所有者对该类财产拥有专属和绝对权利,法律保护其不被公共占用。康奈尔法学院 LII 在线数据库平台给出的解释②为:Property owned by private parties—essentially anyone or anything other than the government。Private property

---

① https://www.law.cornell.edu/wex/personal_property
② https://www.law.cornell.edu/wex/personal_property

may consist of real estate, buildings, objects, intellectual property (for example, copyrights or patents). This is distinguished from Public Property, which is owned by the state or government or municipality. 指私人拥有的财产,可能包括房地产、建筑物、物品、知识产权(例如版权或专利)。这与公共财产(public property)不同,公共财产由国家、政府或市政当局所有。

综上,personal property 应翻译为"个人动产财产";而 private property 重在强调该财产仅为个人所有,包括动产和不动产,应翻译为"私有财产"。

petit treason 与 petty treason

关于这两个术语,《布莱克法律词典》给出的英文释义是:murder of one's employer or husband. Until 1828, this act was considered treason[①] under English law. 维基百科给出的定义[②]为:Petty treason or petit treason was an offence under the common law of England in which a person killed or otherwise violated the authority of a social superior, other than the king.

根据上述定义及其补充的解释可知:petit treason 指相对于 high treason 而言,主要指的是奴仆杀害主人、部下杀害长官、妻子杀害丈夫、教士杀害主教的罪行。其实质在于违反了对个人和家庭所负有的忠诚义务,而叛国罪(treason)则是违反了对国家的忠诚义务。所以该术语常被译为"轻叛逆罪",但这并不恰当。1828 年后英国对该罪改按谋杀罪处理,但该罪行现已被大多数英美法国家废除。

---

① 《布莱克法律词典》(Black's Law Dictionary, 9th Edition, p. 1667)进一步补充道:The frequent reference to higher treason is a carry-over from an ancient division of the offense that has long since disappeared. In the feudal stage of history the relation of lord to vassal was quite similar to the relation of king to subject. The relation of husband to wife came to be regarded in the same category, as also did the relation of master to servant, and that of prelate to clergyman. And just as it was high treason to kill the king, so a malicious homicide was petit treason if it involved a killing of (originally, lord by vassal, and later) husband by wife, master by mistress or servant, or prelate by clergyman. When the special brutality provided by the common law for the punishment of petit treason disappeared, this crime became merged with murder and only one crime of treason remained.

② 维基百科的定义中也进一步补充道:In England and Wales, petty treason ceased to be a distinct offence from murder by virtue of the Offences against the Person Act 1828. It was abolished in Ireland in 1829. It never existed in Scotland. It has also been abolished in other common-law countries. 参见 https://en.wikipedia.org/wiki/Petty_treason。

在我国,杀人主要分为故意杀人和过失杀人两种。而我国《刑法》中并没有为杀害主人或杀害丈夫的行为而定罪的罪名。根据该词的源语释义可将其译为"杀主罪;杀夫罪"。

plea bargain

根据《布莱克法律词典》,plea bargain 也称作 plea agreement, negotiated plea, sentence bargain,其具体含义为:A negotiated agreement between a prosecutor and a criminal defendant whereby the defendant pleads guilty to a lesser offense or to one of multiple charges in exchange for some concession by the prosecutor, usu. a more lenient sentence or a dismissal of the other charges. 由此可知 plea bargain 指在刑事诉讼中检察官和刑事被告人之间的协商协议,被告人做有罪答辩(guilt plea),承认较轻的罪行或多项指控中的一项,以换取检察官的一些让步,被告人从而获得更宽大的判决或撤销其他指控。由《元照英美法词典》的解释可知:检察官与被告人达成的此类协议经法院批准后即可执行。该做法在出现之初引起了人们的争议。20 世纪 60 年代美国最高法院宣布其为合法,从而得到广泛采用。

该术语经常被译为"诉辩交易",但"交易"一词不仅有碍法律语言的严肃性,而且也有损法律维护公平正义的理念。plea bargain 其实不是一种交易,从美国的法律文化角度来考查,这其实是一个非常科学和人性化的做法。

综上,将 plea bargain 译为"认罪协商"更好。

polygamy

《布莱克法律词典》给出的 polygamy 英文释义是:1. The state or practice of having more than one spouse simultaneously. 2. Hist. The fact or practice of having more than one spouse during one's lifetime, though never simultaneously. Until the third century, polygamy included remarriage after a spouse's death because a valid marriage bond was considered indissoluble. 第一层含义:同时有一个以上配偶的状态或做法。也称作 simultaneous polygamy,plural marriage。第二层含义:一个人一生中拥有不止一个配偶的事实或做法,但并非同时拥有。直到 3 世纪,polygamy 还包括配偶去世后再婚。

也称作 successive polygamy, serial polygamy, sequential marriage。

polygamy 常被译为"一夫多妻制",但究其根本,此译文并不恰当。由上述释义可知:polygamy 的第二层含义属于历史概念,现在多使用其第一层含义,即同时存在多个配偶,与数人存有婚姻关系。所以其既可指一夫多妻,也可指一妻多夫。此外,polygamy 的译文中不宜加入"罪",因为其在欧洲和美国虽构成犯罪,但在有些国家则为合法。综上,将其译为"多配偶"更为合适。

presumption of death

根据《布莱克法律词典》,该术语的定义是:A presumption that arises on the unexpected disappearance and continued absence of a person for an extended period, commonly seven years. 结合《元照英美法词典》的解释可知:该术语指当一个人失踪或离开其惯常住所,在持续的法定期间(在美国一般为 7 年)内杳无音信,或由于其他事情的发生,使得其生存的可能有违常理时,依法推定该人死亡。由此可见,并无确切证明说明其死亡,仅是在达到一定时间后从法律上推定其已死亡。

该术语现多错译为"死亡推定"。应明确汉语"死亡推定"之意。我国法律中有推定死亡之意的法条有,《民法典》第一千一百二十一条规定:继承从被继承人死亡时开始。相互有继承关系的数人在同一事件中死亡,难以确定死亡时间的,推定没有其他继承人的人先死亡。都有其他继承人,辈分不同的,推定长辈先死亡;辈分相同的,推定同时死亡,相互不发生继承。由此可见该条规定了继承开始的时间以及被继承人死亡的推定时间。显而易见,此"死亡推定"与英美法中的 presumption of death 含义完全不同。

我国法律中能够与其含义相匹配的实为"宣告死亡"。

我国《民法典》总则编即第四十六条规定:自然人有下列情形之一的,利害关系人可以向人民法院申请宣告该自然人死亡:(一)下落不明满四年;(二)因意外事件,下落不明满二年。因意外事件下落不明,经有关机关证明该自然人不可能生存的,申请宣告死亡不受二年时间的限制。

由此可见,"宣告死亡"与 presumption of death 的唯一不同之处在于时间限定。

综上所述,可将 presumption of death 翻译为"宣告死亡"。

prize fighting

prize fight 常被译为"拳击大奖赛；带奖金的拳击赛"。《布莱克法律词典》对该术语的英语释义为：Fighting for a reward or prize; esp., professional boxing. Prize fighting was not looked upon with favor by the common law as was a friendly boxing match or wresting match。由此可知，该术语指：为奖励或奖品而战的一种职业拳击。英美法律制度中并不把此种比赛视为友好的拳击比赛或摔跤比赛。

根据法律英语语言应当严谨、简洁的特点，"拳击大奖赛""带奖金的拳击赛"不够准确、言简意赅，结合该术语的含义，可译为"职业拳击赛"或"有奖拳击"。

process

根据《布莱克法律词典》，process 有两层含义：1. The proceedings in any action or prosecution (due process of law). 指诉讼或起诉的程序。2. A summons or writ, esp. to appear or respond in court (service of process). 也称作 judicial process, legal process。指传票或令状，尤指出庭或应诉的传票或令状。

process 的第一层含义译为"诉讼程序"无可争议，争议主要在于其第二层含义。以 service of process 为例，将其译为"传票送达"准而不切。"传票送达"仅是其中一层含义。根据维基百科的解释[①]，Service of process is the procedure by which a party to a lawsuit gives an appropriate notice of initial legal action to another party (such as a defendant), court, or administrative body in an effort to exercise jurisdiction over that person so as to enable that person to respond to the proceeding before the court, body, or other tribunal. Notice is furnished by delivering a set of court documents (called process) to the person to be served. 此句中 court documents(called process)包括传票，但不限于传票，可译作诉讼文书。若以传票全指，一者弃他等文书不顾，二者范围过于狭小，意义不准确。

综上，单以 process 而论，当以具体语境得具体含义；若有搭配，如 service of process 应译作"诉讼文书送达"。

---

① https://en.wikipedia.org/wiki/Service_of_process

pronotary

《布莱克法律词典》对该词的解释为 first notary。根据《元照英美法律词典》和 *The Free Dictionary*①，pronotary 与 prothonotary 同义。《布莱克法律词典》对 prothonotary 的定义是：A chief clerk in certain courts of law. 由此可知该术语指法庭的主要职员。《元照英美法律词典》将其译为"首席书记官"。

但根据维基百科的解释，该词在不同国家具有不同释义。在澳大利亚②，prothonotary 的主要职责有负责审判分庭登记处的所有行政工作，也拥有一些准司法权力，包括讼费征税、进行调解、起诉藐视法官的行为和管理保释。所以此语境下 prothonotary 应该翻译为"原审法官"。在美国③，chief clerk, chief administrative officer 即为该词在美国法律系统中的具体含义。根据词典释义可知：chief 指 the principal or most important part or position。而 clerk 指 a court officer responsible for filing paper, issuing process, and keeping records of court proceedings as generally specified by rule or statute. 这容易联想到中国法庭上的书记员一职。在中国，各级人民法院的书记员由本院院长任免，主要担任审判庭的记录工作、并办理有关审判的辅助性事项，如开庭的准备工作，保

---

① https://www.thefreedictionary.com/Pronotary

② 根据维基百科的解释：the chief clerks of the supreme courts of the Australian states of New South Wales and Victoria are titled "prothonotary". The prothonotary of the Victorian Supreme Court has responsibility for all administrative tasks of the trial division registry. Under the Supreme Court Act 1986 (Vic), and the accompanying rules, the prothonotary also has some quasi-judicial powers including taxation of costs, conducting mediations, prosecuting contempt and administering bail. Much of the work of the prothonotary is delegated to specifically appointed deputy prothonotaries who, under the Supreme Court Act (s108), have the same powers and authority as the prothonotary. 参见 https://en.wikipedia.org/wiki/Prothonotary。

③ 根据维基百科的解释：While the term was once commonly used in the United States, only the courts of Pennsylvania and Delaware still term their chief clerks "prothonotaries." The Unified Judicial System of Pennsylvania titles several of its court administrators prothonotaries. The Supreme Court of Pennsylvania maintains two deputy prothonotaries, one in Philadelphia and the other in Pittsburgh, supplementing the role of the prothonotary in Harrisburg. The Superior Court of Pennsylvania's chief administrative officer is also titled a prothonotary and also maintains offices in Harrisburg, Philadelphia, and Pittsburgh. The Pennsylvania Courts of Common Pleas also title their chief clerks prothonotaries, except for the District of Delaware County, which has a clerk of courts instead of a prothonotary under the terms of its special Home Rule Charter. The Commonwealth Court of Pennsylvania and the minor court (the magisterial district courts, the Philadelphia Municipal Court, and the Pittsburgh Municipal Courts) do not have prothonotaries; their administrators are titled a "Chief Clerk" and "administrators," respectively. 参见 https://en.wikipedia.org/wiki/Prothonotary。

管证据、整理卷宗、处理文书工作、司法统计工作、接待来访、处理来信工作、协助审判人员进行调查以及对政策、法规的宣传工作等。故此语境中可译为"首席书记员"。

provided that

根据《布莱克法律词典》,provided 有三层含义:

1. On the condition or understanding (that) (we will sign the contract provided that you agree to the following conditions). 该含义下指以 provided that 句式后的内容为条件,即"以……为条件"或"只要"。

2. Except (that) (all permittees must be at least 18 years of age, provided that those with a bona fide hardship must be at least 15 years of age). 该含义下指以 provided that 句式后的内容为例外,即"……除外"。

3. And (a railway car must be operated by a full crew if it extends for more than 15 continuous miles, provided that a full crew must consist of at least six railway workers). 该含义下指"以及"。

通过上述释义可知,在英文法律文本中,provided that 常引导状语充当一项限制性条款。翻译该句式时,应采用汉语法律文本中限制性条款的固定表达方式对其进行灵活处理,不必照搬上述译文,比如:

例 1:Provided that the acceptance of rent or mesne profits by the Landlord after the expiration of the term of the tenancy hereby created shall not be deemed to operate as a waiver or breach of any of the terms hereof nor as a new periodic tenancy by way of holding over or otherwise. A new Tenancy shall only be created by a fresh tenancy agreement in writing signed by the Landlord and the Tenant. 如在本合约规定的租期届满后业主接受租金或中间收益,不应被认为是起了放弃或违背本合约的任何条件的作用,也不应认为是起了作为继续租用或者其他的新租期的作用。新租约只能是业主和租户签署的新书面租赁合同。例 2:At the end of the lease term, the parties may renew the lease, provided that the renewed term may not exceed twenty years commencing on the date of renewal. 租赁期间届满,当事人可以续订租赁合同,但约定的租赁期限自续订之日起不得超过二十年。

上句中做"但,只要"尚无不可,试想倘若去之不译,亦无不通。此句中位置不变参入句末,其实过于西化,不符汉语习惯,亦当远乎于法律。

reasonable belief

根据字面意思,易将 reasonable belief 译为"合理的信仰"。在法律语境下,这样直译往往有失偏颇。

康奈尔法学院 LII 在线数据库平台给出对该术语的解释为:When there exists a reasonable basis to believe that a crime is being or has already been committed[①],即有合理依据相信犯罪正在或已经发生。USLegal 网站给出的解释[②]更为详细:Reasonable Belief exists, when there is a reasonable basis to believe that a crime is being or has already been committed. In criminal law, similar to the probable cause standard, it is a subjective standard used to validate a warrantless search and seizure or arrest. And that considers whether an officer acted on personal knowledge of facts and circumstances which are reasonably trustworthy. That would justify a person of average caution to believe that a crime has been or is being committed. 即如果有合理的依据相信犯罪正在或已经发生,则存在 reasonable belief。在刑法中,这是一种主观标准。未取得逮捕证而执行逮捕时,必须根据合理可靠的情报所提供的事实和情况,据此使通常谨慎的人相信犯罪已经发生或正在发生。

综上可知,reasonable belief 是未取得逮捕证而执行逮捕的必要条件,即必须有合理依据相信犯罪已经发生或正在发生。基于此含义,可将其翻译为"合理推测"。

reasonable person

根据《布莱克法律词典》,reasonable person 的定义是:A hypothetical person used as a legal standard, esp. to determine whether someone acted with negligence; specif., a person who exercises the degree of attention,

---

① https://www.law.cornell.edu/wex/reasonable_belief
② https://definitions.uslegal.com/r/reasonable-belief/

knowledge, intelligence, and judgment that society requires of its members for the protection of their own and of others' interests. The reasonable person acts sensibly, does things without serious delay, and takes proper but not excessive precautions. 即法律所拟制的、具有正常精神状态、普通知识与经验及审慎处事能力的想象中的人。有人据此将其译为"通情达理的人"并不妥当。

reasonable person,并非实有其人,法律只是把它作为抽象的、客观的标准,其具有法律所期望的一般人所应有的谨慎和理性。该词常用于侵权行为法和刑法中。"通情达理的人"这一译法实际上将其含义进行了进一步深化,而且"通情达理"实际上是一种道德要求。翻译为"普通正常人"更合适一些。当判断被告(人)行为是否谨慎时,我们要看一个"普通正常人"处在被告(人)所处的情况下会怎样行为,而不是"通情达理的人"该如何行为。

rebate 与 refund

rebate 一词常被译为"回扣",比如在"中国法律法规汉英平行语料库"(以下简称"平行语料库")中 rebate(s)有 7 次被译为"回扣";香港律政司"双语法例资料系统"中 rebate 被译为"回扣"的次数更是多达 17 次①。

rebate 一词到底应如何翻译? 首先还是应了解其源语解释。rebate 在《布莱克法律词典》中的定义是:A return of part of a payment, serving as a discount or reduction.《朗文法律词典》中的解释是:refund; credit; discount。在 Dictionary.com 网站中的定义为:A return of part of the original payment for some service or merchandise; partial refund.

中文语境中的"回扣"是指卖方从买方支付的商品款项中按一定比例返还给买方的价款。按照是否采取账外暗中的方式,回扣可以简单分为两种,即"账内明示"的回扣、账外暗中的回扣。我国国家市场监督管理总局规章《关于禁止商业贿赂行为的暂行规定》第五条第 2 款规定:本规定所称回扣,是指经营者销售商品时在账外暗中以现金、实物或者其他方式退给对方单位或者个人的一定比例的商品价款。据此可以总结出回扣具有以下特征:账外暗中、返还一定比例的价款、收受人为对方单位或个人。

---

① 戴拥军,魏向清."回扣"的法理辨析及其英译探究[J].中国科技术语,2014(05):40—44.

由此，我们可以得知，在多数法律文本中"回扣"一词具有贬义色彩，但是 rebate 一词，本身为中性词，因此贸然将其与多数法律文本中的"账外回扣"相挂钩是不合理的。因此可将 rebate 译为中性意义上的"（作为减免或折扣的）部分退款"，从而保证法律语言的准确严谨。

在上文中提到，《朗文法律词典》中使用了 refund 来解释 rebate。试问 refund 是什么意思？同样地，首先找到 refund 的源语解释，它在《布莱克法律词典》中的解释是：n. 1. The return of money to a person who overpaid, such as a taxpayer who overestimated tax liability or whose employer withheld too much tax from earnings. 2. The money returned to a person who overpaid. 3. The act of refinancing, esp. by replacing outstanding securities with a new issue of securities. —refund, vb. of part of a payment, serving as a discount or reduction. 即作名词时意为：1.将钱返还给多付的人，例如政府退还纳税人多缴纳的款项或其雇主退回从收入中扣缴过多的税款。2.把钱退还给多付的人。3.再融资的行为，尤指用新发行的证券替换未偿付的证券。作动词时意为：退款；指付款的一部分，用作折扣。

对比两词的源语解释，可以很清楚地看到，rebate 是在支付应付金额之后，返还给客户的一种优惠以达到刺激消费等目的；而 refund 则是在客户上缴金额中，对超过应缴部分的返还。在我国法律的英译本中，refund 多用于"退税"的表述中[1]。综上，refund 翻译为"退还多付款项"更合适。

redirect examination

《布莱克法律词典》对该术语的定义是：A second direct examination, after cross-examination, the scope ordinarily being limited to matters covered during cross-examination. 经常将其简写为 redirect，在英国也称作 reexamination。通过该释义可以了解到 redirect examination 即为 a second direct examination。康奈尔法学院 LII 在线数据库平台给出的解释[2]为：A second direct examination

---

[1] 比如，《中华人民共和国外商投资企业和外国企业所得税法》第十条：再投资不满五年撤出的，应当缴回已退的税款。其译文是：In case the reinvestment has been withdrawn before the expiration of five full years, the amount of refunded tax shall be paid back.

[2] https://www.law.cornell.edu/wex/redirect_examination

of a witness which may be performed during a trial after cross-examination is complete,由此可知是对证人的 second direct examination。

通过查阅资料可知:在美国,询问证人的顺序通常为 direct examination,然后进行 cross-examination,在这之后进行 redirect examination①。根据 USLegal 网站②和维基百科③给出的更详细的释义可以得知:redirect examination 是对已经宣誓作证的证人进行的询问。在此阶段,证人将会对在 cross-examination 中对方所提出的问题、证据、证词进行解释。所解释的范围仅限于上一轮 cross-examination 中所提及事项。redirect examination 的发起者为最初发起询问的律师,本阶段律师可以提出额外的问题,意在塑造证人的可信度,或以其他方式弥补在之前的阶段中暴露的证人的缺陷。

通过以上解释,可以较好地理解 redirect examination 的含义了,并且从中可以提取出该术语含义的核心为"做有利于自己的'explain'"。同时可以体会到,在 redirect examination 阶段,律师主动发起询问,主动让当事人解释不利于自己的问题、证据或证词。所以在这一过程中,双方律师通过询问证人的行为是利己行为。因此,"主动"一词在译文中需体现出来。

我国法律系统中无英美法系的直接询问及交叉询问,我国只是在刑事诉讼法确立了庭审中交叉询问证人的基本制度。根据我国刑事诉讼法确立了庭审中

---

① When a witness is presented for testimony in the U. S. judicial system, the order is "direct" testimony, then the opposing attorney does "cross" and then "redirect" from the attorney first offering the witness。参见 https://educalingo.com/en/dic-en/re-examine。

② Redirect examination is the trial process that follows cross-examination and is exercised by the party who called first and questioned the witness. Through a reexamination, the party who offered the witness will get a chance to explain or otherwise qualify any damaging or accusing testimony brought out by the opponent during cross-examination. Redirect examination may be limited to only those areas brought out on cross-examination. 参见 https://definitions.uslegal.com/r/redirect-examination/。

③ Redirect examination, in the United States, is the questioning of a witness who has already provided testimony under oath in response to direct examination as well as cross examination by the opponent. On redirect, the attorney offering the witness will ask additional questions that attempt to rehabilitate the witness's credibility, or otherwise mitigate deficiencies identified and explored by the opponent on cross. For example, the opponent might elicit on cross-examination an admission that the witness did not directly perceive every single part of the events at issue; the proponent will attempt on redirect to establish that the witness perceived enough of those events that the finder of fact can draw reasonable inferences as to the gaps where the witness's perception was obstructed. 参见 https://en.wikipedia.org/wiki/Redirect_examination。

交叉询问证人的基本制度,明确了交叉询问的主体包括公诉人、当事人和辩护人、诉讼代理人,并由法官来决定庭审中询问主体是否可以发问。

在译入语文化中找不到对等概念时,可以进行谨慎且精确的创译,《英美法律术语辞典(英汉双解)》将该术语翻译为"再主询问(最初询问证人的当事人或律师对证人进行再询问)"非常恰当。

remoteness of damage

该术语有几种常见译法,其中出现频率最高的两种翻译分别为"损害之疏远"与"间接伤害"。第一种译法属于直译,读者无法知晓汉语译文的真正含义;而第二种译法则完全是错译。

《牛津高阶英汉双解词典》①对 remoteness of damage 的解释为:The extent to which a defendant is liable for the consequences of his wrongful act or omission. 意思是被告因其不当行为或疏忽造成不利后果因而承当责任的程度。而 Yahoo②上对该术语的解释为 After determining that the defendant did cause damage to the plaintiff, it must be established how far the legal responsibility for that damage ought to be attributed back to the defendant"以及"In between the admitted wrongdoer and innocent victim, it can be argued that the wrongdoer should have to bear the loss. 此处是说被告就其对原告造成损失的赔偿的责任范围。

综上可以看出,该短语是说明被告人应当承担赔偿受害人损害的责任的,因此可以把该术语翻译成"损害赔偿"。

right of fixation

目前,该术语常被译为"录制权"。就 fixation 而言,这个词在各大词典中的解释均与"录制"无关,如《朗文当代高级英语辞典》《牛津高阶英汉双解词典》中都解释为"痴迷""不正常的依恋"及"固着"。

---

① Hornby A S. *Oxford Advanced Learner's English-Chinese Dictionary*,7th ed.[Z]. Beijing: The Commercial Press,2009.

② Remoteness of damage. [2017-07-04]. https://quizlet.com/3133956/remoteness-of-damage-flash-cards/

首先从一段描述中来看这条术语的由来：In 1994, the United States established laws prohibiting the making and distribution of "bootleg" recordings of live music concerts. While strongly criticized by many commentators, these provisions establishing a "right of fixation" for musicians have been upheld against repeated constitutional challenges①。由此可知，结合特定的历史背景，该术语表达的是禁止私自制作和经销现场音乐会音像录制的内容。

维基百科有加拿大相关法律对 fixation 的解释：Under the Canadian Copyright Act (R. S., 1985, c. C-42), there is no definition for fixation nor is it required that every work be "fixed". Under s. 3(1)(1.1), however, any literary, dramatic, musical or artistic work, communicated by telecommunication, "is fixed even if it is fixed simultaneously with its communication."… Today, a live broadcast that is being simultaneously recorded, is protected by copyright. The definition of fixation within Canadian Admiral Corp. v Rediffusion Inc., remains the valid②。从这段话中可以看出，fixation 在版权法领域并没有相关的定义，但是在实际运用当中是指作品经由电信传播过即为 fixed 的状态。Under Part II, Performers' Rights, fixation is also addressed. The performer retains certain rights to reproductions of his/her performance depending on whether the performance was fixed or not. If the performance is not fixed, the performer has the sole right to communicate it to the public by telecommunication, to perform it in public (where it is communicated to the public by telecommunication otherwise than by communication signal), and to fix it in any material form. 这段话强调表演内容若不是 fixed 的状态，则表演者有排他性的权利经由电信手段传播录制的表演内容，或通过直接表演向公众传播。

综上可知，该术语强调的是有无权利传播经由电信播送过的音像节目等内

---

① Hughes J. Understanding (and fixing) the right of fixation in copyright law [J]. *Journal of the Copyright Society of the USA*, 2014, 62 (3): 385-436.

② https://en.wikipedia.org/wiki/Fixation_in_Canadian_copyright_law.

容,而原译"录制权"则表示"录音录像的权利",事实上录音录像如果只供个人学习、研究或者欣赏则属于合理使用范畴,是被法律所允许的,但在录音录像后未经许可传播出去才会涉及是否违法违规①,所以该术语翻译成"录制传播权"要比"录制权"更加准确。

royalty bonus

该术语普遍被译为"超额使用费",其翻译依据是 royalty 在法律英语中的意思是"知识产权使用费",指因使用了他人的知识产权、版权等而缴纳的费用,如 royalty bonus 超额使用费②。

由《布莱克法律词典》对 bonus 的定义③可知,bonus 是指"额外的报酬、补偿费、对价"。同样,此处的解释依然没有体现"超额使用"的情形。

《美国传统词典》(The American Heritage Dictionary)④中关于 royalty bonus 的解释为:A sum of money that is paid by a corporation in excess of interest or royalties charged for the granting of a privilege or a loan to that corporation. 由公司付给因授予特权或贷款给本公司的利息或版税以外的一笔钱。该解释最贴近这个术语的本来意思,但是此释义并未强调多付出的钱是因为"超额使用",却将其解释为"红利"。

另外,Sun 微系统公司的乔尔·珀斯德曼(Joel Postman)指出:Companies that engage in businesses with the potential to generate patents-businesses with engineers, programmers, developers, and designers for example-almost always require employees to agree to assign to the company any patents created on the

---

① 中华人民共和国著作权法. [2017-07-13]. http://www.law-lib.com/law/law_view.asp?id=310803.
② 刘碧波. 实务法律英语词汇精解[M]. 北京,中国法制出版社,2013.
③ A gratuity. A premium paid to a grantor or vendor. An extra consideration given for what is received. Any premium or advantage; an occasional extra dividend. A premium paid by a company for a charter or other franchises. 'A definite sum to be paid at one time, for a loan of money for a specified period, distinct from and independently of the interest.' Association v. Wilcox, 24 Conn. 147. A bonus is not a gift or gratuity, but a sum paid for services, or upon some other consideration, but in addition to or in excess of that which would ordinarily be given. Kenicott v. Wayne County, 10 Wall. 452, 21 L. Ed. 319.
④ William M. The American Heritage Dictionary, 4th ed. [M]. Boston: Houghton Mifflin Co, 2000.

job. Many companies will pay an employee who is awarded patent in connection with their work a small bonus. While this can be seen as employee recognition, or reward for a job well done, it is often done for an entirely different reason. Although there is some debate on this point, many attorneys believe that the bonus constitutes "consideration" (a term in contract law) and strengthens the company's claim to ownership of the patent.① 通过这段话可以得知,公司通过给付报酬来获得雇员在工作中有可能取得的专利技术。

《元照英美法词典》中对这个术语的解释为:"指油、气租约中约定以比通常情况更高的使用费作为对价。"很明显,该辞典的解释不全面。就 royalty 这个词而言,英文意思是指知识产权方面,而中文翻译则是油气租约方面,中英文的解释并不对应。

综上,royalty bonus 这个术语翻译成"超额使用费"并不准确,译成"知识产权使用津贴"或者"专利使用补贴"更加准确。

rubber check

根据《布莱克法律词典》rubber check 与 bad check 同义,具体指:A check that is not honored because the account either contains insufficient funds or does not exist,指一种因账户资金不足或不存在而无法兑现的支票。因此它常被译为"空头支票"。

通过查阅资料②得知,在美国,无意开出无法兑付(原因为资金不足 insufficient funds 或停止支付通知单 a stop-payment order)的空头支票不属于犯罪,但是也会产生罚款,例如通常由银行收取的透支费(overdraft fees)。但银行也出台了一些透支保护政策,使得不小心开出空头支票的人无须就此支付费用。在有些情况下,空头支票的接收方(receipt)会对开票方(sender)索取罚金或要求其支付利息,这种情况发生的前提一般是双方之间存在某种先前的合同关系(pre-existing contractual relationship)。虽然一般来说无意中开出的空头

---

① Do any companies give a bonus for patents or trademarks filed? If so, how much? [2017-07-04]. https://www.quora.com/Do-any-companies-give-a-bonus-for-patents-or-trademarks-filed-If-so-how-much

② 参见 https://www.qidulp.com/question/676/answer/705。

支票不受法律惩罚,但故意或多次开空头发票的行为(willful or repeat offenders)则会受到法律的惩罚。银行和其他金融服务提供商可以通过一些数据库监控某个人或公司开空头支票的频率,频率越高,这种支票被拒绝的可能性就越大,同时,也有可能会被视为诈骗 fraud,受到法律的惩罚,这种开空头支票的行为也叫 check kiting①。

satisfaction

根据《布莱克法律词典》,satisfaction 共有 5 种含义:

1. The giving of something with the intention, express or implied, that it is to extinguish some existing legal or moral obligation. Satisfaction differs from performance because it is always something given as a substitute for or equivalent of something else, while performance is the identical thing promised to be done. 即通过明示或暗示的手段有意图的给予某物,用于消除某些现存的法律义务或道德义务。satisfaction 不同于履约(performance),因为 satisfaction 行为总是通过给予等值的替代物来实现,而履约行为总是需要给予与允诺完全一致的目标物来实现。也称作 satisfaction of debt。

2. The fulfillment of an obligation; esp., the payment in full of a debt,即义务的履行,特指债务的履行。

以上两个语境中的 satisfaction 具有相似含义,均指义务的履行,如果用于债务中则为"(债务)的清偿"。由此可引出英美合同法中的一个原则,即 accord and satisfaction 和解与清偿。和解与清偿原则用于解除债务,和解(协议)用于履行义务,清偿为双方当事人同意的对价。一份有效的和解协议应不解除先前的合同,反之根据和解协议的条款终止强制执行合同的权利,(债务的)清偿,或是合同的履约将解除原合同与和解后的合同。若债务人违反和解协议,则债权人即可举证和解(协议)的存在以防止出现任何针对他的行为。中国法律体系

---

① Check kiting is a form of fraud involving the sloshing of theoretical funds between two bank checking accounts. A check written to the criminal from one bank is deposited, and more importantly credited, to an account at a second bank. Because that second bank now shows a positive balance, the criminal can withdraw enough money to deposit back into the first bank before the check bounces for lack of funds. 指向银行开出支票,但其银行账户的存款不足以支付该款项,出票人的意图是希望在支票被向银行提示之前,会有必需的资金存入其账户。

中,《民法典》合同编和侵权责任编等有对债务清偿的相关规定。但是中国法律中并没有和解与清偿原则,关于合同中的债权仅有中止履行,提前履行,部分履行等,其翻译使用 performance。故 satisfaction 的翻译应注意仅处于英美法的语境下且用于 accord and satisfaction 原则中。其他语境下的(债务)履行应使用 performance。

3. satisfaction plece. 也称作 certificate of discharge。具体指:A written statement that one party (esp. a debtor) has discharged its obligation to another party, who accepts the discharge. 即一方(尤其是债务人)已向另一方解除义务的书面声明,另一方接受解除义务。该语境下可翻译为"义务解除证明"或"债务解除证明"。

4. wills & estates. The payment by a testator, during the testator's lifetime, of a legacy provided for in a will. 和 advancement① 同义。即遗嘱人在其有生之年支付遗嘱中规定的遗产。结合 advancement 的释义以及《元照英美法词典》的解释可知,这是衡平法中的一项原则,适用于遗嘱人或赠与人的行为或语言或语词暗示了抵销的情形。这样,如果父母用信托馈赠(portion)的方式将一份遗产馈赠给子女,其后(比如,该子女结婚时),又以信托馈赠的方式赠与他(她)一笔钱,则后面一笔钱被视为完全或部分地抵销了前者。也就是说,当父母去世时,该子女不能再要求继承遗产。因此该语境下 satisfaction 和 advancement 应翻译为"预付遗产"。

5. wills & estates. A testamentary gift intended to satisfy a debt owed by the testator to a creditor. 指一种遗嘱赠与,旨在清偿立遗嘱人欠债权人的债务。结合《元照英美法词典》的解释可知,如果一个遗嘱人将一份遗产给予其债务人,在这份遗产的数额等于或多于其债务而且没有其他意思表示时,该遗产被认为对债务的抵销。因此该语境下 satisfaction 应翻译为"用遗产偿债"。

值得注意的是,遗产、信托馈赠和债的抵销原则(即含义 4 和 5)意味着:一

---

① 根据《布莱克法律词典》(Black's Law Dictionary, 9th Edition, p. 89), advancement 的含义是:A payment or gift to an heir (esp. a child) during one's lifetime as an advance share of one's estate, with the intention of reducing or extinguishing or diminishing the heir's claim to the estate under intestacy laws. In some jurisdictions, the donor's intent is irrelevant if all the statutory elements of an advancement are present. A few jurisdiction define the relationship between the donor and donee to include inter vivos transfers between ancestors and descendants.

项有明示或暗示意思表示的馈赠,将被视为全部或部分地消除了某项先前的债权或要求。当然,赠与人也可以明确宣布其后来的赠与是对先前要求的抵销,以防止受赠人对两者都提出权利主张。

Sea Law 与 Law of the Sea

Sea Law 到底应译为"海商法"还是"海洋法"或是"海事法"? 它与 Law of the Sea 有何区别?

根据《布莱克法律词典》,sea law 与 maritime law,admiralty,admiralty law 同义,具体释义为:The body of law governing marine commerce and navigation, the carriage at sea of persons and property, and marine affairs in general; the rules governing contract, tort, and worker's-compensation claims or relating to commerce on or over water. 指调整海洋商业和航行、海上人员和财产运输以及一般海洋事务的法律体系;管理合同、侵权和工人赔偿索赔的规则,或与水上或水上商业有关的规则。

Merriam-Webster 网站对 Law of the Sea 的定义是:a body of international law promulgated by United Nations convention and covering a range of ocean matters including territorial zones, access to and transit on the sea, environmental preservation, and the resolution of international disputes[①]。指由联合国公约颁布的一套国际法规则,涵盖一系列海洋事务,包括领土区、海上进出和过境、环境保护和国际争端的解决。《联合国海洋法公约》的英文名称即为 United Nations Convention on the Law of the Sea,所以 Law of the Sea 应翻译为"海洋法"。

在我国,"海事法"是"海商法"的同名词,并认为在当代,"海事法"称谓比"海商法"更确切。因为"海商法"形成于航运发展早期商航一体,又称"船货一家"的年代,即船舶所有人在装货港购买商品,作为货物装于其自有的船舶上,运输至卸货港销售,以赚取商品买卖的商业利润,船舶只是其实现商品买卖的运输工具,即船舶所有人从事的是商业活动。19 世纪初,产业革命推动了国际贸易和航运的发展,"商航一体"逐渐解体,出现了"商航分家",又称"船货分家",即船舶

---

① https://www.merriam-webster.com/legal/law%20of%20the%20sea

所有人不再从事商品流通领域的货物买卖,其船舶运输他人的货物,赚取的是运费而非商品买卖的商业利润。至此,船舶所有人实现的只是商品在流通领域中的位移,这种活动被认为是生产活动,或者说是生产过程在流通过程内的继续。从而"海商法"一词的"商"字已不能适应船舶所有人从事的活动的性质从商业活动到生产活动的转化。因此,现代"海商法"已不再调整商业性活动,"海商法"的名称也应正名为"海事法"。综合上述释义,应将 Sea Law 翻译为"海事法"。

sea power

sea power 常见的译文是"海权",而中文语境中的"海权"也常被回译为 sea power。但这并不准确,甚至由于这种跨文化译介传播中原文原义与译入语概念语义的错位,导致了中西跨文化间的误读误识及其引发的诸如西方的"中国威胁论"炒作[①]。

首先我们应了解 sea power 的源语释义。《大英百科全书(在线版)》(*Encyclopedia Britannica Online*)对 sea power 的定义[②]是:sea power, means by which a nation extends its military power onto the seas. Measured in terms of a nation's capacity to use the seas in defiance of rivals and competitors, it consists of such diverse elements as combat craft and weapons, auxiliary craft, commercial shipping, bases, and trained personnel. 由此可知 sea power 指一个国家将其军事力量扩展到海洋的手段和能力。通常以一个国家在对抗对手和竞争者的情况下使用海洋的能力来衡量,它由作战艇和武器、辅助艇、商船、基地和训练有素的人员等多种要素组成。sea power 的主要目的[③]有:保护己方或友军免受敌人攻击,摧毁或阻碍敌人的商业和军事船只;在战时拥有海上指挥权,有

---

① 曲畅,任东升.跨文化互译中的概念误读——以海权为例[J].读书,2021(12):82-88.

② 参见 https://www.britannica.com/topic/sea-power。

③ The capacity for sea power depends upon such factors as population, character of government, soundness of economy, number and quality of harbours and extent of coastline, and the number and location of a nation's colonies and bases with respect to desired sea traffic. The main purpose of sea power has always been to protect friendly shipping from enemy attack and to destroy or hinder the enemy's shipping—both commercial and military. When one belligerent or the other has virtual control of surface shipping in portions of the seas, he is said to have command of the seas, with the ability both to defend his own sea communications and to deny communications to the enemy. 参见 https://www.britannica.com/topic/sea-power。

能力保护自己的海上通信；阻止战争所需商品的进口，对敌人施加军事和经济压力；通过阻止中立国与敌人进行贸易从而封锁贸易等。

由此可见，sea power 实际指向的是"一国的海上军事力量"。此外，根据《牛津高阶英汉双解词典》(第8版)可知，power 具有 the ability to control people or things 以及 political control of a country or an area 之意。因此 sea power 也会被解读为"海洋军事霸权"。

而中文语境中的"海权"又指什么呢？现代意义上的"海权"概念"简单说来就是国家的海洋综合国力，是衡量国家海洋实力和能力的重要指标，其内容涉及政治、经济、军事、文化、科技等社会发展各领域"(刘中民,2013:76)①。"海权"一词确实是从 sea power 演变而来，但经过本土化后，"在中国已成为体现中国特色核心价值观的综合性概念"②，体现中国和平发展的理念，与"中国构建和谐世界的国家战略和对外战略高度一致"(张炜,2012:34)③。

由此可见，sea power 与"海权"的概念内涵并不对等，在外译"海权"时应切忌将其翻译为 sea power。除了上文对 power 本身的词义分析外，power 在西方外交学词典里"是指国际体系中拥有支配他国权力的国家，其标准是强权政治、军事实力和战争能力"(杨明星,2015:101)④。将"海权"翻译为 sea power 无疑是跳入了西方的话语陷阱，抹黑了中国法治外交的形象。

security agreement

security agreement 通常译为"担保协议"，内容囊括动产担保与不动产担保。但在美国的法律文本中，security agreement 的含义范围与中国法律中的"担保合同"并不对等。

《布莱克法律词典》对 security agreement 的定义为：An agreement that creates or provides for an interest in specified real or personal property to guarantee the performance of an obligation. It must provide for a security

---

① 刘中民.中国海洋强国建设的海权战略选择——海权与大国兴衰的经验教训及其启示[J].太平洋学报,2013(08):74-83.
② 高玉霞,任东升.概念话语引进与再输出良性互动探究：以 sea power 为例[J].外语研究,2020(05):75-83.
③ 张炜.中国特色海权理论发展历程综述[J].人民论坛·学术前沿,2012(06):28-35.
④ 杨明星."新型大国关系"的创新译法及其现实意义[J].中国翻译,2015(01):101-105.

interest, describe the collateral, and be signed by the debtor. The agreement may include other important covenants and warranties. 即通过该协议,在特定的动产或不动产上创设或提供某种权益,以担保债务的履行。该协议中必须提供担保权益,指明抵押品,并由债务人签字。该协议可能还包括其他重要的约定和保证。很明显"security"的范围既包括动产亦包括不动产。

美国《统一商法典》中对于 security agreement 适用范围定义在第九编 109 条:This article applies to: a transaction, regardless of its form, that creates a security interest in personal property or fixtures by contract(以合同在动产或不动产的附着物上创设担保物权的交易,而不考虑该交易形式如何)"。与之类似,由 security agreement 而产生的 security interest(担保权益)在《统一商法典》中的范围也仅限于动产、动产契据等("Security interest" means an interest in personal property or fixtures which secures payment or performance of an obligation. "Security interest" includes any interest of a consignor and a buyer of accounts, chattel paper, a payment intangible, or a promissory note in a transaction that is subject to Article 9)。在《牛津法律大辞典》中,security interest 项下另注有 "Security interest under the Uniform Commercial Code, security interests are limited to personal property and fixtures. See1-201",这也可以佐证 security agreement 在 UCC 中的范围。即在美国《统一商法典》中,security agreement 适用于第一大类是货物,它是有形动产的总称,包括四个种类:即消费品、农产品、库存品和设备;第二大类是准有形财产,包括三种,即票据、所有权凭证、动产证书;第三大类是无形财产,由两类财产构成,即账款和一般性无形财产[1]。

我国《民法典》第三百八十八条第 1 款规定:设立担保物权,应当依照本法和其他法律的规定订立担保合同。担保合同包括抵押合同、质押合同和其他具有担保功能的合同。根据此款规定只要有担保功能的合同,均属于担保合同。该条体现了我国在推动担保制度现代化上的尝试,原因之一是其扩大了担保合同的范围,并承认了各类担保合同的效力[2]。之所以有这样的变化,是为了进

---

[1] 徐洁,简评美国《统一商法典》第九篇担保制度[J],当代法学,2007(04):99-103
[2] 参见王利明.担保制度的现代化:对《民法典》第 388 条第 1 款的评析[J].法学家,2021(01):30-39+192.

一步完善担保物权制度,为优化营商环境提供法治保障①。

基于以上分析发现,美国《统一商法典》中所提及的 security agreement 的范围远小于"担保协议"这一词在汉语中的范围。由此可见 security agreement 译为"担保协议"并不能达到完全对等。因此在翻译与美国《统一商法典》相关的文件时,应将其译为"动产担保协议",以消弭在美国《统一商法典》背景下 security agreement 与"担保协议"的词义差距。而在其他情况下,即不涉及美国《统一商法典》时,可以直接译为"担保协议"。

sleeping partner 与 silent partner

sleeping partner 容易与 silent partner 混淆,我们首先有必要通过了解其源语释义厘清两者区别。

根据《布莱克法律词典》,sleeping partner 与 secret partner 同义,指:A partner whose connection with the firm is concealed from the public. 即对公众隐瞒与公司关系的合伙人。

《布莱克法律词典》对 silent partner 的定义是:A partner who shares in the profits but who has no active voice in management of the firm and whose existence is often not publicly disclosed. 与 dormant partner 同义,即分享利润但在公司管理中没有积极发言权的合伙人,其存在通常未公开披露。根据词典中引述的判例规则②也可知:该合伙人通常在企业中投资以换取利润份额,其保留参与日常管理决策的权利,在某种程度上可能实际参与也可能根本不参与日常管理决策,甚至可能在很长一段时间内并不了解公司的实际运作。

---

① 参见王晨:"关于《中华人民共和国民法典(草案)》的说明——2020 年 5 月 22 日在第十三届全国人民代表大会第三次会议上",《中华人民共和国全国人民代表大会常务委员会公报》2020 年特刊,第 188 页。

② "It is worth emphasizing that control does not necessarily mean active involvement. One of the most interesting figures in partnership law, in fact, is the 'silent' partner——typically a person who has invested in a business in return for a profit share, and who reserves the right to, and to some extent may in fact, participate in routine management decisions, may participate in no decisions at all, and may even be unaware of what is happening in the business for long periods of time. The fact of the person's financial interest in the partnership may be a secret from everyone except the other partners (indeed, such secrecy may be vital). Such a person is nonetheless a partner like any other for purposes, among other things, of personal liability for the debts of the partnership. The law simply does not distinguish between active and passive partners.", William A. Klein & John C. CoffeeJr., Business Organization and Finance 64 (2002).

通过以上释义可看出 sleeping partner 重在强调公众不知该合伙人的存在；而 silent partner 重在强调其在公司日常管理中的不积极作为。通过查阅资料可以进一步厘清两者区别：Silent partners in a business are known to the world and their investments aren't discreet. Secret partners (sleeping partner) on the other hand participate discreetly in the business, may assume more operational responsibilities and financial liabilities than a Silent Partner but stay behind the scenes. Their participation is anonymous, not limited[①]. 由此可知 silent partner 是公众知晓的存在，且其投资并不谨慎。而 sleeping partner 谨慎地参与业务，可能比 silent partner 承担更多的运营责任和财务责任，但其参与是匿名的，通常躲在幕后。

综上，结合 sleeping partner (secret partner)"匿名"的特点，可将其翻译为"秘密合伙人"；结合 silent partner (dormant partner)"被知晓""不积极作为"但"参与利润分配"的特点，可将其翻译为"隐形合伙人"。

Solicitor General

《布莱克法律词典》给出的该术语的定义是：The second-highest ranking legal officer in a government (after the attorney general); esp., the chief courtroom lawyer for the executive branch. 由此可知 Solicitor General 是仅次于司法部长(Attorney General)的在政府中级别第二高的法律官员；尤其指行政部门的首席法庭律师。

结合维基百科[②]和《元照英美法词典》的详细解释可以发现，Solicitor General 在各国扮演的职能稍有不同，以下仅以美国和英国为例。

在美国，Solicitor General 是在司法部中地位仅低于首席检察官或司法部长(Attorney General)的法律官员，由总统经参议院提议并同意后任命。其主要职责是在涉及美国国家利益的案件中代表联邦政府出庭(尤其是在联邦最高法院)，决定联邦政府对哪些案件应提出上诉，监督最高法院办理涉及联邦政府的事项等。而在美国各州，一个州的 Solicitor General 通常是代表该州、该州的行

---

① 参见 https://thebusinessprofessor.com/en_US/business-governance/silent-partner-definition。
② https://en.wikipedia.org/wiki/Solicitor_general

政人员和官员以及该州的立法机构的最高上诉律师。在许多州，Solicitor General 也在美国最高法院审理的重大州外案件中塑造其所在州的法律地位①。

在英格兰，国王律师(King's Solicitor)的职位始于 1460 年，从 1515 年起使用现在的名称 Solicitor General。其源起与衡平法院有密切的联系。现在 Solicitor General 为地位仅次于总检察长(Attorney-General)的政府法律官员，除法律职责外，兼具政治职责，一般总是下议院的议员担任此职位。其任务主要是为内阁和各部部长提供法律咨询，将法律议案提交议会审议和通过。自 1895 年以后，Solicitor General 便不能再以私人名义执业。总检察长职位空缺时，通常但并不总是由其继任。在其离职后，经常会被任命为法官。在苏格兰，国王律师(King's Solicitor)首次出现于 17 世纪，自 18 世纪初期起该职位便一直延续下来。在 17 和 18 世纪时，通常有两名 Solicitor General 共同履行职责，但后来经常只有一名。其在政府中为较低级别成员，随政府的更替而离职。现在，他为总检察长(Lord Advocate)的副职和首席助理，履行总检察长的全部职责，尤其是在有关财税(Exchequer)的案件中代表政府出庭，但他不能依职权(jure officii)提出控诉，除非总检察长已去世或离任。按惯例，在法庭上他有权坐在围栏以内法官席的左侧。在总检察长职位空缺时经常由其继任。

综上所述，无论是在英国或是美国，抑或是其他适用英美法体系的国家，Solicitor General 都是在 Attorney General 之下的政府官员，只不过在各国的行政体系中承担不同的职能。

综合考虑其适用的语境，可将其翻译为：(英)副检察长；(美)副司法部长。

specific performance

该术语经常被根据其字面意思误译为"具体履行"或"特定履行"，但这并不是其真正含义。

《布莱克法律词典》对 specific performance 的定义是：The rendering, as

---

① In states in the United States, a state's Solicitor General is usually the top appellate advocate on behalf of the State, its executives and officials, and its legislature (sometimes referred to as State Solicitor, or Appellate Chief, depending upon the particular state). In many states, the Solicitor General also formulates a state's legal position in significant out-of-state cases before the Supreme Court of the United States. 参见 https://en.wikipedia.org/wiki/Solicitor_general。

nearly as practicable, of a promised performance through a judgment or decree; specif., a court-ordered remedy that requires precise fulfillment of a legal or contractual obligation when monetary damages are inappropriate or inadequate, as when the sale of real estate or a rare article is involved. Specific performance is an equitable remedy that lies within the court's discretion to award whenever the common-law remedy is insufficient, either because damages would be inadequate or because the damages could not possibly be established. 也称作 specific relief。由此可知这是衡平法上对违反合同的一种救济，指强制被告实际履行其合同义务，即令其完全按原合同中他所承担从事之事来履行清偿。

因此，应将该术语翻译为"强制履行"。根据《元照英美法词典》的解释可知：强制履行是一种对人诉讼，如果被告不在管辖区内，则强制履行令就不能发出。强制履行只适用于依普通法赔偿损失的方法对其损失不能充分补偿的合同，该合同应该是肯定的合同，对其赔偿损失尚非足够补偿；该合同应是一个待履行的合同，而不是已履行完的合同；而且该合同必须在各个实质性的方面具体确定，必须不是非法或不平等、不公平、不合理的合同。如果合同涉及连续的行为而需法院加以监督时，法院就不强制合同之履行；此外，对个人之承揽与服务、不能交互执行之合同、纯从属于一份不能执行之主合同的合同、给付金钱之合同，或者强制履行令将是无意义的，或者金钱赔偿之偿付将是合适的等情况，法院也都不会执行强制履行。在某种场合，原告可能在某些完全按约履行属于非物质的不能时，以强制履行获得赔偿。在法院能命令强制履行时，法院可以判令损失赔偿以替代强制履行，或在强制履行之外另加损失赔偿。

statement of affairs

根据《布莱克法律词典》，statement of affairs 的含义有两层：

1. 与 statement of financial affairs 同义，属于破产（bankruptcy）领域的概念，即：A document that an individual or corporate debtor must file to answer questions about the debtor's past and present financial status. 指个人或公司债务人必须提交的文件，以显示有关债务人过去和现在的财务状况。因此该含义下应将其翻译为"债权清册"，以反映破产债务人通过该文件反应有关的财务状况、破产情况、账目以及债务情况。

2. A balance sheet showing immediate liquidation values (rather than historical costs), usu. prepared when insolvency or bankruptcy is imminent. 这其中有一个重要概念 balance sheet,《布莱克法律词典》给出的定义是：A statement of an entity's current financial position, disclosing the value of the entity's assets, liabilities, and owners' equity. 即反映某实体当前财务状况的报表,披露其资产、负债和股东权益状况,通常称之为"资产负债表"。所以该层含义下 statement of affairs 指在破产程序中必须提交的、载明有关债务人即时清算价值（而非历史成本）的资产负债表,通常在即将发生破产或支付不能时要准备好该文件。

综上所述,此处的 statement of affairs 应翻译为"（破产时的）资产负债结算表"。

statement of income

根据《布莱克法律词典》,statement of income 与 income statement, profit-and-loss statement, earnings report 同义,其具体释义为：A statement of all the revenues, expenses, gains, and losses that a business incurred during a given period. 即反映企业在一定时期内产生的所有收入、费用、收益和损失。

维基百科给出了更详细的解释①：It indicates how the revenues (also known as the "top line") are transformed into the net income or net profit (the result after all revenues and expenses have been accounted for). The purpose of the income statement is to show managers and investors whether the company made money (profit) or lost money (loss) during the period being reported. 由此可知,statement of affairs 主要计算及显示公司的盈利状况,它显示收入如何转化为净收入或净利润（所有收入和费用都已入账后的结果）。该表的目的是向经理和投资者展示公司在报告期内是盈利还是亏损。

综上,可将该术语翻译为"损益表",从而突出其可直观反映公司是盈利还是亏损的特征。

---

① https://en.wikipedia.org/wiki/Income_statement

status offense

《布莱克法律词典》对该术语的定义是：

1. 与 status crime，personal-condition crime 同义。A crime of which a person is guilty by being in a certain condition or of a specific character. An example of a status crime is vagrancy. 即因处于某种状态或具有某种特征而被判有罪的罪行，比如因流浪行为而被判有罪。

2. A minor's violation of the juvenile code by doing some act that would not be considered illegal if an adult did it, but that indicates that the minor is beyond parental control. Examples include running away from home, truancy, and incorrigibility. 指一种轻微违反青少年行为准则的行为，该行为对于成年人而言不属于违法，但这表明未成年人的行为已经超出了父母的控制范围，比如离家出走、逃学、故意破坏等。

《美国联邦量刑指南》中(Federal Sentencing Guideline)U. S. S. G. §4A1. 2(c)(2). 规定，青少年身份犯罪对成年人来说并不构成犯罪：Sentences for the following prior offenses and offenses similar to them, by whatever name they are known, are never counted：…Juvenile status offenses and truancy… 比如，个人持有枪械武器，其行为本身对于成年人来说并不构成犯罪。在一些州身份犯罪一词特指青少年犯罪；怀俄明州法律中，身份犯罪特指由年龄在十八岁以下的犯罪①。与此同时，欧洲与英国对此种 status offense 行为称为 regulatory offense。在其他情形下，身份犯罪可适用于其他类别的身份，如禁止重罪者持有枪械武器，对于非重罪者而言，持枪是合法的。

综上可知，status offense 本身指的是特定身份的犯罪者实施的犯罪。其特点是仅对该特定身份者视为犯罪，而对于其他身份者不视为犯罪。但是在美国部分州的法律中，身份犯罪特指青少年犯的一些对于成年人来说并不构成犯罪的行为。因此，此处的"身份犯罪"不应直接翻译为"青少年犯罪"，只是由于中国法律语境下的青少年犯罪其罪行并没有与成年人犯的罪行有区分②。在中国的法律语境下，青少年杀人被称为青少年犯罪，但在美国的定义中青少年犯罪不能

---

① Juvenile justice amendments, Wyoming State Bill, 07LSO－0076. W2.
② 魏俐,刘忠文.中美两国青少年犯罪问题之比较研究[J].辽宁警察学院学报,2001(04):56－59.

被称作 status offense，应与成年人杀人一视同仁，均称为 homicide 或 manslaughter 等。而属于美国法律语境下的 status offense 的，如结交罪犯朋友等行为，在中文法律语境下并不视为"青少年犯罪"。由于《未成年保护法》等以及中国传统文化教育观念的存在，这些行为更多地被视为青少年的道德作风问题，并未上升到犯罪的高度[①]。

综上所述，Status offense 在没有相关语境的情况下应翻译为"（美国法）身份犯罪"；若有相关语境确指以青少年这种特殊身份而构成犯罪的应翻译为"青少年身份犯罪"，与中国法律语境中的青少年犯罪区分开。

statutory

《布莱克法律词典》对该术语的定义是：1. Of or relating to legislation (statutory interpretation). 属于立法或与立法相关的（法律解释）。2. Legislatively created (the law of patents is purely statutory). 通过立法创造的（知识产权法是纯粹的成文法）。3. Conformable to a statute (a statutory act). 符合法令的，符合法规的（合法法案）。

statutory 源于 statute，所以在翻译 statutory 构成的术语前，我们有必要先研究一下其原形 statute。根据《布莱克法律词典》，其定义为：A statute is a formal written enactment of a legislative authority that governs a state, city or country. Typically, statutes command or prohibit something, or declare policy. Statutes are rules made by legislative bodies; they are distinguished from case law or precedent, which is decided by courts, and regulations issued by government agencies. 指由立法机关制定的正式的书面文件用于统治管理州、市或国家。其典型内容有命令或禁止某事，或是宣布一项政策。它是由立法机关制定的规则；不同于判例法或先例，其由法庭裁定，也不同于（行政）规定，其由政府机关制定。

statute 其义要注意几点，首先 statute 是指由立法机关颁布的法令、法案、法规，对于英美国家来说，立法机关有联邦、州、县（市）三级的议会（美国），大不列颠及北爱尔兰－苏格兰/英格兰/威尔士/北爱尔兰－地方三级的议会（英国）。由于英美国家遵循三权分立的原则，因此行政机关、司法机关也可以通过法律文

---

① 魏俐，刘忠文.中美两国青少年犯罪问题之比较研究[J].辽宁警察学院学报，2001(04)：56－59.

件。statute 区别于司法机关的判例法以及行政机关的行政法规。但是在大陆法系国家,司法机关并没有权力通过法官造法来行成判例法,所有的法律法规均为制定法。而中文中对于法规法令法案等词的混用更使得在提及法案、法令、法规时对于其颁布的机关不敏感,在翻译过程中应注意提示予以区分①。对于中国来说,立法机关有全国人大,省/自治区/直辖市人大,地方人大,行政部门与司法部门制定的规定仅能称为规定、规章、解释、要求、意见等。

综上,对于 statutory 的翻译首先要明确 statutory 所指的主体为美国法律语境下的由立法机关制定的法规②。面对 statutory＋名词构成的术语首先要查阅资料,确定其"法定"指的是泛指的法定,还是成文法或制定法法定的特殊行为③。若是成文法特定的,一定要尽量标注成文法定或是制定法定。另外由于 statutory law 有成文法和制定法两个中文翻译,翻译时一定要注意前后对照,统一规范。而在中译英时,中国的法定均指的是由立法机关各级人大制定的法律,行政机关或司法机关所做的规定、通知、意见、条例、解释均不能翻为"法定",宪法规定的也不能翻译成"法定",应为"宪法定"即 constitutional。而中国法律语境中不存在判例法或普通法,因此 common law,case law 均不存在,并不存在 statutes 与 case law 的对立。因此中文中的法常直接使用泛指的 law,法定也简单翻为 legal。

tacit mortgage

根据《布莱克法律词典》,tacit mortgage 是民法中的概念,有两层含义。

其一,与 legal mortgage 同义,即 a creditor's mortgage arising by operation of law on the debtor's property。即依照法律规定而在债务人财产上设定的抵押。该层含义下常见的译法就是直译为"默示抵押",意思大抵相同,但不够准

---

① 赵维贞.美国成文法与传统大陆法系成文法立法理念比较研究[J].西南政法大学学报,2004(02):119−122.

② 这类法规比较典型的有 APA(American Patent Act),UCC(Unified Commercial Code),CCPA(Consumer Credit Protection Act)等,因此在英翻中过程中比较常见。

③ 某些术语,如 statutory contract,其含义等同于 contract。因为合同如果生效受法律保护,其必然合法。而另外一些术语,如 statutory lien,其含义不等同于 lien。因为 lien 物权担保在普通的契约中也可存在或产生,这种担保物权受到普通法/判例法的保护而并非由制定法确认或普通法中不存在而由制定法创设的物权担保。因此,statutory lien 应翻译为制定法上的担保物权,指的是在特殊情况或条件下产生于制定法(statutes)的留置权,质权或抵押权。与契约产生的担保物权相区分。

确,未能突出其依法而定,依法而行的特点。应将其翻译为"依法推定的抵押"。

其二,与 tacit hypothecation 同义,即 a type of lien or mortgage that is created by operation of law and without the parties' express agreement。指根据法律规定而非当事人明确约定所创设的留置权或抵押权。USLegal 网站的定义更为详细:a particular kind of a mortgage。It means a lien or mortgage that is created by the operation of law and without the parties' express agreement. Before being abolished in Louisiana, it was used to give rights to another, such as a creditor, over the property of his debtor, as security for payment of a debt, also giving the power of having the property seized and sold in default of payment. 主要出现在借贷双方之间,作为借贷的一种担保。并且如果借方未按时履行付款义务,贷方可扣押并抛售其抵押资产。这一权利与中国法律体系中的"法定抵押权"相似。所谓法定抵押权,是指当事人依据法律的规定而直接取得的抵押权,一般来说,抵押都是由当事人双方通过订立抵押合同并登记而取得的,但是在特殊情况下,法律为保障债权人的利益而设定了法定抵押权。两者区别在于是否签订抵押合同。因此该含义下可以直接译作"法定抵押权",但要补充说明无须当事人双方约定,即"法定抵押权(无须当事人双方约定)"。

tainted evidence

该术语容易被按照字面意思直译为"瑕疵证据"或"污点证据",也有人根据其含义将其翻译为"非法证据",到底哪个译文更准确呢?首先还是应了解其源语释义。

根据《布莱克法律词典》,该术语的定义是:Evidence that is inadmissible because it was directly or indirectly obtained by illegal means. 指因通过非法手段直接或间接获得而不被采信的证据。

根据康奈尔法学院 LII 在线数据库平台给出的更为详细的解释可知,在刑事审判中只有这些证据支持的定罪将被推翻[①]。然而,这一原则也有例外,在以

---

① In a criminal trial, tainted evidence, also referred to as evidence of taint, is evidence that was acquired by illegal means. For example, if authorities gather evidence using a wiretap without a proper warrant, the evidence will be deemed tainted. Because of Fourth Amendment implications, tainted evidence is generally inadmissible, and convictions supported solely by such evidence will be reversed. 参见 https://www.law.cornell.edu/wex/tainted_evidence。

下情况中即使使用了 tainted evidence,也可据此定罪。

第一,在一些司法管辖区(比如纽约),如果 tainted evidence 是从独立来源获得的,而不是通过非法搜查得到,那么它可能会像正常证据一样被接受①。第二,如果能够证明即使没有进行非法搜查,也不可避免地会通过合法活动找到证据,则可以维持通过 tainted evidence 而定的罪。这一例外被称为 inevitable-discovery rule。比如,最高法院认为如果警方非法获得一级谋杀的自证其罪陈述,那么最终的定罪仍然可以维持,因为在正常事件过程中会发现该非法活动的证据。② 第三,如果 tainted evidence 是"无害"的,就可以维持通过 tainted evidence 定的罪,或者换句话说,不管 tainted evidence 是否被采信,被告都会因其行为被定罪。最高法院认为,证据是否无害取决于多个因素,包括证据对控方案件的重要性、证据是否累积以及控方案件的整体实力。例如,弗吉尼亚州最高法院认定,在绑架案的审判中,即使提出了 tainted evidence,最终的定罪也可以维持,因为无论证据如何,所有其他采信的证据都足以满足定罪要求。③ 最后,最高法院认为,tainted evidence 仍有可能被用于证明刑事被告人的可信度

---

① First, in some jurisdictions, like New York, if the tainted evidence was obtained from an independent source, as opposed to an illegal search, then it may be admitted like normal evidence. For example, evidence that would be deemed tainted if confiscated by illegal search will not be tainted if found after it is abandoned by the defendant. 参见 https://www.law.cornell.edu/wex/tainted_evidence。

② Second, a conviction found on tainted evidence may be sustained where it can be shown that the evidence would have inevitably been found by lawful activity even if no illegal search had taken place. This exception has been referred to as the "inevitable-discovery rule." For example, the Supreme Court has held that where self-incriminating statements to first-degree murder was illegally obtained by police, the resulting conviction could nonetheless be upheld on the basis that evidence of the illegal activity would have been discovered in the course of ordinary events. 参见 https://www.law.cornell.edu/wex/tainted_evidence。

③ Third, a conviction found on tainted evidence may be sustained where it can be shown that the tainted evidence was "harmless," or in other words, the defendant would have been convicted regardless of the admission of the tainted evidence. The Supreme Court has held that whether evidence is harmless depends on multiple factors, including the importance of the evidence to the prosecution's case, whether the evidence was cumulative, and the overall strength of the prosecution's case. Determinations made under this standard are highly fact dependent. For example, the Supreme Court of Virginia has found that, in a trial for abduction, the resulting conviction could be upheld even though tainted evidence was presented, because regardless of the evidence, all other fairly admitted evidence would have been sufficient to satisfy the requirements for the conviction. 参见 https://www.law.cornell.edu/wex/tainted_evidence。

有限。①

根据上述定义和解释可以发现，tainted evidence 是因其通过非法手段直接或间接而获取的证据，通常不被采信，但存在一些例外情况。所以"污点证据"或"瑕疵证据"此类译文通过"瑕疵"和"污点"寓意该证据存在一些缺陷，和该术语的含义也较为符合。

在我国是否存在类似的证据呢？2010 年我国《关于办理刑事案件排除非法证据若干问题的规定》和《关于办理死刑案件审查判断证据若干问题的规定》（下称两个证据规定）颁布后，证据学中明确提出了"瑕疵证据"的概念。刑事诉讼法及相关司法解释也吸纳了两个证据规定中关于"瑕疵证据"和"非法证据"的有关规定。根据陕西省人民检察院副检察长王英杰发表在我国最高人民检察院官网上题为"瑕疵证据与非法证据的界定和处理"②一文可知，实际上在这两个证据规定出台之前，只有合法证据和非法证据之分，没有瑕疵证据的概念。这种划分方法显然抹杀了违法取证手段在违法程度上的差异，掩盖了不同程度的违法手段所取得的证据在证据能力上的区分，从而无法区别情况进行排除或补救。在新的证据体系下，我们所讲的非法证据，显然只应是与瑕疵证据相区别的狭义的非法证据。首先，我们可将证据按照是否合法，区分为合法证据和不合法证据。其次，将不合法证据按照违法的程度区分为严重违法证据（即非法证据）和轻微违法证据（即瑕疵证据），前者包括刑讯取得的口供以及采用暴力、威胁等非法方法收集的证人证言、被害人陈述，后者包括不符合法定程序收集的、可能严重影响司法公正的物证、书证等。这样，证据就被划分为三类：合法证据、非法证据和瑕疵证据。与此相对应，这三类证据在证据能力上也被区分开来，分别是具有证据能力、无证据能力和证据能力待定。

在新的证据规则下，瑕疵证据只有轻微违法性，例如，在勘查笔录、搜查笔录、提取笔录、扣押清单上遗漏侦查人员签名或物品名称、特征等，在讯问或询问笔录上遗漏侦查人员签名、讯问或询问起止时间等。其证据形式有瑕疵，但证据本身具有客观真实性和关联性，完全可以弥补，从而使其从效力待定的状态转化

---

① Lastly, the Supreme Court has held that tainted evidence may still be used for the limited purpose of impeaching a testifying criminal defendant's credibility. 参见 https://www.law.cornell.edu/wex/tainted_evidence。

② 参见 https://www.spp.gov.cn/llyj/201405/t20140512_71999.shtml。

为合法有效的证据。而非法证据则由于其严重违法的特点,决定了其客观性受到严重影响,如刑讯取得的供述,其客观真实性受到严重破坏,根本无法补救,必须直接予以排除。

在我国非法证据与瑕疵证据均属于广义上非法证据的范畴。在新的证据体系下,我们所讲的非法证据,显然只应是与瑕疵证据相区别的狭义的非法证据。综上所述可以看出 tainted evidence 的概念范畴大于我国的"瑕疵证据",更符合广义上的"非法证据"概念。但是 tainted evidence 显然存在一些例外情况,即特定条件下仍然可以被采信。而"非法"二字容易否认其可采信,建议进行解释性翻译,以区别与我国的"瑕疵证据"和"非法证据"的不同。综合考虑,可将其翻译为"非法手段获取的证据",只强调其获取的手段非法,而不对其性质进行定性。

tax foreclosure

在《布莱克法律词典》中,这一术语的英文定义为:A public authority's seizure and sale of property for nonpayment of taxes. 指政府对不纳税者的财产实施扣押和出售。如果单独搜索"foreclosure"的定义,会发现它的具体定义为:A process in chancery by which all further right existing in a mortgagor to redeem the estate is defeated and lost to him, and the estate becomes the absolute property of the mortgagee; being applicable when the mortgagor has forfeited his estate by non-payment of the money due on the mortgage at the time appointed, but still retains the equity of redemption. 强调的是取消并终止抵押人的抵押品赎回权。如抵押人在要求的时间期限内未能清偿债务,将丧失物件赎回的权利。所以这一术语的完整概念,还应当包括政府可以终止拖欠税款公民的财产回赎权。这一点也在《元照英美法词典》对 tax foreclosure 的解释中得到了印证。

在中国,未按照规定期限缴纳税款及滞纳金,经税务机关责令限期缴纳,逾期仍未缴纳的纳税人,主管税务机关可以对已扣押、查封的财物进行拍卖、变卖,以拍卖、变卖所得抵缴税款、滞纳金或罚款。

综上,该术语译为"(因逃漏税)依法强行处置"比较合适。

tenancy at will 与 tenancy at sufferance

tenancy at will 和 tenancy at sufferance 这两个术语容易被混为一谈，都解释为"不定期租赁"，但如果了解其源语释义后会发现这两者是不同的概念。

《布莱克法律词典》对 tenancy at will 的定义是：A tenancy in which the tenant holds possession with the landlord's consent but without fixed terms (as for duration or rent); specif., a tenancy that is terminable at the will of either the transferor or the transferee and that has no designated period of duration. Such a tenancy may be terminated by either party upon fair notice. 也称作 at-will tenancy 或 estate at will。即承租人在征得出租人同意的情况下持有所有权，但并未商定租赁的固定期限（如租赁时长或租金）；如欲确定租赁期限或终止租赁的日期，须经各方的一致同意，或任何一方均可随时通知对方，终止租赁。

《布莱克法律词典》对 tenancy at sufferance 的定义是：A tenancy arising when a person who has been in lawful possession of property wrongfully remains as a holdover after his or her interest has expired. A tenancy at sufferance takes the form of either a tenancy at will or a periodic tenancy. 也称作 holdover tenancy 或 estate at sufferance。指租户或保有人在其租赁或保有不动产合法占有权终止以后继续占有该不动产，而土地所有人既未反对亦未明确表示同意时的租赁或保有状况。tenancy at sufferance 的形式可以是 tenancy at will 也可以是 periodic tenancy。这里又引申出一个新的概念 periodic tenancy。

根据《布莱克法律词典》，periodic tenancy 的定义是：A tenancy that automatically continues for successive periods, usu. month to month or year to year unless terminated at the end of a period by notice. A typical example is a month-to-month apartment lease. This type of tenancy originated through court rulings that, when the lessor received a periodic rent, the lease could not be terminated without reasonable notice. 也称作 tenancy from period to period; periodic estate; estate from period to period; 或者可以具体到 month-to-month tenancy (or estate); year-to-year tenancy (or estate)。通常指自动连续租期的租赁，是对按周、按月或按年租赁的通称。这类租赁的效力在每次租赁期满时自动顺延至下一期，但事先通知终止租赁的除外。

综上，根据 tenancy at will 的英文定义，可以看出房东和租户之间是有协议的，但是时间是不确定的，里面含有默许的成分。而从 tenancy at sufferance 的英文定义看出，表示租赁期满，承租人继续使用租赁物。因此，应将 tenancy at will 译为"不定期租赁"；而 periodic tenancy 可译为"周期性租赁"或"定期租赁"；tenancy at sufferance 可译为"宽容租赁"，通过"宽容"一词意指土地所有人既未反对亦未明确表示租户或保有人可以继续占有或者终止占有该不动产。

tenancy in common

该术语在英美法律制度中与资产有关。通过查阅《布莱克法律词典》，可知其与 common tenancy，estate in common 同义，定义为：A tenancy by two or more persons, in equal or unequal undivided shares, each person having an equal right to possess the whole property but no right of survivorship. 即所有共有人对资产（包括动产或不动产）都拥有所有权。并且这种共有，是不确定份额的共有，各个共有人对于共同财产虽然拥有大小不等的份额，但是享有同等的权利，承担同等的义务。但不享有生存者财产权（right of survivorship）。

为了更好理解 tenancy in common 的含义，要注意区分 tenancy in common 与 joint tenancy 之间的差异。根据《布莱克法律词典》可知 joint tenancy 的定义是：A tenancy with two or more coowners who take identical interests simultaneously by the same instrument and with the same right of possession. A joint tenancy differs from a tenancy in common because each joint tenant has a right of survivorship to the other's share (in some states, this right must be clearly expressed in the conveyance—otherwise, the tenancy will be presumed to be a tenancy in common). 结合《元照英美法词典》的相关解释可知 joint tenancy 指两人以上以同一名义共同保有某一地产，他们所享有的这种地产权是统一的一项权利，由同一地产转让契据创设，其权利同时开始，并不加分割地共同占有。其最大的特点是当共同保有人之一死亡时，该共同保有的地产并不予以分割，而是仍作为整体由生存者或遗属（survivor）继续共同保有，直至最后一个共同保有人。也就是说 joint tenancy 中保有人之间彼此享有 right of survivorship（在某些州，这种权利必须在转让书中明确表达。否则，财产的共有方式将被推定为 tenancy in common）。

两者的主要区别在于共有人之间彼此是否享有 right of survivorship。《布莱克法律词典》对 right of survivorship 的定义是：A joint tenant's right to succeed to the whole estate upon the death of the other joint tenant，即共同保有人在另一共同保有人死亡后继承其之前共同保有权益的权利，通常翻译为"生存者财产权"。比如甲和乙共同出资以 tenancy in common 方式购得某一地产，每人支付一半的价金，那么在乙死后，他的权益归他的继承人而非甲。如果甲乙双方以 joint tenancy 方式共有财产，乙死后其生前享有的权益归甲而不是归乙的继承人。

我国的法律概念中有"共同共有"，指两个或两个以上的人基于共同关系，共同享有一物的所有权。共同共有是不确定份额的共有，只要共同共有关系存在，共有人就不能划分自己对财产的份额。只有在共同共有关系消灭而对共有财产进行分割时，才能确定各个共有人应得的份额。共同共有的共有人平等地享有权利和承担义务。各个共有人对于共有物，平等地享有占有、使用、收益、处分权，并平等地承担义务。我国《物权法》还特别规定，共有人对共有的不动产或者动产没有约定为按份共有或者共同共有的，或者约定不明确的，除共有人具有家庭关系等外，视为按份共有。

综上，joint tenancy 符合"共同共有"的含义，可将其翻译为"共同共有财产权"。而翻译 tenancy in common 时应突出其 each person having an equal right to possess the whole property 的特点，因此可将其翻译为"分别共有财产权"。

termination hearing

如果不考察 termination hearing 的源语释义，大部分人可能会直接将其翻译为"终止听审""终止听证"，但了解其源语释义后发现此类译文和其真实含义相差甚远。

根据《布莱克法律词典》可知，这是美国《家事法》中的概念，是 termination-of-parental-rights 的简写形式。其具体解释为：a trial or court proceeding, usu. initiated by a state agency, that seeks to sever the legal ties between a parent and child, usu. so that the child can be adopted. The standard of proof in a termination-of-parental-rights hearing is clear and convincing evidence. 由国家机构发起的审判或法庭程序，通常指试图切断父母和子女之间的法律联系的程

序。经过此程序后孩子就可以被收养。此程序中需有明确且令人信服的证据。

《英美法律术语辞典(英汉双解)》中提供的解释为：a hearing held in the family division of the circuit court to determine if the parental rights are to be taken away from the parties involved, and therefore the child will become a ward of the court. The prosecutor is required to attend. This is the final scheduled hearing of a neglect/abuse case. 由此可知该程序用于在巡回法院家事庭中用以决定是否终止父母监护权而进行的听审。如果法院判决终止父母监护权，则孩子成为法院的受监护人。此类听审一般出现在虐待或疏忽照顾儿童案件的最后听审阶段。

同时在查阅《布莱克法律词典》后，发现几个来源于《家事法》里面与 hearing 该词条相关的术语，都是在《家事法》中与父母监护权相关的术语，例如 custody hearing, disposition hearing, shelter hearing, neglect hearing 以及 permenency hearing。hearing 是法律英语术语中经常看到的一个词，其源语解释为：In law, a hearing is a proceeding before a court or other decision-making body or officer, such as a government agency or a Parliamentary committee. 经常翻译为"听审"或"听证"。指就争议问题提供证据、陈述理由并由有裁判权的个人或机关做出裁决的相对正式的程序。听审的目的在于为争议各方，尤其是可能被剥夺权益的一方，创造陈述意见的机会。听审不限于由司法机关举行，立法机关和行政机关也可以进行听证。包括通知在内的听审是公正程序的基本组成部分。英国的自然公正原则和美国的宪法都有此明确的要求。

在充分理解源语释义之后，可以发现如果仅仅只是简单地按照字面意思翻译为"终止听审""终止听证"的话就会产生漏译甚至是完全错译的现象。因此应当将 termination hearing 这个词的涵义缩小到具体的适用范围中。

综上所述，应将其翻译为"终止父母监护权的听证/听审"。

third degree

大部分译者会将 third degree 直接翻译成诸如"第三等级""第三级别"之类的意思。例如，third-degree burns 三度烧伤，third-degree murder 三级谋杀，这是将 third degree 作为形容词来修饰名词。但用于法律语境时，third degree 的含义则大相径庭。

《布莱克法律词典》对它的定义是：The process of extracting a confession or information from a suspect or prisoner by prolonged questioning, the use of threats, or physical torture (the police gave the suspect the third degree).由此，可以得出其含义：为了获取信息或者让嫌疑人坦白，公检法机关进行长时间严苛的讯问，适用威胁(threats)或 physical torture。为了深入了解其含义，有必要再查询下 torture 一词的含义。根据《布莱克法律词典》，torture 指 the infliction of intense pain to the body or mind to punish, to extract a confession or information, or to obtain sadistic pleasure,即对身体或精神施加强烈的痛苦，以惩罚、逼供或获取信息，或获得施虐的快感。

该含义容易使人联想到中文语境中的"刑讯逼供"。刑讯逼供是指国家司法机关工作人员(含纪检、监察等)采用肉刑或变相肉刑乃至精神刑等残酷的方式折磨被讯问人的肉体或精神，以获取其供述的一种极恶劣的刑事司法审讯方法。我国《刑法》第二百四十七条第一款规定：刑讯逼供罪、暴力取证罪是指司法工作人员对犯罪嫌疑人、被告人实行刑讯逼供或者使用暴力逼取证人证言的，处三年以下有期徒刑或者拘役。我国刑讯逼供罪的构成要件有：1.本罪为身份犯，行为主体必须是司法工作人员，即有侦查、检察、审判监管职责的工作人员；2.行为对象是侦查过程中的犯罪嫌疑人和起诉、审判过程中的刑事被告人；3.必须采用刑讯方法，即必须使用肉刑或者变相肉刑；4.必须有逼供行为，即逼迫犯罪嫌疑人、被告人做出某种供述(包括口供与书面陈述)。

综上所述，third degree 与我国刑讯逼供罪中描述的行为极为相似，但在 third degree 的源语释义中并未发现已将其确定为一项罪名，所以翻译时不宜加入"罪"字，将其翻译为"刑讯逼供"即可。

trademark 与 tradename

trademark 易与 tradename 混淆使用，此处将通过了解其源语释义厘清两者的区别。

根据《布莱克法律词典》，trademark 的含义有两层。其一：A word, phrase, logo, or other graphic symbol used by a manufacturer or seller to distinguish its product or products from those of others. The main purpose of a trademark is to designate the source of goods or services. In effect, the trademark is the commercial substitute for one's signature. To receive federal protection, a trademark must be (1) distinctive rather than merely descriptive or generic; (2) affixed to a product that is actually sold in the marketplace; and (3) registered with the U.S. Patent and Trademark Office. In its broadest sense, the term trademark includes a servicemark. Unregistered trademarks are protected under common-law only, and distinguished with the mark "TM." Often shortened to mark. 结合《元照英美法词典》的解释可知：trademark 通常简写为 mark，指制造商或销售商用于将其产品与其他产品区分开来而使用的单词、短语、标志或其他图形符号。此为狭义的、亦是最常用的含义。通常将其翻译为"商标"。在广义上，该词还可以泛指表示商品或服务来源的任何形式，包括服务商标（servicemark）。商标最初是以普通法进行保护，只要该标识与特定的个人或组织所生产、拣选或销售的商品相联系且具有显著性，则无须注册即受普通法保护。在美国，规定商标注册与保护的联邦制定法是 1946 年的《兰哈姆法》（Lanham Act）。商标获得联邦保护的条件是：(1)具有显著性；(2)与市场上实际销售的某一产品相联系；(3)已在联邦专利与商标局（U.S. Patent and Trademark Office)进行注册。未注册商标仅受普通法保护，并与商标"TM"区分开来。其二：The body of law dealing with how businesses distinctively identify their products. Abbr. TM. 即涉及企业如何区分其产品的法律体系，可翻译为"商标法"。

《布莱克法律词典》对 tradename 的定义也有两层。其一：A name, style, or symbol used to distinguish a company, partnership, or business (as opposed to a product or service); the name under which a business operates. A trade name is a means of identifying a business—or its products or services to establish goodwill. It symbolizes the business's reputation. 指在经营过程中用以确认和区分某一公司、合伙或其他经营组织的名称、记号或标志。tradename 是识别企业或其产品或服务以建立商誉的一种手段，它象征着企业的声誉。其二：A trademark that was not originally susceptible to exclusive appropriation but has acquired a secondary meaning. Also termed brand name; commercial name. 即最初不易被独占的商标，但又拥有了第二层意义。也称为 brand name 或 commercial name。

综上可见，tradename 与 trademark 在功能上有所不同：trademark 具有区

别商品来源的功能,将本商品与其他商品通过 trademark 进行区分;而通过 tradename 可识别企业或其产品或服务以建立商誉。因此 tradename 就是我们日常生活中接触最广泛的"品牌名称"或"商号";而 trademark 是"商标",受法律的保护程度更高,两者不能混为一谈。

traditional waiver

如果不查阅源语释义,可能大部分译者会感觉 traditional waiver 不知所云、不知其意,甚至无从下手翻译。这时候我们就需要了解该术语的法律文化内涵。

在查阅相关资料过程中,发现 traditional waiver 相关的上位词 waiver of jurisdiction,其源语释义为 The process through which the family division of the circuit court relinquishes its jurisdiction over a juvenile who has committed a criminal offense, and transfers the case to the criminal division of the circuit court. There are two types of waivers: automatic waiver and traditional waiver[①]. 根据其释义,可以得知该过程为巡回法院家事庭放弃对犯有刑事犯罪的未成年人的管辖权的过程,并将案件移交给巡回法院的刑事庭。查阅相关资料得知:在美国,处理未成年人犯罪的法律程序与正常的刑事法律程序不同,因为它们是根据未满 18 岁的青少年的特点而设计。每个州都运用不同的制度来处理青少年事务。一些州还设有专门的青少年法庭,而其他州将青少年法律事务放在家庭或遗嘱法庭里面处理,不过当被控的犯罪非常严重时,拥有就青少年法律事务进行聆讯的司法管辖权的大多数法庭可能将案件转入审判法庭。转移未成年人犯罪案件的过程被称为 waiver of jurisdiction。它有两种实现形式:automatic waiver 和 traditional waiver。

此处又引申出一个新术语:automatic waiver,其源语释义为:if a juvenile between ages 14 and 17 is charged with certain violations specified in statute(e. g. murder, armed robbery, first degree criminal sexual conduct), the prosecutor may file a complaint charging the juvenile as an adult. Such cases automatically come under the jurisdiction of the criminal division of the circuit

---

① 张法连. 英美法律术语辞典(英汉双解)[Z]. 上海:上海外语教育出版社,2014.

court. Automatic waivers are sometimes referred to as prosecutorial waivers[①].

而 traditional waiver 的源语释义为:if a juvenile between ages 14 and 17 is charged with any felony, the prosecutor may file a motion requesting the family division of the curcuit court to waive jurisdiction. If the prosecutor's motion is granted, the case is transferred to the criminal division of the circuit court and the juvenile is tried as an adult。

根据上述释义后可以发现 automatic waiver 和 traditional waiver 的区别在于:automatic waiver 指 14 岁至 17 岁的未成年人一旦被控进行了某些违法行为(例如谋杀,持械抢劫,一级犯罪行为),检察官可以直接将其视为成年人而提出控告;这些案件自动交由巡回法庭刑事庭管辖。而 traditional waiver 指 14 岁至 17 岁的未成年人被指控犯有重罪时,检察官要提出申请要求法庭的家事庭放弃管辖权;如果检察官的申请获得批准,案件将移交给巡回法庭的刑事庭,未成年人则作为成年人受审。前者直接将未成年人视为成年人进行控告;而后者需先申请家事庭放弃管辖权,获批后未成年人才作为成人受审。

查阅源语释义,我们发现中国的法律制度不存在此类的法律术语。我们还需进一步了解该术语相关的法律制度。在美国大多数州,达到 18 周岁的门槛才能进入成年人司法体系接受审判。但同时,美国所有州均有在成人司法体系中处理 18 岁以下的未成年人刑事案件的规定。决定未成年人是否需要进入成年人司法体系处理的基本标准主要是犯罪的严重性和是否有犯罪前科,一般不考虑未成年被告人的最低年龄。这种标准实质上是基于对少年犯在未成年人法院体系内矫正的可能性之大小的估计,矫正的可能性大的应当留在未成年人法院体系内,反之,则可以交由成年人司法体系处理[②]。

在分析了美国法律对于处理未成年人犯罪的形式程序以及上述几个词条的

---

① 张法连. 英美法律术语辞典(英汉双解)[Z]. 上海:上海外语教育出版社,2014.

② 具体说来,未成年人案件由成人法庭审判的有四种情况:一是强制性司法管辖权放弃或者说法定排除。按照 38 个州的法律规定,对有些特定类型的案件,通常是暴力重罪案件,少年法院必须移交给成人法庭进行审判。二是裁量性司法管辖权放弃。有 45 个州可以由少年法院法官运用裁量性司法管辖权,放弃对少年案件的管辖。三是检察官裁量向成人法庭起诉的。15 个州可以由检察官裁量直接向成人法庭提起诉讼,检察官向成人法庭起诉的,少年法院失去管辖权。四是推定放弃管辖权。有 15 个州,某些案件可被作为推定放弃,即出现某种情形时推定少年法院放弃管辖权;一旦成立推定放弃,未成年人必须说明理由否定推定,才能避免移交成人法庭。

具体源语涵义后,可以将该词的范围定为"未成年人犯罪"这个术语下,方便目的语读者能够更好地明白,因此可以将上位词 waiver of jurisdiction 翻译为"放弃(未成年人犯罪)司法管辖权";将 automatic waiver 翻译为"自动放弃(未成年人犯罪)司法管辖权";将 traditional waiver 翻译为"经申请获批后放弃(未成年人犯罪)司法管辖权"。

transferred intent

《布莱克法律词典》对 transferred intent 的定义是:Intent that the law may shift from an originally intended wrongful act to a wrongful act actually committed. For example, if a person intends to kill one person but kills another inadvertently, the intent may be transferred to the actual act。即最初的意图的不法行为可能转变为实际实施的不法行为。例如,如果一个人打算杀死一个人,但无意中杀死了另一个人,则该意图可能会转移到实际行为中。该解释有些费解,可以再了解下康奈尔法学院 LII 在线数据库平台给出的解释:Transferred intent is used when a defendant intends to harm one victim, but then unintentionally harms a second victim instead. In this case, the defendant's intent transfers from the intended victim to the actual victim and can be used to satisfy the mens rea element of the crime that the defendant is being charged with. The transferred intent doctrine is only used for completed crimes, and is not used for attempted crimes. 指被告人意图伤害某人,但无意中伤害了另一名被害人。因此被告人的意图从意图被害人转移到实际被害人,并可用于满足被告人被指控的犯罪意图(mens rea)要素。transferred intent doctrine 仅适用于已完成的犯罪,不适用于未遂犯罪。

《元照英美法词典》给出的解释为:此术语为刑法中的概念。指在犯罪故意的驱使下所做出的非法但无故意的行为,依然被认定为故意犯罪行为;即犯罪人最初的犯罪故意从意图被害人转移到实际被害人身上。例如犯罪人企图谋杀甲,却因错误或疏忽而杀害了乙,此时犯罪人仍应被认为犯有故意谋杀罪。在侵权行为法上亦然,如果侵权人企图对某人实施侵权行为,但实际上使第三人受损,则该第三人可以故意侵权而要求行为人承担责任,尽管其对第三人并无侵权故意。

《英美法律术语辞典(英汉双解)》将该术语翻译为"犯意转化"①,从而指明在故意犯罪过程中,犯罪故意发生转化的情况。该译文简明扼要地体现了源语的含义,较为合适。

turf and twig

对该术语做出定义的法律词典较少,通过查阅 Ballentine's Law Dictionary② 得知:A clod of turf, or a twig or bough growing on the land, the usual symbolic means by which livery of seisin was effected, one of these being delivered on the land by the feoffor to the feoffee. 理解该释义可以结合《元照英美法词典》给出的解释:将一块草皮或一根树枝作为拟制的土地让渡的方式,交与土地受让人或受领人,以此作为不动产转移的方式。

上述英文释义中提到了一个概念 Livery of Seisin,根据维基百科的介绍③可得知:Livery of Seisin 出现在中世纪的英国,后流传至美洲殖民地,是一种古老的土地转让方式,一直延续到 17 世纪末期。它的简要概念为 transfer of possession. The concept behind livery of seisin, therefore, was the symbolic transfer of the possession of land. 即通过封地占有移交仪式传递一定数量的土壤、树枝或其他属于该土地上的东西,从而完成土地占有权的转移。

在中国的法律体系中,与土地相关的主要权利分别是土地所有权和土地使

---

① 根据《英美法律术语辞典(英汉双解)》的解释:犯意转化会导致行为人的行为方式、性质产生变化,因而影响犯罪故意内容的认定。犯意转化主要分为两种:第一种情况是,行为人以此犯意实施犯罪的预备行为,却以彼犯意实施犯罪的实行行为。根据重行为吸收轻行为的原则认定犯罪。例如,行为人在预备阶段具有抢劫的故意,但进入现场后实施了盗窃行为。第二种情况是,在实行犯罪的过程中犯意改变,导致此罪与彼罪的转化。例如,甲在故意伤害他人的过程中,改变犯意,意图杀死他人。又如,乙见他人携带装有现金的提包,起抢夺之念,在抢夺过程中转化为使用暴力,将他人打倒在地,抢走提包。再如,丙本欲杀死他人,在杀害过程中,由于某种原因改变犯意,认为造成伤害即可,没有致人死亡。详细内容参见张法连. 英美法律术语辞典(英汉双解)[Z]. 上海:上海外语教育出版社,2014.

② https://ballentine.en-academic.com/38480/turf_and_twig

③ Livery of seisin is an archaic legal conveyancing ceremony, formerly practised in feudal England and in other countries following English common law, used to convey holdings in property. The term livery is closely related to if not synonymous with delivery used in some jurisdictions in contract law or the related law of deeds. The oldest forms of common law provided that a valid conveyance of a feudal tenure in land required physical transfer by the transferor to the transferee in the presence of witnesses of a piece of the ground itself, in the literal sense of a hand-to-hand passing of an amount of soil, a twig, key to a building on that land, or other token. 参见 https://en.wikipedia.org/wiki/Livery_of_seisin.

用权,与之搭配大多是动词"转移"等;相关可供参考的还包括不动产交付。我国法律对土地所有权的规定是:城市的土地属于国家所有。农村和城市郊区的土地,除由法律规定属于国家所有的以外,属于集体所有;宅基地和自留地、自留山,也属于集体所有。土地使用权由县级以上人民政府确定,土地管理部门具体承办。不动产的占有移转给受让人的法律事实。交付就是占有的移转,也被称为占有的交付。交付的法律意义在于公示,即表示不动产物权的设立、变更及移转的法律事实。

结合以上分析,可将该术语译为"土地所有权交付"。

tutorship by nature

该术语的常见译法为"当然监护权",如果不了解其准确的法律内涵,很有可能产生误解。

《布莱克法律词典》对该术语的定义是:1. Tutorship of a minor child that belongs by right to a surviving parent,指对未成年子女的监护权属于尚存父母,即父母一方死亡,另一方拥有对未成年子女的监护权。2. Tutorship of a minor child that belongs to the parent under whose care the child has been placed following divorce or judicial separation. If the parents are awarded joint custody, both have cotutorship and equal authority, privileges, and responsibilities. 指父母离婚或分居(经法庭判决的分局)后,由与未成年子女共同生活或受托照顾未成年子女的一方负责监护。如果指定由父母共同监护未成年子女,则父母双方拥有平等的监护权。

《元照英美法词典》等词典均将该术语译为"当然监护权",可能是受 nature 之意的影响。考虑到该术语的含义中规定此种监护权的取得依其具有父或母的身份,可将该术语翻译为"血亲监护权"。

unclean hands

根据《布莱克法律词典》可知,unclean hands doctrine 的意义与 clean hands doctrine 的意义相同。其具体解释为:The principle that a party cannot seek equitable relief or assert an equitable defense if that party has violated an equitable principle, such as good faith. Such a party is described as having "unclean hands". For example, section 8 of the Uniform Child Custody Jurisdiction Act contains an unclean-hands provision that forbids a court from exercising jurisdiction in a child-custody suit in certain situations, as when one party has wrongfully removed a child from another state, has improperly retained custody of a child after visitation, or has wrongfully removed a child from the person with custody. The clean-hands doctrine evolved from the discretionary nature of equitable relief in English courts of equity, such as Chancery. —Also termed unclean-hands doctrine. 由此可知,如果一方违反了公平原则,如诚信原则,则该方不能寻求公平救济或主张公平辩护的原则。这样的一方被描述为 unclean hands。例如,美国《统一儿童监护管辖权法案》(Uniform Child Custody Jurisdiction Act)第 8 节包含一项 unclean hands 条款,禁止法院在某些情况下对儿童监护权诉讼行使管辖权。比如当一方错误地将儿童从另一个州带走,在探视后不当地保留对儿童的监护权;或错误地将一名儿童从有监护权的人手中带走。该原则源于英国衡平法。

根据《元照英美法词典》,clean hands 的意思是:指某人在其起诉他人之事项上,其行为是正当的、合法的。由此可以援引出 unclean hands 强调对清白正直、诚信善良主体进行保护,对双方行为予以限制,意即向法庭提起诉请的人不仅需要证明自己有正当合理的诉讼理由,而且需保证自身清白可信。其实质是要求主张权利、请求保护之人善良正直,不得从事与其诉讼请求相矛盾之行为,不得欺诈法庭,隐瞒重要事实。该原则与不正当行为原则、禁止权利滥用原则、禁止反悔原则、禁止权利懈怠规则等规则具有相通之处,通常都被申请人或被告使用以针对原告诉讼请求进行有效抗辩。该原则不仅适用于诉讼程序领域,要求行为人诚实守信,不得欺诈法庭和滥用权利,而且适用于实体领域,要求其正直善良,不得从事不当行为,尤其是与诉讼请求相悖的事。违反该规则,可能导致其主张无法获得司法救济。与此同时,我们需要意识到,该原则在美国法中主要应用于专利侵权领域。

综上,unclean hands 强调的是一种处理相关的法律情境时采取的原则,可直译为"不洁之手原则",当涉及具体的法律背景,再结合具体情况解释该原则下的具体行为,从而能够更好地体现法律的准确严谨。

unconscionability

该术语在《布莱克法律词典》中的定义为：1. Extreme unfairness. Unconscionability is normally assessed by an objective standard：(1) one party's lack of meaningful choice, and (2) contractual terms that unreasonably favor the other party. 2. The principle that a court may refuse to enforce a contract that is unfair or oppressive because of procedural abuse during contract formation or because of overreaching contractual terms, esp. terms that are unreasonably favorable to one party while precluding meaningful choice for the other party. Because unconscionability depends on circumstances at the time the contract is formed, a later rise in market price is irrelevant. 由此可知该术语的两层含义分别指：一种极度不公平的状态和一种原则。即法院根据该原则可以以合同缔结中的程序滥用或以与合同内容相关的实体滥用为由拒绝强制执行不公平或压迫性合同，任何一种滥用都是以显失公平为基础的。对合同是否存在 unconscionability 的基本检验标准是，根据缔约时的环境和通常的商业背景以及特定交易的商业要求，确定合同条款是否不合理地使一方当事人受益，从而压迫另一方当事人或对另一方当事人不公平。如果一方当事人未能对合同内容做出有实质意义的选择却使另一方不合理地受益，则存在 unconscionability。因此，该术语可以翻译为"显失公平（原则）"。

美国《统一商法典》(U.C.C.)第 2－302 条规定：1.如果法院作为法律问题发现合同或合同的任何条款在缔约时显失公平，法院可以拒绝强制执行，或仅执行显失公平以外的其他条款，或限制显失公平条款的适用以避免显失公平的后果。2.由于一方当事人主张或法院认为合同或合同的任何条款有可能属于显失公平时，应给予另一方当事人合理的机会提供证据，证明缔约的商业背景、合同的目的和效果，以帮助法院做出决定。《美国合同法重述（第二版）》(Restatement of Contracts, Second)第 208 条亦有相同规定。在英国，它是衡平法中的传统术语，与公平(good conscience)相反，衡平法院通常对显失公平的交易不予认可。

underlying stock

查阅《剑桥商务英语词典》，underlying stock 与 underlying shares 同义，解

释为 the shares, etc. to which something such as an option (= the right to buy or sell them at a particular price by or on a future date) relates; With prices falling, the stock index futures were below underlying share prices。

对 underlying stock 的翻译有"标的股票"或"基准股票"。通过查阅资料发现:"基准股票"又称标的股票,是可转换债券的标的物,是债券持有人将债券转换成发行公司的股票。"标的股票"的搜索结果缺乏权威的解释,不够明确。而在万律中国数据库中,与 underlying stock 对应的含义是"标的股票",例如《上海证券交易所关于扩大融资融券标的股票范围的通知》这一标题的翻译为 the Notice of the Shanghai Stock Exchange on Expanding the Scope of Underlying Stocks for Margin Trading and Securities Lending。同时,该通知正文表明:"……上海证券交易所(以下简称'本所')决定扩大融资融券标的证券(以下简称'标的股票')范围 (decided to expand the scope of underlying securities for margin trading and securities lending (hereinafter referred to as the 'Underlying Stocks')"。此外,在北大法宝数据库中搜索"标的股票",能够检索出113篇中央法规司法解释,且其释义及语境与 underlying stock 的含义相近;而"基准股票"在北大法宝数据库中的搜索几乎没有结果。同时,为达到使译文清楚、简洁的目的,"标的股票"的表述也优于"融资融券标的证券"。因此,将 underlying stock 译为"标的股票"较为合适,不应译为"基准股票"或"融资融券标的证券"。

undue influence

在《布莱克法律词典》中,undue influence 的源语意思有两层。其一,也称作 implied coercion 或 moral coercion。具体含义为:The improper use of power or trust in a way that deprives a person of free will and substitutes another's objective. Consent to a contract transaction, or relationship or to conduct is voidable if the consent is obtained through undue influence. 其二,也称作 improper influence。是 Wills 和 estates 中的概念。具体指:Coercion that destroys a testator's free will and substitutes another's objectives in its place. When a beneficiary actively procures the execution of a will, a presumption of undue influence may be raised, based on the confidential relationship between the influencer and the person influenced.

通过以上源语释义并结合《元照英美法词典》中的解释可知,undue influence 在英国法中,指一种影响、压力或控制力,使得一方当事人由此而不能自由、独立地就自己的行为做出选择。它作为衡平法的原则,是推定欺诈原则的组成部分。一方当事人从合同中获利或接受另一方当事人的赠与,如果对方当事人在交易中因受该方当事人的影响而无从进行自由、独立的判断,则该交易是可撤销的。一般当双方当事人之间具有信任关系时,例如监护人和被监护人、医生和病人、律师和当事人等之间的关系,可推定存在 undue influence,但这一推定是可以被推翻的。在其他情况下则可以由主张者提供证据加以证明,而认定存在 undue influence。在选举事务中,它指任何外力、暴力、限制或伤害、胁迫、恐吓,以诱使任何人报案或不报案。美国法亦认为,如果某一合同、交易、关系或行为的同意是在 undue influence 下做出的,则其属于可撤销的。在遗嘱与遗产继承中,它指破坏立遗嘱人自由意志的胁迫。如果由遗嘱受益人实际上执行遗嘱,则可以基于立遗嘱人与影响人之间的信任关系而推定 undue influence 的存在。同时《英美法律术语辞典(英汉双解)》中也提到 undue influence 是确认合同效力的制度,指一方当事人利用其优越地位、意志或思想,在精神或其他方面向另一方当事人施加非正当的间接压力,从而迫使对方签订合同的一种非法行为。

根据《英汉法律用语大词典》,undue 解释为不当的,过分(度)的,非法的,(期票等)未到期的,未到支付期的等。① 因此结合语境可以将 undue 翻译成"不正当";根据《元照英美法词典》influence 意思为:影响;作用;势力;权势;支配力;在某些隐含意义例如劳动关系中,指可腐蚀或压倒主观意愿的压力,至少是一种超越了雇主与雇员之间单纯关系和友好交往的影响力。再结合源语意思,我们可以看出 influence 的翻译难点主要在于是翻译成"压力"还是"影响",查阅《新华字典》,对于影响的解释是①对别人的思想和行动起作用(如如影随形,响之应声)②对人或事物所起的作用。③传闻的;无根据的。② 而维基百科中对于压力的解释是:压力是心理压力源和心理压力反应共同构成的一种认知和行为体验过程。压力是一个外来词,来源于拉丁文 stringere,原意是痛苦。现在表示

---

① 宋雷. 英汉法律用语大辞典(第 2 版)[Z]. 北京:法律出版社,2019.
② 中国社会科学院语言研究所词典编辑室. 新华字典(第 10 版)[Z]. 北京:商务印书馆,2004.

压力的单词是"distress（悲痛、穷困）"的缩写。由此可以总结，压力比影响更强调消极影响，为了更好地反映源语涵义，因此翻译成"压力"更能体现其不正当性，正好呼应 undue。

综上所述，undue influence 翻译成"不正当压力"更能体现源语的意思。

unilateral contract

《布莱克法律词典》对 unilateral contract 的定义是：A contract in which only one party makes a promise or undertakes a performance; a contract in which no promisor receives a promise as consideration for the promise given. 根据源语解释可知，unilateral contract 指仅由一方当事人做出允诺，而另一方当事人以行为的作为或不作为所达成的合同。它与由双方当事人均做出允诺而达成的双方合同相对。例如①，甲对乙说，"如果你从布鲁克林大桥上走过去，我给你 100 元。"则甲对乙做出了一个允诺，而并没有要求乙也做出一个允诺作为对价。甲要求乙执行，而并不是一个承诺。因此这个合同就是 unilateral contract。乙不能许诺跨过大桥而接受要约。如果乙履行了合同，那就必须接受要约。因为没有相对允诺，任何时候乙都要履行。如果乙履行了承诺，涉及甲乙两方的合同达成，但是由于只有一方负有义务，该合同为 unilateral contract。

综上所述，考虑到 unilateral contract 中仅有一方做出允诺，可将其汉译为"单诺合同"更能体现其内涵。

unqualified audit report 或 unqualified auditor's report

unqualified 的一般含义有"不合格的""不能胜任的""无资质的"等，但在 unqualified audit report/auditor's report 的翻译中，这些释义难以适用。

---

① 原文参见《布莱克法律词典》(Black's Law Dictionary, 9th Edition, p.402) 对该词条的补充解释："Many unilateral contracts are in reality gratuitous promises enforced for good reason with no element of bargain." "If A says to B, 'If you walk across the Brooklyn Bridge I will pay you $100,' A has made a promise but has not asked B for a return promise. A has asked B to perform, not a commitment to perform. A has thus made an offer looking to a unilateral contract. B cannot accept this offer by promising to walk the bridge. B must accept, if at all, by performing the act. Because no return promise is requested, at no point is B bound to perform. If B does perform, a contract involving two parties is created, but the contract is classified as unilateral because only one party is ever under an obligation."

根据《布莱克法律词典》的定义,auditor's report 指 An independent auditor's written statement, usually accompanying a company's financial statement, expressing the auditor's opinion of the accuracy of the company's financial condition as set forth in the financial statement. 即独立审计师的书面声明,通常随附于公司财务报表,表达审计师对财务报表中所述公司财务状况准确性的意见。

通过查阅网络资料①得知:An unqualified audit report is an audit report that confirms that, in the opinion of the auditor, the financial statements of the entity represent a true and fair view of its financial position. An unqualified audit report does not note any discrepancy or any adverse observations with respect to the financial reporting of the entity. Such a audit report is therefore also termed as a clean audit report. When the auditor is satisfied with audit evidence gathered by him and is satisfied that all accounting standards and rules have been duly followed while preparing books of accounts and reporting in financial statements, he issues an unqualified or clean audit report. 即在该报告中审计师确认某实体的财务报表真实、公允地反映了其财务状况。unqualified audit report 不会指出与实体财务报告有关的任何差异或任何不利意见。因此,这种审计报告也被称为 clean audit report。审计师如果对其收集的审计证据感到满意,并且在编制账簿和财务报表时,对所有会计准则和规则都得到了适当遵守感到满意,便会出具 unqualified audit report。

北大法宝数据库和万律数据库将 unqualified audit report/unqualified auditor's report 译为"无保留意见的审计报告"。审计报告是会计师事务所、上市公司、监管部门和投资者等密切关注的一个重要信息载体,其及时性好坏直接关系到决策有用性的大小②。无保留意见意味着注册会计师经过审计以后,认为被审计单位的会计报表的反映是合法且公允的③。根据上述分析,将其翻译为"无保留意见的审计报告"是恰当的。

---

① https://www.termscompared.com/qualified-vs-unqualified-audit-report/
② 陈高才. 会计师事务所特征影响审计报告时滞吗[J]. 财经论丛,2012(01):91—96.
③ 李敏. 浅析带说明段的无保留意见审计报告与保留意见审计报告的区别[J]. 注册会计师通讯,1997(07):17—18.

utmost good faith

由于该术语在权威法律词典中找不到定义,可以先对 good faith 进行了解。《布莱克法律词典》对 good faith 的定义是:A state of mind consisting in (1) honesty in belief or purpose, (2) faithfulness to one's duty or obligation, (3) observance of reasonable commercial standards of fair dealing in a given trade or business, or (4) absence of intent to defraud or to seek unconscionable advantage. 也称作 bona fides。指一种精神状态,包括:(1)信仰或目的上的诚实;(2)对自己的职责或义务的忠诚;(3)在特定行业或业务中遵守公平交易的合理商业标准,或(4)没有欺诈或寻求不合理利益的意图。根据维基百科,good faith 作为法律术语的解释是:In contract law, the implied covenant of good faith and fair dealing is a general presumption that the parties to a contract will deal with each other honestly, fairly, and in good faith, so as to not destroy the right of the other party or parties to receive the benefits of the contract[1]. 即在合同法中,普遍推定合同交易遵循诚实信用和公平交易,即合同当事人将诚实、公平、善意地进行交易,不损害另一方或另一方获得合同利益的权利。

同时,维基百科显示,utmost good faith 是拉丁语词组 uberrima fides 的释义:Uberrima fides (sometimes seen in its genitive form uberrimae fidei) is a Latin phrase meaning "utmost good faith" (literally, "most abundant faith"). It is the name of a legal doctrine which governs insurance contracts. This means that all parties to an insurance contract must deal in good faith, making a full declaration of all material facts in the insurance proposal. This contrasts with the legal doctrine caveat emptor ("let the buyer beware")[2]. 由此可知 utmost good faith 是一个适用于保险领域的法律术语,旨在表明双方在签订保险合同时完全诚信、诚实地对有关事项进行说明。

综上可知,utmost good faith 在保险领域所表达的含义是诚实、诚信,而结合具体知识可以发现,保险合同法中,这一词组对应的理解应为"最大诚信原则"。保险最大诚信原则适用于整个保险法领域,是要求人们在保险活动中善

---

[1] https://en.wikipedia.org/wiki/Good_faith#Law
[2] https://en.wikipedia.org/wiki/Uberrima_fides

意、诚信和有信用地行使权利、履行义务的法律原则。它包括两个方面:第一,要求保险合同当事人订立保险合同及在保险合同的有效期内应依法向对方提供影响对方做出缔约决定的全部实质性重要事实,同时绝对信守合同信用的约定与承诺,诚实履行合同义务;第二,要求保险业者应当诚信经营,维持良好的经营和充足的抵御风险的能力,要求其他保险活动的辅助者,如保险经纪人、保险代理人及保险评估机构,诚信、真实地参与保险活动,禁止利用自身条件参与或者为保险欺诈提供便利条件。最大诚信原则是保险法的首要原则①。因此应将 utmost good faith 翻译为"(保险)最大诚信原则"。

verdict

verdict 通常被翻译为"裁定",判断该译文是否准确,还需先了解其英文释义。

根据《布莱克法律词典》,verdict 的定义有:1. A jury's finding or decision on the factual issues of a case. 2. Loosely, in a nonjury trial, a judge's resolution of the issues of a case.

将该释义与《元照英美法词典》中的解释结合可知,verdict 在英美法律体系中有两种用法。第一,陪审团就提交其审理的事项所做的正式裁决。通常可分为概括式(general verdict),即确定原告胜诉还是被告胜诉(民事案件中)或被告人有罪还是无罪(刑事案件中)和特别式(special verdict),即陪审团仅对案件中的特定事项做出裁决,而将对该事实适用法律的问题留给法官解决。通常只有在很特殊的案件中才会做出 special verdict。在英国,特别根据 1974 年 Juries Act,民事案件中的 Jury's verdict 必须是一致的(unanimous verdict),除非当事人双方同意接受(majority verdict);刑事案件中的 verdict 在某些情况下,法庭可以接受 majority verdict。在苏格兰,民事诉讼中的 verdict 可以是 general verdict 或 special verdict;刑事诉讼中的 verdict 则包括 guilty,not proven 和 not guilty 三种,其中后两者都具有宣告无罪的效力。在美国,传统上要求 Jury's verdict 必须是一致的,但现在已有所改变。第二,无陪审团审判时法官的裁决。这种用法仅在非严格意义上讨论。

而在中国法律语境中,"裁定"指"法院在诉讼过程中就程序问题或部分实体

---

① 张永强. 论保险最大诚信原则及实现机制[D]. 山东大学,2006.

问题所做的决定"。裁定在中国法律体系中使用的情形主要包含三种:民事诉讼、刑事诉讼以及行政诉讼。在中国,民事裁定适用于下列范围:不予受理;对管辖权有异议的;驳回起诉;财产保全和先予执行;准许或者不准许撤诉;中止或者终结诉讼;补正判决书中的笔误;中止或者终结执行;不予执行仲裁裁决;撤销仲裁裁决;不予执行公证机关赋予强制执行效力的债权文书;其他需要裁定解决的事项。其中不予受理、对管辖权有异议和驳回起诉的裁定,可以上诉。诉讼保全和先行给付的裁定,当事人如果不服可以申请复议一次,复议期间,不停止裁定的执行。刑事裁定主要用于解决诉讼过程中的程序问题,也用于减刑、假释、驳回自诉等实体问题。行政诉讼裁定主要用于解决程序问题,以驳回起诉、准许或不准许撤诉以及其他由裁定解决的事项。裁定书一般以书面形式做出,由审判人员、书记员署名,加盖人民法院印章。口头裁定的,需记入笔录。第二审人民法院及最高人民法院做出的裁定,第一审依法不准上诉或者超过上诉期没有上诉的裁定,是发生法律效力的裁定。

可以看出,裁定在我国审判系统中主要是就诉讼过程中的程序性问题的决定,裁定的主要作用在于指挥诉讼活动,推进诉讼的进程。这与英美法语境中 verdict 的真实含义是极不相符的。裁定适用于程序性问题,而英美法中的 verdict 则是对事实问题的裁断。究其原因,还是在于中外的审判体制区别。英美的法官解决的是法律适用问题,而事实问题的判断(如判断刑事案件的被告有罪或无罪)则由陪审团来承担;然而在中国,法官不仅要解决事实问题,还要解决法律适用,所以用法上难免出现无法一一对应的问题。

verdict 在英美法律文化中蕴含了对法律事实的一种判断,是对一个人有罪与否的初步的、朴素的判断。因为 Jury 常由不具备专业法律知识的普通公民担任,所以我们可以假设:verdict 是一个理性人对于一个事实是否有罪的朴素的判断。如果继续使用"裁定"容易造成中文法律术语的混淆,所以应合理创造一个专门与 verdict 相对照的法律术语,便于理解也避免歧义。在此基础上,可将其翻译为"(法官或陪审团的)裁断"。"裁"在汉语中有衡量、思量之意思,与"Jury 根据理性、经验进行衡量考评"一意相近;"断"字在汉语中意味着"最终、终局"的含义。正如在英美法律体系中,一旦 Jury 做出了 guilty 的 verdict,那么法官只能判定其有罪,再在有罪的基础上定罪量刑;一旦 Jury 做出了 not guilty 的 verdict,即便事后查明其有罪,也只能判其无罪(如辛普森杀妻案),所以

verdict 不能上诉,具有终局决定之意义,恰与"断"字相吻合。

waiting period

在有些英汉法律词典中,waiting period 被译为"上诉时效"。判断该翻译是否准确,首先还是应了解其在英美法中的源语释义。

《布莱克法律词典》中 waiting period 的定义是: A period that must expire before some legal right or remedy can be enjoyed or enforced. For example, many states have waiting periods for the issuance of marriage licenses or the purchase of handguns. 在某些法律权利或补救措施得以享有或执行之前必须等待一段时间。例如,许多州发放结婚证或购买手枪时要求必须有 waiting period。很显然,waiting period 并不指"诉讼时效"。

根据维基百科对 waiting period 更详细的解释[①]可知:waiting period 是指从请求或授权采取行动到行动发生之间的一段时间。在美国,该术语通常用于枪支管制,因为美国一些州要求从经销商处购买或预订枪支后需等待一定天数,然后才能实际拥有枪支。在 waiting period 期间,州政府会对购买人或预订人进行背景调查,以确认购买者合法拥有枪支。waiting period 也用于购买新的保险单,尤其是医疗保险和洪水保险,在此期间发生的事件不可索赔。该术语还可以指从提出索赔到支付索赔之间的时间。在商业金融语境中,waiting period 是指进行首次公开募股(IPO)的公司必须对其保持沉默的时间,以免人为地抬高股票价值。其他可能需要等待的事情包括离婚和合并程序。设置 waiting period

---

① A waiting period is the period of time between when an action is requested or mandated and when it occurs. In the United States, the term is commonly used in reference to gun control, as some U. S. states requires a person to wait for a set number of days after buying or reserving a firearm from a dealer before actually taking possession of it. This waiting period allows the state to reform a background check to confirm that the purchaser is legally permitted to possess a firearm. In theory, waiting periods may also be in place to serve as a "cooling off" period for potential buyers who may wish to commit crimes in the "heat of the moment". Waiting periods are also used for new insurance policies, particularly health insurance and flood insurance. Incidents, which occur during this time, are not claimable. The term may also refer to the time between the making of a claim and the payment of it, also called the elimination period. In business finance, a waiting period (or quiet period) is the time in which a company making an initial public offering initial public offering (IPO) must be silent about it, so as not to inflate the value of the stock artificially. It is also called the cooling-off period. Other things potentially subject to waiting periods include divorce and merger proceedings. 参见 https://en. wikipedia. org/wiki/Waiting_period。

的目的在于使当事人冷静(cooling off)。我国《民法典》中婚姻家庭编中也有类似的规定①,即关于"离婚冷静期"的规定。

综上,可将 waiting period 翻译为"冷静期"或者按其字面意思译为"等待期",既传达了其含义,也不会产生歧义。

waiver of jurisdiction

通过查找英文源语法律词典,我们得知 Waiver of jurisdiction 及其相关术语的释义是:Waiver of jurisdiction refers to an order of the juvenile court that waives the case to a court that would have jurisdiction had the act been committed by an adult. Waiver is for the offense charged and all included offenses. There are three types: discretionary waiver, where the judge in a juvenile court has some discretion in deciding whether a juvenile defendant will be transferred to criminal court or not; presumptive waiver, where if the crime falls under a particular category, it is presumed that a waiver is appropriate; and mandatory.

Concurrent jurisdiction waiver, also called concurrent jurisdiction, direct file waivers occur when the prosecutor has the option of filing the case in either juvenile court or adult court. Discretionary Waiver. A form of judicial waiver that is the oldest and most common type in the United States.

研究源语释义,我们发现中国的法律制度不存在此类法律术语。我们还需进一步了解该术语背后的法律制度。在美国大多数州,青少年达到18周岁的门槛才能进入成年人司法体系接受审判。但同时,美国所有州均有在成年人司法体系中处理未成年人刑事案件的规定。决定未成年人案件是否需要进入成年人司法体系处理的基本标准主要是犯罪的严重性和是否有犯罪前科,一般不考虑未成年被告人的最低年龄。这种标准实质上是基于对少年犯在未成年人法院体系内矫正的可能性之大小的估计,矫正可能性大的应当留在未成年人法院体系内,反之,则可以

---

① 我国《民法典》第一千零七十七条规定:自婚姻登记机关收到离婚登记申请之日起三十日内,任何一方不愿意离婚的,可以向婚姻登记机关撤回离婚登记申请。前款规定期限届满后三十日内,双方应当亲自到婚姻登记机关申请发给离婚证;未申请的,视为撤回离婚登记申请。

交由成年人司法体系处理①，这个过程即为 waiver of jurisdiction。

综上，应将该术语中暗含的适用对象翻译出来以求更符合源语的内涵，所以应将 waiver of jurisdiction 翻译为"放弃未成年人犯罪的司法管辖权"。

waiver of tort

waiver of tort 是否可以理解为其字面意思"放弃侵权行为"呢？首先还是应了解其源语释义。

《布莱克法律词典》对 waiver of tort 的定义为：The election to sue in quasi-contract to recover the defendant's unjust benefit, instead of suing in tort to recover damages. 指某人受到侵权后享有选择救济方式的权利，并且选择以准合同（quasi-contract）起诉，以要求被告返还不当得利，而不是在侵权中起诉以获得损害赔偿。根据《元照英美法词典》的补充解释也可知，在此情况下，侵权之诉并未消灭。实际上，这两种救济方式是"无之则不然"（sine qua non）的关系，原告均应证明侵权行为之存在。

《布莱克法律词典》为了进一步解释清楚 waiver of tort 的含义，还将其与 waive the tort② 进行了比较。通过比较发现无论采取侵权损害赔偿或是不当得利返还的补救方式，仍然必须证明侵权行为的存在。若翻译成"放弃侵权行为"，这个表述便容易产生歧义。若一开始就"放弃侵权行为"，或在还未产生侵权效力之前就"放弃侵权行为"，那么此处"侵权行为"便不是侵权行为。既然没有损害原告的利益，被告也没有不当得利（unjust benefit），"侵权行为"也就不存在了，因此不符合 waiver of tort 的定义。

---

① 具体说来，未成年人案件由成人法庭审判的有四种情况：一是强制性司法管辖权放弃或者说法定排除。按照 38 个州的法律规定，对有些特定类型的案件，通常是暴力重罪案件，少年法院必须移交给成人法庭进行审判。二是裁量性司法管辖权放弃。有 45 个州可以由少年法院法官运用裁量性司法管辖权，放弃对少年案件的管辖。三是检察官裁量向成人法庭起诉的。15 个州可以由检察官裁量直接向成人法庭提起诉讼，检察官向成人法庭起诉的，少年法院失去管辖权。四是推定放弃管辖权。有 15 个州，某些案件可被作为推定放弃，即出现某种情形时推定少年法院放弃管辖权；一旦成立推定放弃，未成年人必须说明理由否定推定，才能避免移交成人法庭。

② A person upon whom a tort has been committed and who brings an action for the benefits received by the tortfeasor is sometimes said to "waive the tort." (Restatement of restitution, 1937: 525) "Waiver of tort" is a misnomer. A party only waives a tort in the sense that he elects to sue in quasi-contract to recover the defendant's unjust benefit rather than to sue in tort to recover damages; he has a choice of alternative remedies. But the tort is not extinguished. Indeed it is said that it is a sine qua non of both remedies that he should establish that a tort has been committed. (The Law of Restitution, 1986: 605) waiver of tort 最早出现在 1776 年 Hambly v. Trott (1776)一案中,主审法官曼斯菲尔德勋爵(Lord Mansfield)为受侵害人开辟了这样一条补偿途径,以期能规避侵权诉讼中的免责条款,为受侵害人的利益提供合法保护。即受侵害人通过"认可"侵权行为的合法性,而将案件的诉由从不法行为转变为对允诺的不履行,适用"简约之诉(assumpsit)",①要求侵权人归还通过不法行为获得的利益。这种做法后来在英国法中被称为 waiver of tort。由此可见,这是对因违反合同或允诺而取得的不正当利益的返还,而不再是因侵权行为对受侵害人造成伤害的损害赔偿,是一种有别于传统损害赔偿的救济方式。

综上,通过分析 waiver of tort 的定义发现该定义强调的是放弃对侵权行为的起诉,而提起要求恢复原状的诉讼(即返还不正当获利)。② 由于英国法中认为不可为同一损失收取双重救济,双重违法行为在法律上的效果也是一个违法行为,只能获得一次满足。因此,在因侵权行为而获利的案件中,如果同一个事实既符合侵权又符合准契约(quasi-contract)的构成要件时,受侵害人无需再大费周章地认可被告的侵权行为而拟制出一个允诺来请求返还获利,完全可以自由选择依据不法行为提起损害赔偿或是直接依据不当得利的事实要求返还不当得利。如果选择了后者,根据同一个违法行为不能获得两次救济的原则,也就意味着自然放弃了侵权的主张。因此,将 waiver the tort 译为"放弃侵权之诉"比较合适。如果翻译为"放弃侵权行为",会让人误以为其行为的发起者是侵害人,即被告人停止他对受侵害人即原告人的侵权行为,但显然这种解读是错误的。因为就 waiver of tort 的定义来看,其行为发起人很明显是原告。另外"放弃侵

---

① Waiver of tort 产生的历史背景是"简约之诉(assumpsit)"的发展。assumpsit 的英美法定义是:An express or implied promise, not under seal, by which one person undertakes to do some act or pay something to another (an assumpsit to pay a debt). (Garner,2009:133)基于英国法早期违约即为欺诈的理念,简约之诉的基础是在受允诺人基于相信允诺人的允诺,而允诺人不适当的履行(mis-feasance)侵权了受允诺人的人身或财产,因此违约行为也可以被视为是一种不法行为,通过简约之诉要求允诺人承担侵权的损害赔偿责任(tort liability)。简约之诉不断发展,开创了现代英国法上准契约(quasi-contract)的法律制度。简约之诉不仅可以适用请求侵权损害赔偿的救济方式,还可以适用请求利益返还,即英国后来发展起来的不当得利(unjust benefit)返还的救济方式。

② 举个例子,被告侵占原告的货物,原本市场价值 1 万元,为他使用或者出售,此时市场价格上涨,出售所得 2 万元。如果原告凭借侵占他人财产行为起诉被告,他作为赔偿所能得到的只是侵占货物行为之时的货物的价值,即 1 万元;但是如果他放弃对侵权行为的起诉,把被告视为曾作为他的受托人出售了货物,因此可以凭借准契约追回出售所取得的利润,即 2 万元全部取回。而如果货物的市场价格下降,他仍然可以凭借侵权起诉,得到出售这些货物时的价值,即原本的 1 万元。

权行为"也会让人误以为是侵权人侵权行为的责任承担方式。根据我国《民法典》侵权责任编的相关规定,侵权责任承担的方式有:停止侵害、排除妨碍、消除危险、返还财产、恢复原状、赔偿损失、赔礼道歉、消除影响、恢复名誉。而在实施侵权行为过程中,从开始侵权行为,到中止侵权行为,再到终止侵权行为,都没有"放弃侵权行为"这种说法。

warrantless arrest 与 warrantless search

这两个术语容易被分别翻译为"非法搜查"和"非法逮捕",但是仔细考究该术语的源语释义以及适用情景发现,这两个法律术语中 warrantless 是否含"非法/非正当的"之意要视情况而定。

《布莱克法律词典》对 warrantless arrest 的定义是:A legal arrest, without a warrant, based on probable cause of a felony, or for a misdemeanor committed in a police officer's presence. 也称作 arrest without a warrant。指不需持有逮捕令而逮捕某人,即基于重罪或有警察在场的轻罪,在没有逮捕令的情况下进行的合法逮捕。根据《元照英美法词典》对该词条补充的解释可知:以上是美国适用 warrantless arrest 的情境。在英国,任何人有权对犯有或正在实施可捕罪(arrestable offence)或有合理根据怀疑其犯有或正在实施可捕罪的任何人进行 warrantless arrest。由此可知,在特定情境下,warrantless arrest 属于 legal arrest,因此结合上述释义,warrantless arrest 应翻译为"无证逮捕"。

《布莱克法律词典》对 warrantless search 的定义是:A search conducted without obtaining a proper warrant. Warrantless searches are permissible under exigent circumstances or when conducted incident to an arrest. 指未获得正当搜查令而进行的搜查。在紧急情况下,或在发生逮捕事件时,允许进行无搜查令的搜查。因此,warrantless search 应翻译为"无证搜查"。在美国,无证搜查受到《美国宪法第四修正案》相关规定的限制[①]。

---

① "In the United States, warrantless searches are restricted under the Fourth Amendment to the United States Constitution, part of the Bill of Rights, which states. The right of the people to be secure in their persons, houses, papers, and effects, against unreasonable searches and seizures, shall not be violated, and no Warrants shall issue, but upon probable cause, supported by oath or affirmation, and particularly describing the place to be searched, and the persons or things to be seized." 参见 https://en.wikipedia.org/wiki/Warrantless_searches_in_the_United_States。

with average

通过查阅资料①得知 with average 的释义为：A marine insurance term meaning that a shipment is protected from partial damage whenever the damage exceeds 3 percent (or some other percentage). If the ship is involved in a major catastrophe, such as a collision, fire or stranding, the minimum percentage requirement is waived and the insurance company pays for all of the damage. 由此可知这是海上保险术语，同 with particular average，意思是当货物的部分损坏超过3%（或其他百分比）时，货物将受到保护，免受部分损坏。如果船舶发生重大灾难，如碰撞、火灾或搁浅，则免除最低百分比要求，保险公司赔偿所有损失。

该术语的正确译文为"水渍险"，是海洋运输保险的一种。水渍险又称"单独海损险"（简称 WA 或 WPA）。这里的"海损"指自然灾害及意外事故导致货物被水淹没，引起货物的损失。水渍险负责被保险货物由于恶劣气候、雷电、海啸、地震、洪水等自然灾害所造成的部分损失。具体来说还分为是海水浸渍还是雨水浸渍。所以，水渍险是对海洋运输中自然灾害和意外事故而导致的货物被水淹没，引起货物损失的一种保护措施。

withdrawal（in criminal law）

withdrawal 常被译为"撤回/取钱"，但是在刑法中，withdrawal 的含义却并非如此。比如在 withdrawal from a crime 中，若译为"撤回犯罪"，显然不太能让读者理解。

在 legal-dictionary（online）中，withdrawal 的一个定义为：in criminal law, leaving a conspiracy to commit a crime before the actual crime is committed, which is similar to "renunciation". If the withdrawal before any overt criminal act the withdrawer may escape prosecution. 根据以上英文解释可知 withdrawal 是 stop committing crime，可理解为"犯罪中止"。

我国《刑法》第二十四条第一款界定了"犯罪中止"的概念："在犯罪过程中，自动放弃犯罪或者自动有效地防止犯罪结果发生的，是犯罪中止。"犯罪中止存在两种情况，一是在犯罪预备阶段或者在实行行为还没有实行终了的情况下，自

---

① https://www.tradeport.org/index.php/library/trade-units-and-terms? id=150

动放弃犯罪;二是在实行行为实行终了的情况下,自动有效地防止犯罪结果的发生。作为故意犯罪的未完成形态的犯罪中止,是指行为人已经开始实施犯罪而又中止了犯罪的形态。犯罪中止形态与犯罪中止行为本身具有密切关系:没有中止行为就不可能有犯罪中止的形态,中止行为是犯罪中止形态的决定性原因。犯罪中止形态与中止行为本身又具有区别:中止行为本身不是犯罪,而是刑法所鼓励的行为;犯罪中止形态则是犯罪的状态,应当负刑事责任。换言之,中止行为之前的行为属于犯罪行为,是行为人应当负刑事责任的事实根据,中止行为本身属于刑法所鼓励的行为,是应当免除或者减轻处罚的根据。

基于中英文语境下对该术语的定义比较,在刑法中将 withdrawal 翻译为"犯罪中止"更为合适。

words of purchase

如果单从字面意思理解该术语,很容易将其译为"购买用语",但其实这个术语和购买毫无关系。

《布莱克法律词典》对该术语的定义是:Language in a deed or will designating the persons who are to receive the grant. For example, the phrase "to A for life with a remainder to her heirs" creates a life estate in A and a remainder in A's heirs. 即指定将来谁通过契约或遗嘱获得地产的话语。例如,"由甲终身享有地产且剩余地产权(remainder)由其继承人享有",这句话即 words of purchase,通过这句话使得甲终身享有地产,且甲的继承人享有剩余地产权(remainder)。根据 USlegal 网站上给出的范例,可以帮助理解该术语使用的语境①。words of purchase 应该是一种统称,指的是在财产受让没有前提条件或限制条件时表明受让人的词句。可概括译为"财产转让中表明受让人的词句"。

可以进一步了解和 words of purchase 一起出现的另一个术语 words of

---

① A word of purchase is a language seen in a will which refers to the persons who are to receive the grant under the will. For instance, the word "children", in its primary or natural sense, is always a word of purchase, and not a word of limitation; and the word "issue" is very frequently a word of purchase also. Similarly, when the ancestor by any gift or conveyance takes an estate of freehold, and in the same gift or conveyance an estate is limited, either moderately or immediately to his heirs in fee or in tail, "the heirs" are words of limitation of the estate and not words of purchase.

limitation，以做区分。《布莱克法律词典》对 words of limitation 的定义是：Language in a conveying instrument—often nonliteral language—describing the extent or quality of an estate. For example, under long-standing principles of property law, the phrase "to A and her heirs" creates a fee simple in A but gives nothing to A's heirs. 指地产权转让证书或遗嘱中影响地产权存续期间的用语。如规定将地产转让给甲和其继承人，其中"和其继承人"等词就是 words of limitation，它表示甲取得的是非限嗣继承地产权（estate in fee-simple）。通过分析定义，可以发现 words of limitation 和 words of purchase 不同之处在于：words of limitation 指的是对财产转让的限制，即给财产转让增加了一个附加条件。通过了解其出现的语境①可知，words of limitation 和 words of purchase 一样，也是一个统称，但它指的是财产转让中的附加条件，这个附加条件可以是对财产转让合同的有效时间的限制，也可以是对接受财产的人的限制。words of limitation 的含义和我国《合同法》（现已废止）中第四十五条②和第四十六条③的"附生效条件""附生效期限"的含义相近。我国《民法典》第一百五十八条规定：民事法律行为可以附条件，但是根据其性质不得附条件的除外。附生效条件的民事法律行为，自条件成就时生效。附解除条件的民事法律行为，自条件成就时失效。因此，可以把 words of limitation 译为"财产转让中的限制条件"。

yardstick theory

yardstick theory 是美国反垄断法中的一个术语，有人将其译为"标尺比较法"。想要准确严谨地翻译该术语，首先要清楚它在美国法中的具体含义。

《布莱克法律词典》对 yardstick theory 的定义是：antitrust. A method of determining damages for lost profits (and sometimes overcharges) whereby a

---

① Land given "to X and his heirs", the words of limitation are "and his heirs", indicating X's quantum of interest, but giving nothing to heirs by direct gift. Strict words of limitation must be used to create a fee tail. Land given "to X and his heirs", the words of limitation are "and his heirs", indicating X's quantum of interest, but giving nothing to heirs by direct gift. Strict words of limitation must be used to create a fee tail.
② 第四十五条规定：当事人对合同的效力可以约定附条件。附生效条件的合同，自条件成就时生效。附解除条件的合同，自条件成就时失效。
③ 第四十六条：当事人对合同的效力可以约定附期限。附生效期限的合同，自期限届至时生效。附终止期限的合同，自期限届满时失效。

corporate plaintiff identifies a company similar to the plaintiff but without the impact of the antitrust violation. 由此可知 yardstick theory 是美国反垄断法中一种确定原告在垄断侵害期间所丧失之应得利益(有时是超过支付额)的方法。该方法将与原告经济状况类似但未受到垄断侵害的公司作为参照的"标尺",原告在垄断侵害期间遭受损失即为"标尺"(未受到垄断侵害)的经济状况与原告(受到垄断侵害)经济状况之间的差额。该方法具有一定的局限性,主要适用于发生在地区性同源市场下的垄断侵害,如果范围过大,可能不存在近似的市场条件下的市场主体作为比较。

将 yardstick theory 译为"标尺比较法"不妥,原因有二。一是因为 yardstick theory 作为一种美国反垄断法独有而中国法律体系中缺失的概念,直接翻译为"标尺比较法"容易使人感到一头雾水,不能直接把握该术语的确切含义;二是因为"标尺比较法"会使人联想到更加广为人知的管理学领域概念"标尺竞争"(yardstick competition),因而造成不必要的误解。

yardstick theory,before-and-after theory 以及 market-share theory 三者是处于相同级别上的概念,即同为确定垄断侵害致损金额的三种不同方法,后两者的一般译法为"前后比较法"和"市场份额法"。"前后比较法"是将受损人在垄断侵害发生前或侵害结束后的经济状况与受到侵害期间的经济状况作比较(杨蓉,2015:98—99)[①]。"市场份额法",顾名思义指的是根据原告因垄断侵害而丧失的市场份额来计算损失的方法(杨蓉,2015:99)。三者综合来看,所谓的"标尺比较法"的参照系是其他市场主体,而"前后比较法"的参照系是以受损人自身的时间轴为前提的,二者的主要差别在于参照系的不同;而"市场份额法"是一种独立的计算方法,与前两者使用的参照系无关。三者在实际运用过程中是相辅相成的关系,经常是以所谓的"标尺比较法"为主,辅以"前后比较法",用来强调计算金额的真实性,当无法找到合适"标尺"或缺乏前后比较的时间轴时,就可以独立使用"市场份额法"进行计算。

根据《中华人民共和国反垄断法》第六十条规定,经营者实施垄断行为,给他人造成损失的,依法承担民事责任。但在反垄断民事损害赔偿中,据以计算损失的价格包括了时间和市场多种不可重置的历史因素,要准确界定原告的损失是

---

① 杨蓉.美国垄断致损赔偿责任制度研究[D].湖南大学,2015.

否是因为垄断行为导致的,难度很大(李志刚、徐式媛,2011:77)①。在中国法律体系中暂时没有一套系统性的理论指导垄断损害的计算,实际案例中使用的计算方法也较为单一。

鉴于国内目前在垄断侵害损失计算方面并未形成统一的理论,对某些美国反垄断法中的法律术语的翻译也未形成统一标准,在此拟对 yardstick theory 进行意译,译作"相似市场主体比较法",和"前后比较法"(before-and-after theory)形成概念上的对比,从而避免读者产生错误联想或者不知所云。

Year-and-a-day Rule

《布莱克法律词典》对该术语的定义是:Criminal law. The common-law principle that an act causing death is not homicide if the death occurs more than a year and a day after the act was committed. 拉丁语为 annus et dies。由此可知这是适用于刑事案件中的规则。具体指:在普通法上,因死亡提起的诉讼必须在死者死后一年零一天内提出。根据《元照英美法词典》的解释也可知:除非被害人在被告人的不法行为发生之日起一年零一天内死去,被害人的死亡不能归责于被告人。这是因为当时缺乏必要的医疗手段,在经历了如此长的时间后,无法精确地确定死亡的原因,也无法查明是否是其他外来原因导致被害人死亡。但现在随着医学发展,该规则似乎已经过时而应当舍弃。在美国,有些司法管辖区已通过立法或司法判例舍弃,但大多数司法管辖区尚保留。

通常,在适用该规则时要确定:时间的长度是比一年多一天,即从足足一年时间的第二天开始算起。在我国也有相似的法律规定,例如:签订的劳动、工作合同,驾驶执照上会有一年期满的说法。

综上,可将该短语翻译为"满一年规则",从而突出"一年期满"这个特点。

years of discretion

《布莱克法律词典》对 discretion 的定义有:1. Wise conduct and management; cautious discernment; prudence. 2. Individual judgment; the power of free decision-making. 3. Criminal & tort law. The capacity to

---

① 李志刚,徐式媛. 反垄断法上的民事赔偿责任[J]. 人民司法,2011(07):76-82.

distinguish between right and wrong, sufficient to make a person responsible for his or her own actions. 4. A public official's power or right to act in certain circumstances according to personal judgment and conscience, often in an official or representative capacity. 即 1. 明智的行为和管理；谨慎的洞察力；谨慎；2. 个人判断；自由决策的能力。3. 刑法和侵权法中：行为人若具有辨别正确和错误、合法和非法、明智和愚蠢的能力，就应对自己的行为负完全责任；4. 指公务人员根据授权法的规定，在特定的环境下根据自己的判断和良心执行公务，不受任何他人干涉或控制的权力或权利。

根据柯林斯在线词典可知 years of discretion 与 age of discretion 同义，具体含义为：the age at which a person becomes legally responsible for certain acts and competent to exercise certain powers①。指一个人对某些行为负有法律责任并有能力行使某些权力的年龄。由此可见此处的 discretion 符合其定义中的第二和第三层含义。

我国类似的表述有"刑事责任年龄"②，"民事行为年龄"③。由此可见，我国法律语境中的"责任年龄"与 years of discretion 都是对某人到了某个年龄而应负法律责任或可以为某行为而做出的年龄规定。因此可以将该术语翻译为"责任或行为年龄"。

yellow knight

yellow knight 是一个经济领域中与企业并购相关的术语，有人将其直译为"黄色骑士"，但这种翻译形在神散，仅仅译出了字面的意思。更重要的是，在汉

---

① https://www.collinsdictionary.com/dictionary/english/age-of-discretion
② 比如我国《刑法》第十七条规定：已满十六周岁的人犯罪，应当负刑事责任。已满十四周岁不满十六周岁的人，犯故意杀人、故意伤害致人重伤或者死亡、强奸、抢劫、贩卖毒品、放火、爆炸、投放危险物质罪的，应当负刑事责任。已满十四周岁不满十八周岁的人犯罪，应当从轻或者减轻处罚。因不满十六周岁不予刑事处罚的，责令其父母或者监护人加以管教；在必要的时候，依法进行专门矫治教育。
③ 根据《民法典》相关规定，十八周岁以上的成年人，以自己的劳动收入为主要生活来源的十六周岁以上的未成年人，视为完全民事行为能力人。可以独立实施民事法律行为。八周岁以上的未成年人、不能完全辨认自己行为的成年人为限制民事行为能力人。实施民事法律行为由其法定代理人代理或者经其法定代理人同意、追认；但是，可以独立实施纯获利益的民事法律行为或者与其智力、精神健康状况相适应的民事法律行为。不满八周岁的未成年人、不能辨认自己行为的成年人、不能辨认自己行为的八周岁以上的未成年人，为无民事行为能力人。由其法定代理人代理实施民事法律行为。

语语境下"黄色骑士"并不是一种约定俗成的说法,不具备引申义,不能被人所理解,所以将 yellow knight 译为"黄色骑士"不可取。要想使译文忠实于原文,就要清楚该术语在源语语境下的具体内涵。

Black's Law Dictionary Free Online Legal Dictionary 2nd Ed. 对 yellow knight 给出的定义是:Corporation with plans to takeover a company in hostile manner①。首先,我们可以看到定义中出现了 takeover 和 hostile 两个关键词,由此可以联想到 hostile takeover,《布莱克法律词典》给出的定义是:A takeover that is resisted by the target corporation. 即受到目标公司抵制的收购行为。其次,在汉语语境下有"敌意收购"一词,"上市公司敌意收购,也称非合意收购或恶意收购,是指并购方在目标公司管理层对并购意图不明确或对并购行为持反对态度的情况下,对目标公司强行进行的并购(中国证券监督管理委员会,2009:5)②。可见 hostile takeover 一词与敌意收购的内涵是重叠的。根据以上两点可以得出结论:yellow knight 指代意图敌意收购目标公司的某家公司。

明确类似术语的含义有助于对 yellow knight 的理解和翻译。在 hostile takeover(敌意收购)的相关术语中,black knight 以及 white knight 和 yellow knight 构词方式相似。black knight 指 a raider that makes a bid unwelcome by management③"。《布莱克法律词典》对 white knight 的定义是:A person or corporation that rescue the target of an unfriendly corporate takeover, esp. by acquiring a controlling interest in the target corporation or by making a competing tender offer. 前者是在目标公司不愿意的情况下,通过使用各种策略迫使目标公司同意收购的袭击者;而后者则是和袭击者竞争、通过提出更优惠的条件,收购目标企业的友好企业。

综合分析 yellow knight 的具体内涵,可将 yellow knight 译作"计划敌意收购的公司"。

---

① Black's Law Dictionary Free Online Legal Dictionary 2nd Ed. What is YELLOW KNIGHT? [EB/OL]. https://thelawdictionary.org/yellow-knight/.
② 中国证券监督管理委员会. 中国上市公司并购重组发展报告[Z]. 中国经济出版社,2009.
③ Black's Law Dictionary Free Online Legal Dictionary 2nd Ed. What is BLACK KNIGHT? [EB/OL]. https://thelawdictionary.org/black-knight/.

yellow sheets

yellow sheets 的源语释义①为：A daily listing of bid and ask price quotes for over-the-counter bonds. Yellow Sheets are a product of the National Quotation Bureau. 指美国全国报价局（National Quotation Bureau）出版的一种黄色小册子，意思为场外交易债券的日常报表。

通过查阅资料②进一步了解到：与 yellow sheets 相对的有 pink sheets，之所以如此称呼是因为两个不同股权市场所采用的打印纸的颜色不同，股票报价打印在粉色纸上，而债券价格则在黄色纸上，为了方便区分直接以颜色来命名。

国内的证券市场不常使用这个术语，正因为它的涵义是建立在美国独特的历史和市场行情上的，所以在解释或翻译该术语的时候应更加注重受众的理解程度。因此，在翻译时可以省略颜色给它的最初定义，而翻译为"债券报价册"。

yield net

根据 USLegal 网站的释义③，yield net 又称 net yield，具体指：the rate of return of profit or loss on an investment or security after deducting all appropriate loss reserves and expenses such as commissions, costs of purchase, and taxes. Municipal bonds are quoted on a net yield basis. With respect to bonds, it means the rate of return after taking into account the purchase price, the coupon rate, and number of years to maturity. 即扣除所有损失准备金和费用（如佣金、购买成本和税费）后得到的投资或证券的利润或亏损回报率。市政债券以 net yield 为基础报价。就债券而言，它是指在考虑购买价格、票面利率和到期年数后的回报率。

---

① https://businessdictionary.info/definition/yellow-sheets/
② A United States bulletin that provides updated bid and ask prices as well as other information on over-the-counter (OTC) corporate bonds (also called "corporate"). Companies issue corporate bonds to raise money for capital expenditures, operations and acquisitions. Similar to the Pink Sheets that track non-exchange-traded OTC micro-cap stocks, the yellow sheets are a key source of information for investors who follow OTC bonds or fixed income securities. The yellow sheets also provide a list of brokerages that make a market in the particular bonds. Today's investors can still receive hard copies of the yellow sheets. However, the information is also available in electronic form. 参见 https://www.financereference.com/yellow-sheets/.
③ https://definitions.uslegal.com/n/net-yield/

yield 这个词本身有收益、利益的意思，与 net yield 相似的有 gross yield，但是两者又有不同：Gross yield is everything before expenses. It is calculated as a percentage based on the property's cost or market value divided by the income generated by the property.①而 Net yield is everything after expenses. It takes into account all the fees and expenses associated with owning a property. As such, it is a far more accurate way of calculating actual yield. It is also much harder to calculate as most costs are variable.②两者的主要差别在于是否刨除成本的费用，所以在翻译的时候，都翻译为"净收益"是不准确的，由于 net yield 是去除以后的，所以它所得的收益结果更为纯净，因此可以将 yield net 或 net yield 翻译为"实际净收益"；而 gross yield 可以翻译为"毛收益"。

young offender

判断 young offender 译为"青年违法者"或"青年犯"是否妥当，首先还是应了解其源语释义。

根据《布莱克法律词典》，young offender 与 youthful offender 同义，有两层含义：

1. A person in late adolescence or early adulthood who has been convicted of a crime. A youthful offender is often eligible for special programs not available to older offenders, including community supervision, the successful completion of which may lead to erasing the conviction from the offender's record. 指在青春期晚期或成年早期被判有罪的人。这类罪犯通常有资格获得成年罪犯无法获得的特殊项目，比如社区监督，如表现良好，即可消除其犯罪记录。美国联邦和各州的法律确定青年违法者的身份旨在通过在监狱中为其提供就业、教育、咨询等服务，防止他们接触其他年长且有经验的罪犯，以便使其成功地回归社会。

2. A minor who is guilty of criminal behavior, usu. punishable by special

---

① https://www.urban.com.au/expert-insights/investing/59646-net-yield-gross-yield-what-s-the-difference

② https://www.urban.com.au/expert-insights/investing/59646-net-yield-gross-yield-what-s-the-difference laws not pertaining to adults. 指犯有犯罪行为的未成年人，通常受到与成年人不同的特别法律惩罚。根据《元照英美法词典》补充的解释可知，该术语指未达到特定年龄的违反刑事法律或有不良行为的未成年人，需要对其治疗、改造、管理。在美国，某些州的法律将有下列行为的少年儿童视为有不良行为者：1.违反联邦或州的法律，或违反市政当局或其他地方性法规；2.无正当理由离家出走或离开其合法的、当局认可的住所地；3.脱离父母或其他监护人监护的；4.有下流或不道德行为的；5.经常逃学或在校期间屡次公开违反校规校纪的；6.违反法庭命令的。

由此可见，第一层含义强调"已被定罪"，应将其译为"未成年犯"；而第二层含义中强调其"犯有不法行为"，应译为"未成年违法者"。

zipper clause

zipper clause 是美国合同法术语，目前对 zipper clause 的汉译主要有三个："拉链条款""完全同意条款"和"不能重开谈判条款"。要判断这三个译文是否准确，首先应当了解该法律术语在英语语境下的涵义。

《布莱克法律词典》对 zipper clause 的定义是：A contractual provision that operates both as an integration clause and as a no oral-modification clause. 通过查阅更详细的释义①得知：联邦劳动法要求劳资双方代表就工资、工作时间以及其他条款等问题进行磋商或谈判。在加州，公共部门的雇主应当遵循诚信善意的原则进行讨价还价或磋商。集体谈判是雇主和工会代表之间的谈判过程，目的是达成协议，规范工作条件。zipper clause 是在集体谈判协议中所列的条款，强调在书面合同中达成的协议即为双方对此事件的完整的协议，任何合同规定内的内容都不算做协议内容。在合同中加入此类条款通常是为了防止协议双方就合同中未包括的事项再行协商，也就意味着免除了协议双方后续的再协商义务。

---

① A zipper clause is a term in an employment agreement that "purports to close out bargaining during the contract term and to make the written contract the exclusive statement of the parties' rights and obligations." It is the provision included in collective bargaining agreements to emphasize that the written document contains the complete agreement negotiated by the parties to it, and that nothing that is excluded is agreed to unless it is put into writing, is signed by all parties, and is attached to the main agreement. 参见 https://encyclopedia.lexroll.com/encyclopedia/zipper-clause/。

zipper clause 有两类。一类是完整或完全同意条款,这种类型的条款表示凡合同所涉及的事项,无论是在合同协商期间或合同签署时已经协商过的事项,还是虽未协商过但在代表权利范围内的任何其他事项,双方均放弃要求对其进行再谈判或协商的权利。雇员或工会都不能在含有该条款的合同的有效期内要求对该合同进行重新谈判。由于雇员和工会放弃了这项权利,雇主则可变更合同中的事项,规定可进行谈判的事项除外。这类条款并不常见,因为大部分雇员都不会同意。另一类比较常见的 zipper clause 是在劳资协议和谈判中被撤销的问题上终止谈判的条款。这类条款并没有放弃就合同中未涉及的事项进行谈判的权利。换句话说,雇主和工会将被要求就不包括在当前合同中的讨价还价的强制性问题进行谈判。从 zipper clause 目前已有的汉译来看,"完全同意条款"和"不能重开谈判条款"均含有其所表达的意思,前者更趋向于第一类,而后者更趋向于第二类,如何更精准地对该术语进行翻译,可参考与该术语相关的其他术语。

　　与 zipper clause 相似的一个术语为 merger clause。确切地说,zipper clause 是 merger clause 的一种,运用于雇佣合同中,通常情况下二者意思相同。merger clause 是当事人在书面合同中约定的表明其书面合同即为当事人的完整的意思表示,该书面协议是完整的,排除了用此前或同时的证据来补充、修改或对抗书面合同的可能性,为双方的交易关系提供确定性和可预见性,以确保交易安全,减少交易费用。其定义为:"一种合同条款,该条款声明合同体现了双方当事人全部和最终的协议且取代了所有与合同标的有关的非正式和口头协定"①。

　　由此看来,与 merger clause 意思相同,对于 zipper clause 更常见的理解是该条款表示双方放弃对合同涉及的事项,即在谈判或签署时已商讨过的事项,申请重开谈判的权利,不能以此前或同时的证据来补充、修改或对抗当事人之间的书面协议,该书面协议即为双方意思表示的全部内容,则译为"不能重新谈判条款"更为合适,其中的"重新谈判"表示当事人此前已对某事项协商过,任何一方

---

① 根据《布莱克法律词典》(Black's Law Dictionary, 9th Edition, p. 908) merger clause 也称作 integration clause,其定义为: A contractual provision stating that the contract represents the parties' complete and final agreement and supersedes all informal understandings and oral agreements relating to the subject matter of the contract.

不得再以任何证据来对该事项申请重新谈判。而"完全同意条款"虽体现了该合同为当事人全部的意思表示,但也在一定程度上表明双方对合同未涉及的事项完全同意。因此,应用更广的 zipper clause 翻译为"禁止重新谈判条款"更为合理。

附录一 常见美国法引证缩写

Abbreviation	Title	Contents
A., A. 2d	*Atlantic Reporter*, 1st and 2nd series	cases from Connecticut, Delaware, District of Columbia, Maine, Maryland, New Hampshire, New Jersey, Pennsylvania, Rhode Island, Vermont
A. L. R., A. L. R. 2d, A. L. R. 3d, A. L. R. 4th, A. L. R. 5th, A. L. R. Fed.	*American Law Reports*, 1st, 2nd, 3rd, 4th, 5th, Federal series	cases from Connecticut, Delaware, District of Columbia, Maine, Maryland, New Hampshire, New Jersey, Pennsylvania, Rhode Island, Vermont
Am. Jur. 2d	*American Jurisprudence*, Second	encyclopedia
B. R.	*United States Bankruptcy Reporter*	United States Bankruptcy Courts cases

续表

Abbreviation	Title	Contents
C. F. R.	*Code of Federal Regulations*	federal regulations arranged by subject
Cal. Rptr., Cal. Rptr. 2d	*California Reporter*, 1st and 2nd series	cases from California Supreme Court; California Court of Appeal; and California Superior Court, Appellate Dept.
C. J. S.	*Corpus Juris Secundum*	encyclopedia
Ct. Int'l Trade or Ct. Intl. Trade	*Court of International Trade Reports*	cases from the United States Court of International Trade
F., F. 2d, F. 3d	*Federal Reporter*, 1st, 2nd, and 3rd series	cases from all United States Courts of Appeals
F. App'x	*Federal Appendix* (*Bluebook* citations)	"unpublished" cases from all United States Courts of Appeals
F. Supp., F. Supp. 2d	*Federal Supplement*, 1st and 2nd series	cases from all United States District Courts
F. R. D.	*Federal Rules Decisions*	rulings involving procedural rules, from all United States District Courts
Fed. Appx.	*Federal Appendix* (*ALWD Manual* citations)	"unpublished" cases from all United States Courts of Appeals
Fed. Cl.	*Federal Claims Reporter*	cases from the United States Court of Federal Claims
Fed. R. Civ. P.	*Federal Rules of Civil Procedure*	court rules
Fed. R. Crim. P.	*Federal Rules of Criminal Procedure*	court rules

续表

Abbreviation	Title	Contents
Fed. R. Evid.	*Federal Rules of Evidence*	court rules
Fed. Reg.	*Federal Register*	federal regulations by date
ILCS	*Illinois Compiled Statutes*	Illinois statutes arranged by subject
Ill., Ill. 2d	*Illinois Reports*, 1st and 2nd series	Illinois Supreme Court cases
Ill. Admin. Code	*Illinois Administrative Code*	Illinois regulations arranged by subject
Ill. App., Ill. App. 2d, Ill. App. 3d	*Illinois Appellate Court Reports*, 1st, 2nd, and 3rd series	Illinois Appellate Court cases
Ill. Cl.	*Illinois Court of Claims Reports*	Illinois Court of Claims cases
Ill. Comp. Stat.	*Illinois Compiled Statutes*	Illinois statutes arranged by subject
Ill. Comp. Stat. Ann.	*West's Smith-Hurd Illinois Compiled Statutes Annotated*	Illinois statutes arranged by subject
Ill. Dec.	*West's Illinois Decisions*	cases from Illinois Supreme Court and Illinois Appellate Court
Ill. Laws	*Laws of Illinois*	Illinois statutes by date
Ill. Reg.	*Illinois Register*	Illinois regulations by date
Ill. Rev. Stat.	*Illinois Revised Statutes*	Illinois statutes arranged by subject (previous code)
L. Ed., L. Ed. 2d	*United States Supreme Court Reports, Lawyers' Edition*, 1st and 2nd series	United States Supreme Court cases

Abbreviation	Title	Contents
M. J.	*West's Military Justice Reporter*	cases from the United States Court of Appeals for the Armed Forces and Military Service Courts of Criminal Appeals
N. E., N. E. 2d	*North Eastern Reporter*, 1st and 2nd series	cases from Illinois, Indiana, Massachusetts, New York, Ohio
N. W., N. W. 2d	*North Western Reporter*, 1st and 2nd series	cases from Iowa, Michigan, Minnesota, Nebraska, North Dakota, South Dakota, Wisconsin
N. Y. S., N. Y. S. 2d	*New York Supplement*, 1st and 2nd series	cases from New York Court of Appeals and New York Supreme Court, Appellate Division
P., P. 2d	*Pacific Reporter*, 1st and 2nd series	cases from Alaska, Arizona, California, Colorado, Hawaii, Idaho, Kansas, Montana, Nevada, New Mexico, Oklahoma, Oregon, Utah, Washington, Wyoming
S., S. 2d	*Southern Reporter*, 1st and 2nd series (ALWD Manual citations)	cases from Alabama, Florida, Louisiana, Mississippi
S. Ct.	*Supreme Court Reporter*	United States Supreme Court cases
S. E., S. E. 2d	*South Eastern Reporter*, 1st and 2nd series	cases from Georgia, North Carolina, South Carolina, Virginia, West Virginia
S. W., S. W. 2d, S. W. 3d	*South Western Reporter*, 1st, 2nd, and 3rd series	cases from Arkansas, Kentucky, Missouri, Tennessee, Texas

续表

Abbreviation	Title	Contents
So., So. 2d	*Southern Reporter*, 1st and 2nd series (*Bluebook* citations)	cases from Alabama, Florida, Louisiana, Mississippi
Stat.	*United States Statutes at Large*	federal statutes arranged by date
T. C.	*United States Tax Court Reports*	cases from United States Tax Court
U. S.	*United States Reports*	United States Supreme Court cases
U. S. C.	*United States Code*	federal statutes arranged by subject
U. S. C. A.	*United States Code Annotated*	federal statutes arranged by subject
U. S. C. S.	*United States Code Service*	federal statutes arranged by subject
Vet. App.	*West's Veterans Appeals Reporter*	cases from the United States Court of Appeals for Veterans Claims

附录二　常用法律缩略语

A

A. — Atlantic Reporter (USA)

ABA — American Bar Association

A. B. L. R. — Australian Business Law Review

A. C. — Appeal Cases

ACC — Association of Corporate Counsel

A. J. C. L. — American Journal of Comparative Law

A. J. F. L. — Australian Journal of Family Law

A. J. I. L. — American Journal of International Law

Ala. Admin. Code — Alabama Administrative Code

Ala. Code — Code of Alabama 1975

Alaska Admin. Code — Alaska Administrative Code

Alaska Stat. — Alaska Statutes

A. L. J. — Australian Law Journal

A. L. J. R. — Australian Law Journal Reports

A. L. M. D. — Australian Legal Monthly Digest

A. L. Q. — Arab Law Quarterly

A. L. R. — American Law Reports or Australian Law Reports

A. R. — Alberta Reports (1977—)

A. T. R. — Australian Tax Review

All E. R. — All England Law Reports

All E. R. Rev. — All England Law Reports Annual Review

A. L. R. — American Law Reports

A. L. R. Fed. — American Law Reports, Federal

Am. Jur. — American Jurisprudence

Am. Jur. 2d. — American Jurisprudence, 2nd Series

Anglo-Am. L. R. — Anglo-American Law Review

Anor — Another

Arbitration Int. — Arbitration International

Art. — Article

Ariz. Admin. Code — Arizona Administrative Code

Ariz. Admin. Reg. — Arizona Administrative Register

Ariz. Rev. Stat. — Arizona Revised Statutes

Ark. Code — Arkansas Code

Asap — As Soon As Possible

Atty — Attorney

B

B. A. P. — Bankruptcy Appellate Panel

B. C. C. — British Company Law Cases

B. C. L. C. — Butterworths Company Law Cases

B. C. L. R. — British Columbia Law Reports

BFP — Bona Fide Purchaser

B. J. I. B. & F. L. — Butterworths Journal of International Banking & Financial Law

B. L. — Business Lawyer

B. L. R. — Building Law Reports or Business Law Review

BR or B/R — Bankruptcy (Also the Abbreviation for the United States Bankruptcy Courts Reporter, West's Bankruptcy Reporter)

B. T. R. — British Tax Review

B. Y. I. L. — British Yearbook of International Law

Brit. J. Criminol. — British Journal of Criminology

Bracton L. J. — Bracton Law Journal

Build. L. R. — Building Law Reports

Bull. E. C. — Bulletin of the European Communities

C

c. — Chapter (of Act of Parliament)

C. A. — Court of Appeal

CA — Class Action

C. & S. L. J. — Company and Securities Law Journal

Cal. Code — California Code

Cal. Code Reg. — California Code of Regulations

CB — Casebook

CBJ — California Bar Journal

C. B. L. J. — Canadian Business Law Journal

C. B. R. — Canadian Bar Review

CC — Commerce Clause

C-C — Counterclaim

CE — Collateral Estoppel

C. C. L. T. — Canadian Cases on the Law of Torts (1976—)

CCR — California Code of Regulations

C. E. C. — European Community Cases

C. F. I. L. R. — Company Financial and Insolvency Law Review

C. F. R. — Code of Federal Regulations

CFR — Call for Response

C. I. L. J. S. A. — Comparative and International Law Journal of Southern Africa

C. J. Q. — Civil Justice Quarterly

CJS — Corpus Juris Secundum

C. L. — Current Law

CL — Common Law

C. L. & P. — Computer Law and Practice

C. L. B. — Commonwealth Law Bulletin

C. L. E. A. Newsletter — Commonwealth Legal Education Association Newsletter

C. L. J. — Cambridge Law Journal

C. L. P. — Current Legal Problems

C. L. Q. — Civil Justice Quarterly

C. L. R. — Commonwealth Law Reports (Australia)

C. L. S. R. — Computer Law and Security Report

C. L. Y. — Current Law Year Book

C. M. L. R. — Common Market Law Reports

C. M. L. Rev. — Common Market Law Review

CNeg — Contributory Negligence

C. O. D. — Crown Office Digest

Cong. Rec. — Congressional Record

C. P. C. — Carswell's Practice Cases

C. T. & E. P. Q. — Capital Taxes and Estates Planning Quarterly

Ct. Cl. — the United States Court of Federal Claims Reporter

C. T. L. R. — Computer and Telecommunications Law Review

Cambrian L. R. — Cambrian Law Review

Can. Bar J. — Canadian Bar Journal

Can. B. R. — Canadian Bar Review

Ch. — Chancery Division

Co. Law — Company Lawyer

Com. Cas. — Commercial Cases

Com. Jud. J. — Commonwealth Judicial Journal

Comp. & Law — Computers and Law

Comp. L. & P. — Computer Law and Practice

Con. L. R. — Construction Law Reports

Const. L. J. — Construction Law Journal

Conv. (n. s.) — Conveyancer and Property Lawyer (New Series)

Cr. App. R. — Criminal Appeal Reports

Cr. App. R. (S.) — Criminal Appeal Reports (Sentencing)

Csl. — Counsel

Crim. L. J. — Criminal Law Journal

Crim. L. R. — Criminal Law Review

Cx — Constitution

Cx-C — Cross-claim

Cxl — Constitutional

D

Δ (Greek Letter Delta) — Defendant

DA — District Attorney

DAC — Days After Contract

DAR — Driving After Revocation

D. & R. — Decisions and Reports of the European Court of Human Rights

DB — Dead Body

DBD — Death by Drowning

DC — Denied Charges

DC — District Court

D. C. — Divisional Court

Denning L. J. — Denning Law Journal

DL — Driver's License

D. L. R. — Dominion Law Reports

DOA — Date of Accident

DOB — Do Our Best

DOD — Day of Death

DOJ — Decree of Justice

DOP — Division of Prison

DOV — Date of Violation

DP — Due Process

DR — Delayed Remedy

DT — Direct Transfer

DTF — Drug Trance Force

DWD — Drunk While Driving

DWS — Driving While Suspended

E

E. B. L. R. — European Business Law Review

E. C. C. — European Commercial Cases

E. C. L. — European Current Law

E. C. L. R. — European Competition Law Review

E. C. R. — European Court Reports

EE — Employee

E. G. — Estates Gazette

E. G. C. S. — Estates Gazette Case Summaries

E. G. L. R. — Estates Gazette Law Reports

E. H. R. R. — European Human Rights Reports

E. I. P. R. — European Intellectual Property Review

E. J. I. L. — European Journal of International Law

E. L. Q. — Ecology Law Quarterly

E. L. R. — European Law Review

E. M. L. R — Entertainment and Media Law Reports

ER — Employer

E. R. — English Reports

et al. — Latin for "and others".

E. T. M. R. — European Trade Mark Reports

Ent. L. R. — Entertainment Law Review

Eur. Access — European Access

F

F. — Federal reporter (USA)

F. App'x — Federal Appendix

F. Cas. — Federal Cases 1789—1880

F. C. R. — Family Court Reporter or Federal Court Reports (Australia) or Federal Court Reports (Canada)

Fed. Reg. (Sometimes FR) — Federal Register

Fed. R. Bankr. P. — Federal Rules of Bankruptcy Procedure

Fed. R. Civ. P. (Sometimes FRCP) — Federal Rules of Civil Procedure

Fed. R. Crim. P. — Federal Rules of Criminal Procedure

Fed. R. Evid. (Sometimes FRE) — Federal Rules of Evidence

F. L. R. — Family Law Reports or Federal Law Reports (Australia)

F. S. R. — Fleet Street Reports

F Supp. — Federal Supplement (USA)

F. Supp. 2d — Federal Supplement, 2nd Series

F. T. L. R. — Financial Times Law Reports

Fam — Family Division

Fam. Law — Family Law

Fin. L. R. — Financial Law Reports

G

GAC — Guilty as Charged

GAS — Gang Anti-social

GATT — General Agreement on Tariffs and Trade

GB — Gun Broker

GC — Grandfather Clause

GC — General Counsel

GCR — General Court Rules

GFA — Grounds for Assault

GI — General Inquiry

GL — Government and Laws

GSW — Gun Shot Wound

GTI — Getting Teenagers Involved

GVR — Grant, Vacate, and Remand

G. W. D. — Green's Weekly Digest

H

HBC — Hit by Car

HBD — Has Been Drinking

HDC — Holder in Due Course

H. L. R. — Housing Law Reports

H. R. L. J. — Human Rights Law Journal

H. R. J. — Human Rights Journal

H. R. Q. — Human Rights Quarterly

HS — Home Search

Harv. L. R. — Harvard Law Review

I

I. B. L. — International Business Lawyer

I. Bull. — Interights Bulletin

I. C. C. L. R. — International Company and Commercial Law Review

I. C. J. — International Court of Justice

I. C. L. Q. — International and Comparative Law Quarterly

I. C. L. R. — International Construction Law Review

I. C. R. — Industrial Cases Reports

I. F. L. Rev. — International Financial Law Review

I. I. C. — International Review of Industrial Property and Copyright Law

I. J. E. C. L. — International Journal of Estuarine and Coastal Law

I. L. & P. — Insolvency Law and Practice

I. L. J. — Industrial Law Journal

I. L. M. — International Legal Materials

I. L. P. — International Legal Practitioner

I. L. R. — International Labour Review or International Law Reports

I. L. R. M. — Irish Law Reports Monthly

I. L. T. — Irish Law Times

I. M. L. — International Media Law

I. P. D. — Intellectual Property Decisions

I. P. Q. — Intellectual Property Quarterly

I. P. R. — Intellectual Property Reports

I. R. — Irish Reports

I. R. L. I. B. — Industrial Relations Legal Information Bulletin

I. R. L. R. — Industrial Relations Law Reports

I. T. E. L. R. — International Trust and Estate Law Reports

I. T. R. — Industrial Tribunal Reports

IALS Bull. — Institute of Advanced Legal Studies Bulletin

Imm. A. R. — Immigration Appeals Reports

Imm. and Nat. L. & P. — Immigration and Nationality Law and Practice

Ind. Sol. — Independent Solicitor

Ins. L. & P. — Insolvency Law and Practice or Insurance Law and Practice

Int. J. Comp. L. L. I. R. — International Journal of Comparative Law and Industrial Relations

Int. J. Law & Fam. — International Journal of Law and the Family

Int. J. Soc. L. — International Journal of the Sociology of Law

Int. Rel. — International Relations

Ir. Jur. — Irish Jurist

Ir. Jur. Rep. — Irish Jurist Reports

J

J — Judge or Justice

J. A. L. — Journal of African Law

J. B. L. — Journal of Business Law

J. C. L. — Journal of Child Law or Journal of Contract Law or Journal of Criminal Law

J. C. L. & Crim. — Journal of Criminal Law and Criminology

J. C. M. S. — Journal of Common Market Studies

J. Ch. L. — Journal of Child Law

J. E. R. L. — Journal of Energy and Natural Resources Law

J. Env. L. — Journal of Environmental Law

J. I. B. L. — Journal of International Banking Law

J. I. F. D. L. — Journal of International Franchising and Distribution Law

J. J. — Jersey Judgments

J. L. H. — Journal of Legal History

J. L. I. S. — Journal of Law and Information Science

J. L. S. S. — Journal of the Law Society of Scotland

J. Law & Soc. — Journal of Law and Society

J. Leg. Hist. — Journal of Legal History

J. M. L. C. — Journal of Maritime Law and Commerce

J. M. L. & P. —— Journal of Media Law and Practice

JMOL —— Judgment as a Matter of Law

JNOV —— Judgment Notwithstanding Verdict

J. P. —— Justice of the Peace Reports

J. P. L. —— Journal of Planning and Environment Law

J. P. J. —— Justice of the Peace Journal

J. R. —— Juridical Review

J. W. T. —— Journal of World Trade

Jx —— Jurisdiction

K

K. B. —— King's Bench

K. C. L. J. —— King's College Law Journal

K. I. R. —— Knight's Industrial Reports

Kingston L. R. —— Kingston Law Review

KOS —— Kill on Sight

KP —— Kidnap and Ransom

KS —— Kill Stealing

KT —— Kid Toucher

L

L. C. —— Lord Chancellor

L. C. News —— Law Centres News

L. C. P. —— Law and Contemporary Problems

L/C —— Letter of Credit

L. Ed. —— United States Supreme Court Reports (Lawyers' Edition)

L. Exec. —— Legal Executive

L. G. Rev. —— Local Government Review

L. I. E. I. —— Legal Issues of European Integration

L. J. —— Law Journal

L. J. R. —— Law Journal Reports

LLC —— Limited Liability Company

LLP — Limited Liability Partnership

L. M. C. L. Q. — Lloyds Maritime and Commercial Law Quarterly

L. Q. R. — Law Quarterly Review

L. S. — Legal Studies

L. S. Gaz. — Law Society's Gazette

L. T. — Law Times

L. Teach. — Law Teacher

Law Lib. — Law Librarian

Law & Just. — Law and Justice

Law & Pol. — Law and Policy

Lit. — Litigation

Liverpool L. R. — Liverpool Law Review

Ll. Rep. — Lloyd's List Reports (Before 1951)

Lloyd's Rep. — Lloyd's List Reports (After 1951)

M

M. L. B. — Manx Law Bulletin

M. L. J. — Malayan Law Journal

M. L. R. — Modern Law Review

McGill L. J. — McGill Law Journal

Mal. L. R. — Malaya Law Review

Marpol — Marine Pollution Conventions

Med. Leg. J. — Medico-Legal Journal

Med. Sci. Law — Medicine, Science and Law

Mel. L. J. — Melanesian Law Journal

MOU — Memorandum of Understanding

MPC — Model Penal Code

N

N. D. — New Directions in the Law of the Sea

NDA — Non-Disclosure Agreement

N. E. — North Eastern Reporter (USA)

NGO — Non-Government Organization

N. I. L. R. — Northern Ireland Law Reports

N. I. L. Q. — Northern Ireland Legal Quarterly

No. — Number

N. Z. C. L. C. — New Zealand Company Law Cases

N. Z. L. R. — New Zealand Law Reports

N. W. — North Western Reporter (USA)

N. Y. S. — New York Supplement

New L. J. — New Law Journal

Nig. L. J. — Nigerian Law Journal

O

OBJ — Objection

O. D. I. L. — Ocean Development and International Law

OFA — Order for Arrest

O. F. L. R. — Offshore Financial Law Reports

O. G. L. T. R. — Oil and Gas Law and Taxation Review

O. J. — Official Journal of the European Communities

O. J. L. S. — Oxford Journal of Legal Studies

OOB — Out on Bail

OOC — Out of Control

OOJ — Order of Justice

OPN — Opinion

OTD — On the Docket

OWO — Only Way Out

Ors — Other

P

■ (Pilcrow) — Paragraph

Π (Greek letter Pi) — Plaintiff

P. — Pacific Reporter

p. — Page

P. — Probate Division or Pacific Reporter (USA)

PA — Power of Attorney

PA — Public Act

P. A. D. — Planning Appeal Decisions

P. & C. R. — Property and Compensation Reports

P. C. C. — Palmer's Company Cases

P. L. R. — Planning Law Reports

P. N. — Professional Negligence

Parl. Aff. — Parliamentary Affairs

PL — Public Law

Pol. J. — Police Journal

pp. — Pages

Prison Serv. J. — Prison Service Journal

Probat. J. — Probation Journal

Proc A. S. I. L. — Proceedings of the American Society of International Law

PSV — Probably Stealing Vehicles

PT — Police Training

PTO — Pretrial Order

PTR — Pretrial Release

Pub. L. — Public Law

Q

Q. B. — Queen's Bench

QCD — Quick Claim Deed

QDRO — Qualified Domestic Relations Order

QEW — Qualified Expert Witness

QLU — Quarterly Legal Update

QPD — Qualified Public Depository

R

R — Rex or Regina

R. A. — Rating Appeals

R. E. or R/E — Real Estate

Rev. Proc. — Revenue Procedure

Rev. Rul. — Revenue Ruling

R. F. D. A. — Revue Française de Droit Aérien et Spatial

R. I. A. A. — Reports of International Arbitral Awards

R. I. D. A. — Revue Internationale du Droit d'Auteur

R J — Recurring Judgement

R. M. C. — Revue du Marché Commun

R. P. C. — Reports of Patent, Design and Trade Mark Cases

R. P. R. — Real Property Reports (Canada)

R. T. R. — Road Traffic Reports

R. V. R. — Rating and Valuation Reporter

Res. B. — Research Bulletin

S

s. or § — Section

sd = Said

ss. or § § — Sections

S. C. R. (or SCR) — Supreme Court Reports (Supreme Court of Canada)

S. Ct. — Supreme Court Reporter (Supreme Court of the United States)

S. E. — South Eastern Reporter

S. E. 2d — South Eastern Reporter, 2nd Series

SCOTUS — Supreme Court of the United States

SI — Statutory Instruments

S/J — Summary Judgment

SMJ — Subject-Matter Jurisdiction

So. — Southern Reporter

So. 2d — Southern Reporter, 2nd Series

SOL — Statute of Limitations

SOR — Statutory Orders and Regulations

S. — Southern Reporter (USA)

Stat. — United States Statutes at Large

S. A. L. J. — South African Law Journal

S. A. L. R. — South African Law Reports

S. A. S. R. — South Australian State Reports

S. C. — Session Cases (Scotland)

S. C. C. R. — Scottish Criminal Case Reports

S. C. L. R. — Scottish Civil Law Reports

S. C. R. — Supreme Court Reports (Canada)

S. E. — South Eastern Reporter (USA)

S. I. — Statutory Instrument

S. J or Sol. J — Solicitors' Journal

S. L. G. — Scottish Law Gazette

S. L. T. — Scots Law Times

S. P. L. P. — Scottish Planning Law and Practice

S. T. C. — Simon's Tax Cases

S. W. — South Western Reporter (USA)

Sol. L. — Socialist Lawyer

Stat. L. R. — Statute Law Review

T

T. D. — Treasury Decision

T. L. R. — Times Law Reports

Tas. S. R. — Tasmanian State Reports

Tax — Taxation

Tax. Int. — Taxation International

TM or TM — Trademark

Top. L. — Topical Law

Tr. L. — Trading Law

Tr. & Est. — Trusts and Estates

Trent L. J. — Trent Law Journal

Tru. L. I. — Trust Law International

U

UCC — Uniform Commercial Code

UCMJ — Uniform Code of Military Justice

U. G. L. J. — University of Ghana Law Journal

U. L. R. — Utilities Law Review

UPC — Uniform Probate Code

USC — United States Code

USCA — United States Code Annotated

USCCAN — United States Code Congressional and Administrative News

USCS — United States Code Service

UST — United States Treaties and Other International Agreements

U. S. — United States Supreme Court Reports

U. T. L. J. — University of Toronto Law Journal

V

VA — Verbal Abuse

VAW — Violence Against Women

V. A. T. T. R. — Value Added Tax Tribunal Reports

V. L. R. — Victorian Law Reports

VIO — Violence

VOC — Victim of Corruption

VOCA — Victims of Crime Act

VOL — Volume

VOP — Violation of Parole

VOV — Victory Over Violence

VR — Violent Rage

W

WA — With Attitude

WB — Wife Beater

WCK — Weapons Check

WCO — Weapons Control Officer

WDR — World Domain Rights

W. I. R. — West Indian Reports

W. L. R. — Weekly Law Reports

W. N. — Weekly Notes

W. W. R. — Western Weekly Reports

Web. J. C. L. I. — Web Journal of Current Legal Issues

Welf. R. Bull. — Welfare Rights Bulletin

WTNS — Witnesses

WTTL — Where the Truth Lies

WTO — World Trade Organization

W. Va. Code — West Virginia Code

X

XIP — Execute in Place

XN — Examination in Chief

XXN — Cross Examination

Y

YA — Young Arrest

Y. B. Eur. L. — Yearbook of European Law

Y. B. W. A. — Yearbook of World Affairs

YJ — Youth Justice

Y. L. C. T. — Yearbook of Law, Computers and Technology

Yb. Int'l. Env. L. — Yearbook of International Environmental Law

YC — Youth Court

Y\N — Yes or No

YSP — Youth Smoking Prevention

Z

ZD — Zero Dignity

ZH — Zero Hum

ZI — Zero Intelligence

ZR — Zero Restriction
ZRM — Zero Releasing Module
ZTZ — Zero Tolerance Zone

附录三　WTO法常用术语

Ad valorem tariff	从价税
Anti-dumping duty	反倾销税
Appeal	（争端解决）上诉
Arbitration	仲裁
ATC — Agreement on Textiles and Clothing	《纺织品与服装协议》
Balance-of-payments（BOP）Provisions	国际收支条款
Bound level	约束水平
Ceiling Bindings	（关税）上限约束
Compensation	补偿
Conciliation	调解
Consensus	协商一致
Countervailing duty	反补贴税
Customs valuation	海关估价
de minimis	微量

续表

Export subsidy	出口补贴
DSB — Dispute Settlement Body	争端解决机构
Dumping	倾销
GATS — General Agreement on Trade in Service	《服务贸易总协定》
GATT — General Agreement on Tariff and Trade	《关税与贸易总协定》
General Exceptions	一般例外
Government procurement	政府采购
Illustrative list	例示清单
Import licensing	进口许可
Import substitution	进口替代
Import surcharge	进口附加税
Infant industry	幼稚产业
Intellectual Property Rights（IPRs）	知识产权
Market access	市场准入
Market price support	市场价格支持
Material injury	实质损害
MFN — Most-favored-nation treatment	最惠国待遇
National treatment	国民待遇
Non-actionable subsidy	不可诉补贴
Non-tariffs Measures（NTMs）	非关税措施
Plurilateral Agreement	诸边协议
Prohibited subsidy	（补贴协议）被禁止的补贴
Protocols	议定书
PSI — Preshipment Inspection	装运前检验
Rules of origin	原产地规则
Safeguard measures	保障措施
Schedule of concessions	承诺减让表
Specific tariff	从量税
SPS — Sanitary and Phytosanitary Measures	动植物卫生检疫措施

续表

Tariff Binding	关税约束承诺
Subsidy	补贴
Tariffication	关税化
TBT — Technical Barriers to Trade	技术性贸易壁垒
TPRM — Trade Policy Review Mechanism	贸易政策审议机制
Transparency	透明度
TRIMS — Trade-related Investment Measures	与贸易有关的投资设施
TRIPS — Trade-related Intellectual Property Rights	与贸易有关的知识产权
TRQ — Tariff rate quotas/tariff quotas	关税配额
Waiver	(WTO义务的)豁免
WTO — World Trade Organization	世界贸易组织

参考文献

Bryan A. Garner. *Black's Law Dictionary*，9th edition[Z]. St. Paul：West Publishing Co.，1999.

Elizabeth A. Martin. *A Dictionary of Law*，5th edition[Z]. New York：Oxford University Press，2003.

Eugene A. Nida. *Toward a Science of Translating*[M]. Shanghai：Shanghai Foreign Language Education Press，2004.

Hornby A S. *Oxford Advanced Learner's English-Chinese Dictionary*，7th edition[Z]. Beijing：The Commercial Press，2009.

Hughes J. Understanding (and fixing) the right of fixation in copyright law[J]. *Journal of the Copyright Society of the USA*，2014，62 (3)：385—436.

James E. Clapp. *Webster's Dictionary of the Law*[Z]. London：Random House，2000.

John Bell. *French Legal Culture*[M]. London：Butterworths，2001.

John M. Mastin, Jr.，Eric L. Nelson，& Ronald G. Robey. *Common Sense Construction Law：A Practical Guide for the Construction Professional*，6th edition[M]. New Jersey：Wiley & Sons, Inc.，2019.

Lawrence M. Friedman. Legal Culture and Social Development[J]. *Law and Society Review*, 1969, 4(01):29-44.

Rene David & John E. C. Brierley. *Major Legal Systems in the World Today*[M]. London: Stevens & Sons Ltd., 1985.

Susan Sarcevic. *New Approaches to Legal Translation*[M]. The Hague: Kluwer Law International, 1997.

陈高才. 会计师事务所特征影响审计报告时滞吗[J]. 财经论丛, 2012(01):91-96.

陈建平. 法律文体翻译探索[M]. 杭州:浙江大学出版社, 2007.

陈庆柏等. 英汉双解法律词典(第2版)[Z]. 北京:世界图书出版公司, 1998.

陈文龙. 夫妻联合申报——个人所得税纳税单位的另一种选择[J]. 科技经济市场, 2007(03):258-259.

程超凡. 英汉汉英双向法律词典[Z]. 北京:法律出版社, 2007.

戴拥军, 魏向清. "回扣"的法理辨析及其英译探究[J]. 中国科技术语, 2014(05):40-44.

高鸿钧. 法律文化的语义、语境及其中国问题[J]. 中国法学, 2007(04):23-38.

高玉霞, 任东升. 概念话语引进与再输出良性互动探究:以 sea power 为例[J]. 外语研究, 2020(05):75-83.

关正义, 李婉. 海商法和海事法的联系与区别——兼论海商法学的建立与发展[J]. 法学杂志, 2012(06):35-39+55.

李敏. 浅析带说明段的无保留意见审计报告与保留意见审计报告的区别[J]. 注册会计师通讯, 1997(07):17-18.

李志刚, 徐天媛. 反垄断法上的民事赔偿责任[J]. 人民司法, 2011(07):76-82.

梁治平. 中国法的过去、现在与未来:一个文化的检讨[J]. 比较法研究, 1987(02):17-32.

刘碧波. 实务法律英语词汇精析[M]. 北京,中国法制出版社, 2013.

刘国生. 法律英语术语误译[J]. 重庆交通大学学报(社会科学版), 2016(03):128-133.

刘瑞玲. 试论法律术语翻译的精确性[J]. 外语学刊, 2010(04):125-127.

刘作翔. 法律文化论[M]. 西安:陕西人民出版社, 1992.

马强. 试论配偶权[J]. 法学论坛, 2000(02):49-57.

斯蒂文·N.苏本等著. 傅郁林等译. 民事诉讼法——原理、实务与运作环境[M]. 北京:中国政法大学出版社, 2004.

宋雷. 英汉法律用语大辞典(第2版)[Z]. 北京:法律出版社, 2019.

田国宝. 论基于推定承诺的行为[J]. 法学评论, 2004(03):133-138.

王建. 影响法律英语翻译的因素[J]. 中国科技翻译, 2003(01):1-5.

王利明.担保制度的现代化:对《民法典》第388条第1款的评析[J].法学家,2021(01):30-39+192.

王霞.论英美法中弃权和禁止反言原则在保险法上的适用[D].对外经济贸易大学,2000.

魏俐,刘忠文.中美两国青少年犯罪问题之比较研究[J].辽宁警察学院学报,2001(04):56-59.

吴如巧.美国联邦上诉程序终局判决规则:内涵、例外与发展[J].人大法律评论,2013(02):225-238.

吴煜晨.民事诉讼中的禁反言规则研究[D].2004.

吴志忠.美国《统一商法典》("货物买卖"篇)评析[J].中南财经政法大学学报,2004(05):123-129.

夏登峻.英汉法律词典(第四版)[Z].北京:法律出版社,2012.

熊云武.《合同法》中的权利瑕疵担保制度研究[J].科教文汇,2007(08):127-129.

徐洁.简评美国《统一商法典》第九篇担保制度[J].当代法学,2007(04):99-103.

薛波.元照英美法词典[Z].北京:北京大学出版社,2017.

薛华业.通用英文合约译解[M].南宁:广西出版总社·广西教育出版社.1993.

杨明星."新型大国关系"的创新译法及其现实意义[J].中国翻译,2015(01):101-105.

杨蓉.美国垄断致损赔偿责任制度研究[D].湖南大学,2015.

张法连.法律语言研究:法律英语翻译[M].济南:山东大学出版社,2014.

张法连.英美法律术语辞典(英汉双解)[Z].上海:上海外语教育出版社,2014.

张法连.英美法律术语汉译策略探究[J].中国翻译,2016(02):100-104.

张法连.中西法律语言与文化对比研究[M].北京:北京大学出版社,2017.

张法连.法律翻译中的文化传递[J].中国翻译,2019(02):165-171.

张炜.中国特色海权理论发展历程综述[J].人民论坛·学术前沿,2012(06):28-35.

张文彬.论普通法上的禁止反言原则[J].长江大学学报(社会科学版),2001(04):48-54.

张永强.论保险最大诚信原则及实现机制[D].山东大学,2006.

赵维贞.美国成文法与传统大陆法系成文法立法理念比较研究[J].西南政法大学学报,2004(02):119-122.

赵信会,谌其艳.美国民事上诉制度析论.东方论坛 2005(01):106-113.

中国证券监督管理委员会.中国上市公司并购重组发展报告[Z].北京:中国经济出版社,2009.

索 引

access right　35

administrative revocation　36

advocate general　38

agency of necessity　39

amicus curiae　40

apparent authority　41

appellate record　42

assignment of error　43

attorney-in-fact　44

bad title　45

bench　46

bias crime　47

bill of indictment　48

bona fide purchaser　49

breach of the peace　50

breaking bulk　51

brief　52

burden of proof　52

bylaw　54

check　54

check fraud　56

community service　57

conjugal rights　58

constructive acceptance　59

count　61

crossed check　61

custodial parent　62

daisy chain　63

damn-fool doctrine　64

dawn raid　64

death-knell doctrine　66

decision　68

declaratory judgment　69

deed of arrangement　70

defendant   71

defense   72

determination   73

domicile   74

due diligence   75

effective vote 与 counted vote   76

election under the will   77

entrapment   77

equal-access rule   79

equitable distribution   79

estoppel   80

European Council   82

execution   83

false arrest   84

false statement   86

family allowance   87

final judgment   88

foreign   89

foreign judgment   89

forward merger   90

friend of the court   92

fruit   92

fundamental law   93

futures   94

futures contract   94

garnishee   95

general demurrer   96

golden parachute   97

good cause   98

graded offense   98

ground lease 与 ground rent   99

halfway house   100

hell-or-high water clause   100

high crime   101

highway by user   102

holistic marketing   102

hornbook   103

hotchpot   104

house law   105

incapacity of physician   106

inchoate offense 与 inchoate crime   106

insider trading   108

instantaneous seisin   109

intrinsic fraud   110

introduced evidence   111

invented consideration   112

involuntary association   113

jactitation of marriage   114

jail breaking   115

jail credit   116

jeopardy   116

Jewell instruction   117

joint petition   118

journeys accounts   119

judicial opinion   120

jus tertii   120

key-man insurance   121

Knock-and-announce Rule   123

knockoff   124

knowingly   125

labes realis   125

land charges   127

law review   128

lawful age   129

legal person　130

legal fiction 与 legal presumption　131

legitimate child　133

Lemon Law　133

libel　134

life imprisonment　135

longevity pay　136

lump-sum agreement　137

malfeasance　138

material evidence　139

memorandum of alteration　139

modification order　140

moral evidence　141

municipal corporation　142

mutual insurance company　142

necessary party　143

necessity doctrine　144

no-contest clause　145

obiter dictum　146

omission　147

one day, one trial　148

opinion evidence　149

O. R. (own recognizance)　150

ordinance　151

outcome responsibility　152

overrule　153

personal property 与 private property　154

petit treason 与 petty treason　155

plea bargain　156

polygamy　156

presumption of death　157

prize fighting　158

process　158

pronotary　159

provided that　160

reasonable belief　161

reasonable person　161

rebate 与 refund　162

redirect examination　163

remoteness of damage　165

right of fixation　165

royalty bonus　167

rubber check　168

satisfaction　169

Sea Law 与 Law of the Sea　171

sea power　172

security agreement　173

sleeping partner 与 silent partner　175

Solicitor General　176

specific performance　177

statement of affairs　178

statement of income　179

status offense　180

statutory　181

tacit mortgage　182

tainted evidence　183

tax foreclosure　186

tenancy at will 与 tenancy at sufferance　187

tenancy in common　188

termination hearing　189

third degree　190

trademark 与 tradename　191

traditional waiver　193

transferred intent　195

turf and twig　196
tutorship by nature　197
unclean hands　197
unconscionability　199
underlying stock　199
undue influence　200
unilateral contract　202
unqualified audit report 或 unqualified auditor's report　202
utmost good faith　204
verdict　205
waiting period　207
waiver of jurisdiction　208
waiver of tort　209
warrantless arrest 与 warrantless search　211
with average　212
withdrawal (in criminal law)　212
words of purchase　213
yardstick theory　214
Year-and-a-day Rule　216
years of discretion　216
yellow knight　217
yellow sheets　219
yield net　219
young offender　220
zipper clause　221